The Indispensable Librarian

The Indispensable Librarian

Surviving and Thriving in School Libraries in the Information Age

Second Edition

Doug Johnson

Illustrations by Brady Johnson

LINWORTH

AN IMPRINT OF ABC-CLIO, LLC
Santa Barbara, California • Denver, Colorado • Oxford, England

Library of Congress Cataloging-in-Publication Data

Johnson, Doug, 1952–
    The indispensable librarian : surviving and thriving in school libraries in the information age / Doug Johnson ; illustrations by Brady Johnson. — Second edition.
        pages cm
    Includes bibliographical references and index.
    ISBN 978-1-61069-239-7 (pbk.) — ISBN 978-1-61069-240-3 (ebook)
  1. School libraries—United States—Administration. 2. School librarians—United States. I. Title.
    Z675.S3J64   2013
    025.1'978—dc23   2012051394

ISBN: 978-1-61069-239-7
EISBN: 978-1-61069-240-3

17 16 15 14 13   1 2 3 4 5

This book is also available on the World Wide Web as an eBook.
Visit www.abc-clio.com for details.

Libraries Unlimited
An Imprint of ABC-CLIO, LLC

ABC-CLIO, LLC
130 Cremona Drive, P.O. Box 1911
Santa Barbara, California 93116-1911

This book is printed on acid-free paper ∞
Manufactured in the United States of America

Chapter 11 contains material from Doug Johnson, "Librarians and Ethics in Use of Technology," chapter 5 in *Ethics in School Librarianship: A Reader* by Carol Simpson. Copyright © 2003. Reproduced with permission of ABC-CLIO, LLC.

This book is dedicated to all librarians who have turned a child on to reading, taught a teacher a new technology skill, and made the world a better place by improving the effectiveness of their schools with great library programs. And of course, to the LWW who does all these things every day.

Contents

List of Figures   xi
Foreword: You Have to Be Mad   xiii
    Joyce Kasman Valenza
Acknowledgments   xv
Introduction to the Second Edition   xvii

Chapter One: The Roles and Missions of the Librarian   1
    The Virtual Librarian   1
    What are the challenges facing our profession?   4
    Seven ways for librarians to remain relevant in a ubiquitous information environment
       full of NetGen learners   7
    Do school librarians have "enduring values"?   10
    Sample professional mission statement and the elevator speech   11
    The Mankato transition: A case study   11
    For reflection: Why are *you* in the profession?   15

Chapter Two: Program Assessment   16
    Creating long-term change   16
    How will you show your program is impacting student achievement?   17
    Why assess your program?   18
    The formal library assessment   18
    Ongoing assessments   25
    Context and focus   28
    A 12-point library program checklist for principals   29
    For reflection: Linking libraries and reading achievement   32

Chapter Three: Planning   35
    Critical elements of a library/technology plan   35
    The planning process   40
    Using goal setting to help in professional evaluations   41
    For reflection: Twenty-plus years of working with advisory groups—what I've learned   42

Chapter Four: Communications and Advocacy   44
    What are the components of an effective communications program?   44
    Speaking where people are listening   51
    Can a good library program be a marketing tool for your school?   52
    What are the basic rules of effective advocacy?   53
    For reflection: What is transparency, and why is it critical to the librarian's success?   55

Chapter Five: Managing Others and Collaboration 57

Working with the library support staff 57

Working with the technology department 60

Working with the teaching staff: The fundamentals of successful collaboration 63

For reflection: What is the secret to successful supervision? 67

Chapter Six: Managing Digital Resources 69

You know you are a 21st-century librarian when . . . 69

How has the library's role changed as information and books go digital? 70

What is cloud computing, and how can librarians take advantage of it? 75

For reflection: E-books and libraries 78

Chapter Seven: Curriculum 81

Putting technology skills in their place 81

Integrating technology skills into an information literacy curriculum 82

Building an information/technology literacy curriculum 84

Elements of projects that motivate 88

What new skills are needed to survive the information jungle? 93

How can librarians support the development of "right brain" skills? 96

For reflection: What does a library for a postliterate society look like? 97

Chapter Eight: Budget 100

Budgeting as a library ethic 100

Ten strategies of effective library budgeters 101

Good purchasing strategies 109

For reflection: Weed 110

Chapter Nine: Facilities 112

Why should I go to the library when the library will come to me? 112

The fundamentals of good school library design and why they are still important 116

Ten common design pitfalls and how to avoid them 118

For reflection: Are there schools that don't need a library? 125

Chapter Ten: Digital Intellectual Freedom 127

Freedom to learn 127

Maintaining intellectual freedom in a filtered world 128

Best practices for meeting CIPA requirements 132

Seven myths about Internet filters 134

For reflection: Getting websites unblocked 135

Chapter Eleven: Ethics and Technology 137

How has technology impacted the ethical practice of librarians? 137

Knowing right from wrong in the digital age 148

For reflection: Guidelines for educators using social and educational networking sites 156

Chapter Twelve: Copyright and Creative Commons 159

Make a copyright u-turn and other audacious statements about copyright 159

Creative Commons and why it should be more commonly understood 164

For reflection: Why students (and adults) satisfice 166

Chapter Thirteen: The Librarian's Role in Effective Staff Development   168

The why, what, and who of staff development in technology and the librarian's role   168

How can we provide effective staff development opportunities for our teachers?   172

For reflection: Top 10 ways to increase your technology skills and knowledge
(and the secret to being perceived as a technology guru)   177

Chapter Fourteen: Surviving Professional Transitions   179

Personal learning networks—Why you can't afford to wait for the next conference   179

Finding the time   181

When your job is on the line . . .   182

For reflection: Prevention   184

Chapter Fifteen: Libraries and the Future   185

A mind-set list for librarians   185

Miles's library: A vision for school libraries   186

For reflection: Prognostications for libraries and schools   195

Afterword: A Day of Ordinary Library Miracles   197

Author's Note   199

Index   203

List of Figures

Images

Image 3-1: Developing ownership of the planning process   39
Image 4-1: Reporting flowchart   48
Image 4-2: Students at computers in the library   49
Image 6-1: There are books and there are books   79
Image 8-1: Budget process   101
Image 9-1: Study carrels and bird noises   119
Image 9-2: Multiple uses   121
Image 9-3: Unsightly wiring   122
Image 9-4: Visual control   123
Image 9-5: Traffic patterns and zones   124
Image 9-6: Misplaced light switches   125
Image 10-1: How filtering policies are made   135
Image 12-1: A cure for satisficing   167

Tables

Table 2-1: Covey's time management matrix   16
Table 5-1: It's not the technology that's good or bad. It's how it is used.   61
Table 8-1: A library budget worksheet   105
Table 13-1: Strengths and weaknesses of technology trainers   170
Table 13-2: The technology upgrade   174

Foreword

You Have to Be Mad

You have to be mad . . .

In chapter eleven, Doug recalls: *A person recently commented to me that one must be mad to go into school librarianship . . . You have to be mad (passionate) for stories, technology, and especially work with kids. You have to be mad (angry) about how poorly our schools underserve too many vulnerable children. And finally, you have to be mad (crazy) enough to believe that you as one little individual have the power to change your institution, your political systems, and especially, the lives of your students and teachers.*

For those of us who are that kind of *mad*, Doug steers a course through the storm.

Some people see this point in time as a perfect storm, for those *nonessential* elements of the school program.

Call me *mad*, but I am truly excited about new possibilities for our profession. In fact, I think this may be the best time in the history of time to be a librarian. Rather than a perfect storm, I see the sweet spot—a ripe moment for teacher librarians to expand the notion of literacy in schools and to introduce richer experiences in using information and creating and communicating with it in ways we never dreamed of even ten years ago. It's a critical time to help grow ethical and engaged digital citizens. And it's a critical time for young learners to have access to powerful school library programs.

Doug Johnson has been making me laugh and pushing me to think bigger and smarter since we met for lunch at my first AASL Conference in Portland in 1997. That was the year Doug initially published *The Indispensible Librarian.*

I left our first lunch together thinking that this was a man who made me want to be a better librarian.

Nearly 20 years later, Doug tells us, *the tools have changed, the mission has not.*

He also sees a sweet spot. In fact, he sees lots of them. Applying both business and library principles, his own quirky humor, clear vision, and practical wisdom, Doug informs and inspires our day-to-day decision making.

Doug guides the in-the-trenches practitioner in asking the right questions, in making the case, and in demonstrating what best practice looks like. He presents a workbook filled with illustrations, diagrams, samples, tools, and checklists. And he addresses the many essential questions about programs that keep us all up at night: how to set goals and objectives; what does effective communication look like?; how to be transparent; how to build a personal learning network; how to incorporate digital resources; how to manage a program and work with others; how to integrate digital/technology literacy skills into curriculum; how to make your program a budget priority; how to plan that *third place* for learners; how to balance school filters with principles of intellectual freedom.

Doug says, *Now, and in the future, the physical room, the title of the person running it, or the kinds of resources provided will not matter. I will know I am in a library by what it values.*

This book is about those values, and it is a pep talk, a road map, a checklist.

The values are a constant, but the game has changed. Shift is no longer optional. Learning to be indispensable is more important than it was back in 1997.

For those of us in the trenches who believe in the *madness* of trying to make permanent, powerful, positive change for learners, for those who also see the sweet spots, Doug asks hard questions, offers encouragement, and shares the secrets of indispensability.

Whether you are new to the field or a seasoned veteran, Doug is an indispensable coach, and *The Indispensable Librarian* could be your indispensable guide.

Joyce Kasman Valenza

Acknowledgments

Acknowledgments are a dangerous thing since it is all too easy to forget individuals who have had a big impact on one's philosophy and practice. But I am going to name some names. Mary Alice Anderson, Jane Prestebak, Mary Meshikomer, Joyce Valenza, and Anne Hanson each read and commented on chapter drafts of this book, making the final product much more insightful than my original. Blue Skunk Blog readers added ideas when I posted bits and pieces of it online while writing. A new generation of library leaders, including Buffy Hamilton, Shannon Miller, Cathy Jo Nelson, and Chris Harris, have pushed me into the future with their writings and presentations. I owe a debt of gratitude to every brave practicing librarian who has shared best practices, exciting projects, and successful experiences by writing blog posts, publishing journal articles, and giving conference presentations.

Introduction to the Second Edition

The skill of writing is to create a context in which other people can think.
— Edwin Schlossberg

The introduction to the 1997 edition of this book began:

> We are a profession that is undergoing radical transformation working in an institution that is undergoing radical transformation serving a society that is undergoing radical transformation.
> This is appealing to some of us, but to many of us it is not.
> Even school media specialists and technology coordinators with the best skills, the highest capacity to learn, and the strongest egos often feel overwhelmed and threatened.

Nearly two decades ago technology was a looming change agent for the profession. The Internet was relatively new. Online databases were radical departures from our print magazine back issues accessed using the *Readers' Guide to Periodical Literature*. In the quiz that began the book, I challenged the reader with questions about HTML coding, viruses, e-mail privacy, spreadsheets, and .pdf files.

As I write this, we are still a profession in transformation—perhaps at an even more rapid pace than in 1997. And while technology is still evolving and challenging to many of us, other forces are asking us to reexamine our professional roles in school as well.

With the passage of the No Child Left Behind Act signed into law in 2002, with dramatic shortfalls in state education budgets, and with education becoming increasingly politicized, librarians are being asked to prove they make an empirically measurable difference in the effectiveness of their schools. Computing is no longer tied to labs and desks. Technology enthusiasts have embraced "21st-Century Skills"—which bear a striking resemblance to what once may have been called information literacy.

Please take a few seconds to complete the following quiz:

1. What technologies best facilitate data-driven decision making?
2. What is a *netbook*, what is *cloud computing*, and what does BYOD stand for? What is a *wiki*, what is *RSS*, what is *microblogging*, what is a *CMS*, and can you *flip a classroom*?
3. What do teachers do that make an interactive whiteboard *interactive*?
4. How do you advise teachers whose students wish to "friend" them on a social networking site?
5. What are the strengths and weakness of online classes?
6. How can students find information online other than using Google? Is Wikipedia a trusted source of information?
7. Why are Creative Commons and Fair Use important to students and teachers?
8. How can one promote intellectual freedom in an institution that uses Internet filtering software?
9. What is the difference between a criterion-referenced test, a norm-referenced test, and a value-added test?
10. Where can one find research on the impact of school library programs on student achievement?

The librarians in my district would do well on this little test. For that, I am proud and grateful, but I also am very aware that the ability to answer questions like these tells us that we need to know more about more things than we have ever needed to know before—important things like curriculum, assessment, politics, facility planning, online safety, and budgeting. We have to learn how to seek out and use the expertise of others in our schools—curriculum area, assessment, reading, and special education experts. We need to know the best practices of not just our field, but in many fields.

If the old adage that "knowledge is power" is true, then we have a tremendous opportunity to provide leadership roles in our schools. In fact, our roles as leaders, as planners, and as communicators are more important than ever if we wish to stay a relevant part of helping all students gain the skills they will need to live and work in a digital, global, and fast-changing world.

This is appealing to some of us, but to many of us it is not.

There is a continuing perception that our profession is in jeopardy. I really don't know. There certainly seems to be a general anxiety among all educators, not just librarians. Perhaps there is a general nervousness among all thinking people.

Yet, there also seem to be other factors at work that indicate that librarians are more in demand than ever. In the job-applicant–glutted field of education, well-prepared librarians find themselves in somewhat short supply. The ALA has a special "recruitment to the profession" task force. I get several calls each spring from principals looking for "really good" librarians for their schools.

Despite what seems to be a return to a "back to the basics" movement with an emphasis on high-stakes testing and "content" rather than "process," national educational organizations still are united in what they consider best practices in the classroom (Zemelman, Daniels, and Hyde 2012). These best practices include:

- Less lecturing and more coaching and hands-on learning
- Less student passivity and more active, collaborative learning
- Less dependence on textbooks and more use of whole books and primary sources
- Less rote memorization and more higher-order thinking skills
- Less one-size-fits-all approaches to learning and more differentiated approaches to instruction to meet the needs of individuals

I look at that these trends and think, "Good grief, all classrooms are going to start operating like good libraries." If you think the library field has undergone cataclysmic change, wait till you see what's in store for the teaching profession.

When every teacher becomes a pretty good librarian, then what do we do? That will take a while, and in the meantime, we as professionals who have practiced these "new" teaching operations can help lead the way. Our role as staff developer, in-service provider, and decision maker is coming to the fore. It's time.

This is appealing to some of us, but to many of us it is not.

Most of us feel overworked, yet many of us feel our positions might be in jeopardy if there were to be even a modest budget reduction. Are we focusing on the right objectives, spending time on the most important tasks?

In many school districts (and even in whole states), there are serious questions as to whether librarians and library programs are necessary. Why do we need a library when we have the Internet? What can a librarian offer that Google doesn't? Aren't small class sizes more important than all these "specialists"? Can't technicians or clerks provide the same services librarians do now?

There is only one way to keep one's profession viable and job meaningful and secure. That is to have important skills and offer critical services no one else in the building can. Simple as that. The question is: What exactly are those skills?

That question is at the heart of all the writings in this book. I have to say that what I offer is only one vision, one path that can be taken. My ideas may or may not be to your liking, but they seem to have worked for me as a building librarian and seem to be working for many of the successful librarians I know. Of one thing you can be assured: I am a pragmatist. I work in real schools with real teachers, real kids, real administrators, and real librarians.

I have organized this material in much the same way I organized the Administration and Management graduate class I taught as "Adjunct of the Last Resort" for a local university. What is interesting to me, however, is how the original syllabus came about—it was modeled after the administration class I took in the mid-1970s—when the personal computer was but a twinkle in Steve Wozniak's eye. Again, what that says to me is that our mission is little changed, but the tools with which we are to accomplish that mission have—quite radically.

So while 90 percent of the material in this new edition is new, the purpose is to still make you, the building librarian, indispensable.

Reference

Zemelman, Steven, Harvey Daniels, and Arthur Hyde. *Best Practice: New Standards for Teaching and Learning in America's Schools* 4th ed. Portsmouth, NH: Heinemann, 2012.

Chapter One

The Roles and Missions of the Librarian

Who can find a virtual librarian?
for her price is far above rubies.
—after Proverbs 31:10

The traditional roles of the librarian are just fine as far as they go. Teacher, information specialist, and program administrator are, and will remain, important roles for our profession. But these tasks have been around for over thirty years in print, and conceptually long before that. Thirty years—an eon in a time when an encyclopedia of information can travel across the globe on a beam of light in the blink of an eye. I suggest we need to add three more roles to our profession: Virtual Librarian, Crowsnester, and Rabblerouser.

The Virtual Librarian

I've helped design or redesign over a dozen new school libraries in my career, but designing one in 1991 was the first time I'd actually bargained *away* floor space. Floor space had always been the *last* thing I'd give up when the inevitable cutbacks were made after construction bids came in. Carpet, air conditioning, more shelving, or display cases could always be added later, but once floor space was relinquished, it was gone, gone, gone. In designing this middle school library, however, I argued that floor space at a certain number of dollars per square foot be traded in for a computer network running throughout the building. Why?

Information has gone digital—no question. The world's information resides primarily in an electronic form. Our libraries already reflect this. Our resources include books that talk, computer games that engage and educate, real-time connections to the outside world through video conferencing, searchable databases of full-text periodicals, and movies and music that are streamed to us. Today's entering librarians no longer remember that the library catalog was once a wooden box of drawers—it has always been a spinning platter of rust-coated plastic accessed with a keyboard and monitor. Information exists ever less in physical space, and ever more in "virtual space" made of electrons, not atoms.

Does physically reducing the size of the library mean our jobs as librarians are becoming less important? That depends on how well our profession accepts the role of Virtual Librarian. One of the beauties of digital information is that it travels extremely well. Connect two computers with copper wire or glass fiber or a wireless interface and the transfer of information between them is nearly instantaneous. If we accept that our resources are legitimate in electronic formats and that they reside in virtual space, stringing wire to all the classroom computers in our school makes *the entire school the library*. Wow! If we connect our services and resources to the Internet, *the entire world becomes our library*. Double wow! If we place a wireless transmitter in a classroom and give students personal devices like laptops, tablets, or smartphones, *every desk in the school becomes our library*. Triple wow! Create library webpages, blogs, and wikis that link to our library's online resources *and our students' homes become our library*. Our physical library may have shrunk, but our virtual library has expanded explosively. Our virtual presence can be everywhere—24/7. Will there be any stopping us? I think *not*.

What might some of the functions of the Virtual Librarian be? Network administrator certainly. Staff trainer in using e-mail, cloud-computing, networked learning tools, and Internet search engines. A digital information evaluator and selector. A teacher who can develop information evaluation skills in her staff and students. Certainly webmaster for the library, if not the school. Social networking director, perhaps. When information is transmitted to a class instead of the class being transmitted to the library, where should the Virtual Librarian be working with students?

I strongly maintain that the only way we will remain viable as a profession (and have any job security) is to offer indispensable services no one else in the school building can or will. The Virtual Librarian delivers such services.

Crowsnester

Our professional literature does a wonderful job of outlining how the librarian can support restructuring and educational reform. Efforts in performance-based assessment, whole language instruction, constructivist education, brain-based teaching, diversity awareness, differentiated instruction, and global citizenship are all getting help from the library profession. Libraries are essential even to "back-to-basics" movements: We have a major impact in making sure all students can read and do well on high-stakes tests.

Yet it seems too often the librarian is one of the last to leap on the tailgate of educational change rather than sit in the driver's seat. And unfortunately we are ignored by some staff development activities altogether because we are not viewed as being "real teachers."

Librarians need to become inhabitants of an educational crowsnest. Like the sailor high atop a ship's mast, a critical role of our profession is to scan the horizon for educational, technological, and societal changes that will affect our students, teachers, schools, and communities. And we must morph our library programs to support those changes.

Crowsnesters read. They read a variety of general professional education periodicals, not just library journals. Crowsnesters know the latest debates on educational listservs and blogs on the Internet. They download challenging newsletters and reports from the web. Crowsnesters form personal learning networks of fellow librarians and educators using a variety of social networking tools. Crowsnesters seek, read, and use research about all best practices in education—not just about librarianship.

Crowsnesters travel. They raid other schools for great ideas. Crowsnesters regularly attend professional conferences and technology workshops. They take classroom teachers and principals and board members and students with them when they travel, so that when exciting things are seen or heard, others share the dreams and visions. Crowsnesters travel virtually as well, participating in learning events online and in videoconferences.

Crowsnesters don't just participate in, but lead, building- and district-level school improvement initiatives. They know their building's goals and how they fit into every program their buildings are implementing to help meet those goals. They collaborate, not just at a classroom level but also at a leadership level with other departments.

Crowsnesters learn and teach and learn some more. Once it was enough for information-technology specialists to garner a body of specialized knowledge and then, like wizards, ration it out to patrons who needed it (which often created resentment in the patron). Advances in technology have made the "wizard" approach to service unethical. Everyone needs not just information, but the ability to harvest it and work with it and use it. *The most valuable person in an organization today is not the one who knows the most, but the one who can learn the best, and can teach that which is learned to others.* The Crowsnester who empowers others through teaching useful skills, concepts, and applications, instead of being resented like the "wizard," is valued and respected and, yes, sometimes even liked.

I strongly maintain that the only way we will remain viable as a profession (and have respect among our fellow professionals) is to offer indispensable services no one else in the educational organization can or will provide. The Crowsnester delivers such services by looking at and adapting to events on the horizon.

Rabblerouser

Librarians write lots of wonderful documents—manifestos, standards, rants, and journal articles. But like inspirational sermons heard only by the choir, do the words in them actually change anyone or anything? Unless the librarian accepts the role of Rabblerouser, visions of improved education will stay only visions.

I have a personal list of things I believe absolutely stink about schools and society, and that something should damn well be done about. Here's a partial list:

- Schools don't serve all children equally, and many children not at all.
- Schools lack leadership, vision, and competent administration.
- Classrooms lack engagement, excitement, and stimulation.
- There is far too much emphasis on high-stakes testing.
- Most learning is not motivating, enjoyable, or relevant.
- Technology is too often purchased for the sake of technology rather than to meet educational goals.
- Children (and sometimes teachers) are treated as second-class citizens, especially in regard to information.
- Library and technology programs (that *are* child-centered) are not adequately funded.
- Censors get too much attention, and promoters of intellectual freedom get too little.
- Ethical and safe use of technology is not taught.
- Children are not being taught to think critically for themselves.

I could go on. One doesn't have to agree with a thing on this list, but I think everyone must believe schools and society can be made better.

The librarian's role as Rabblerouser is not one of critic, but one of builder. Remember the Noah Principle: "No more prizes for predicting rain. Prizes only for building arks." Rabblerousers have a plan, vision, or principle around which the roused rabble can rally. If your budget were magically increased 1000 percent, do you have an improvement plan you could immediately start implementing? If you were suddenly given total control of your school's staff development program, do you know what you'd teach? If you were made King or Queen of your school, what decrees you would immediately enact?

A clear vision well articulated by the librarian can have a tremendous impact on a school. The librarian as Rabblerouser can fill a leadership void. We're especially good Rabblerousers because:

- Our programs impact the whole school climate.
- We advocate information skills and individualized learning for children of all ability levels.
- We have few subject area biases and territories to protect.
- We're extremely charming and wise.

Rabblerousers must challenge the system to be effective agents for change, and do so by working on school governing committees, leading staff development activities, and exemplifying great teaching practices. Rabblerousers are involved in curriculum revision. They write for their district newsletters and talk to their parent–teacher organizations. They hold offices in their unions and other professional associations. Rabblerousers are politically involved. They form strong networks with fellow Rabblerousers inside and outside their profession both in person and virtually.

It's impossible to be a good librarian without being a Rabblerouser. We need to remind those who enter our field that it takes just as much courage to be an educational Rabblerouser as it does to be a police officer, firefighter, or soldier. It's not even a role one adopts only as a librarian, but as a caring, involved member of the human race who has passions beyond one's self. Jerry Garcia once said, "Somebody has to do something and it's just incredibly pathetic it has to be us." But when it is librarians doing "something," it's not pathetic at all.

I strongly maintain that the only way we will remain viable as a profession (and sleep with clear consciences) is to offer indispensable services no one else in society can or will. The Rabblerouser delivers such services.

What are the challenges facing our profession?

> The Chinese use two brush strokes to write the word "crisis."
> One brush stroke stands for danger; the other for opportunity.
> In a crisis, be aware of the danger—but recognize the opportunity.
> —John F. Kennedy, speech in Indianapolis, April 12, 1959

It certainly seems like our profession is in a state of crisis. Various places in various parts of the country are:

- Reducing school library programs and cutting professional and clerical staff.
- Providing minimal budgets for library materials.
- Supplanting library programs with technology initiatives.
- Closing university library education programs.
- Establishing "teach to the test" and "teacher-proof" curricula.

And you can probably add to the list.

However, my sense is that most professions are usually facing one sort of crisis or another much of the time. My sense is that school library programs in general have always been in a crisis situation. But at the same time, my sense is that there are as many vital, successful library programs in schools today as there have ever been.

Let's just face it, good school library programs may never be seen as a permanent part of the educational landscape. Gifted and talented programs, art programs, academic and athletic extracurricular programs, and even school counseling programs—anything in a school that goes beyond one teacher, thirty students, and a textbook—can and will be seen as nonessential by some decision makers.

I am not sure that this is a bad thing. Our very vulnerability demands that we as a profession need to continually find ways to strengthen our programs and roles. I would suggest we take a hard look at the challenges we currently face and see how we can rise to meet them. Below I suggest seven areas where every librarian can and should take action.

1. Tying our library program goals to the larger goals of our educational system

Too many librarians create lovely programs that have very little to do with what transpires in the rest of the school. While I'm sure their library skills and activities do wonderful things for students, teachers and administrators are too often unaware of them and see little impact on the school's overall learning goals. Classroom instruction is and will remain the primary focus of education, and unless we have an impact on it, we will be seen as superfluous. Our library goals must be directly aligned to the instructional goals of the district, building, and classroom. Sometimes I sense that we work very, very hard to climb one mountain only to find the rest of the school on a completely different peak.

While it is probably the most daunting part of our jobs, we must continually enhance our collaborative efforts with teachers. This is the only way that what we do in the library will tie directly to what is happening in the classroom. We need to work with *every* teacher on staff (not just the living, as we like to joke). That will only happen with initiative and persistence. Make it your goal to work one-on-one with four additional teachers *every* year. Hone those interpersonal skills, identify and articulate the areas where you can be seen as someone who can be helpful, and keep at it. Our best librarians are ones who serve on site-based councils, technology committees, curriculum teams, and in other decision-making positions. I call this "collaboration at a higher level." The credibility established by serving as a "leader" often goes a long way in gaining acceptance by teachers in team efforts.

2. Demonstrating and publicizing our effectiveness through accountability

While we certainly have responsibilities that go beyond direct student instruction, our role as a teacher of critical skills is the one that is the most important in an educational setting. In order to be seen as true teachers it is imperative we:

- Establish an integrated information/technology curriculum with clearly defined, measurable skill benchmarks by grade level.
- Collaborate with teachers in designing and teaching units in which students learn, practice, and demonstrate those skills within a content area.
- Collaborate with teachers in designing and administering the student performance assessment that accompanies those units.
- Report attainment of skills to students, parents, and community though progress reports, conferences, and public reports.

Perhaps the most challenging task we have ahead is helping our administrators and public understand how our information literacy curricula complement and support school accountability efforts that use standardized testing as a critical measurement. A publicity effort that informs those outside our profession about the findings of studies like those done by Keith Curry Lance needs to be undertaken by every district.

3. Recognizing the need for a new economic rationale for libraries

The traditional economic rationale for libraries has always been simple: It's less expensive to buy one book and share it than it is to buy a book for everyone. And for centuries this model has given libraries their value. And that worked just fine when information and entertainment were physical and only one person could access one container of information at a time. It worked best when information and entertainment were expensive for the average person. It worked well when people seemed OK with paying taxes to support the common good—like public libraries and public schools.

But for the first time in history we are moving from a time of information scarcity to one of information abundance—even overload. Can we define why libraries are necessary when information is ubiquitous, more scalable, far more convenient, and often free online?

E-books at the time of this writing are just becoming major players in schools and society. Publishers, concerned with unauthorized distribution and the resulting diminution of profits, are not making e-books library-friendly, placing severe restrictions on how often they can be circulated by creating digital rights management schemes and publishing in proprietary formats. There seems to be no "first sale doctrine" that applies to books in electronic format. Traditionally, print books, magazines, CDs, DVDs, video tapes, music albums, etc. have been considered the property of anyone who purchased the material, although the intellectual property contained in them is still owned by the creator/publisher. This has meant that individuals and libraries can loan, give, or resell the *object* to whomever they choose—thus transferring access to the content.

4. Remaining experts in helping others make meaning out of technology

Schools have made a rapid technological transformation. They have gone from institutions devoid of technology to institutions full of underused, rapidly aging technology. Students often seem to have more access to and more comfort in using technology. Teachers need training in not just basic productivity tools such as word processors and webpage design, but also in learning how to construct instructional units that help students master technology skills, content concepts, and higher-level thinking skills.

Thoughtful information literacy units can also teach most if not all technology competencies needed by students. Technology used to locate, assess, synthesize, and communicate information in order to answer questions and solve problems is technology used in its most powerful and meaningful way. Librarians must be seen as the experts in this use. We also need to make sure teachers and students are truly technologically literate: They know when technology is *not* the best solution to a problem as well.

New and changing technologies create a need for exceptional staff development opportunities for school librarians. But if we demonstrate to our administrators that we will teach to our staffs what we have learned though workshops, conferences, and other training opportunities, we can justify receiving those extra staff development dollars.

We can also do some of the technology tasks in our buildings that are rapidly becoming very important. These tasks include webmastering, network management, and technician supervision. Remember that there is rarely a position that is indispensable, but there are specific tasks that *must* be done. Personally, I like to stay valuable by doing jobs no one else is willing or able to do.

5. Retaining our professional teaching status

The most distressing talk I hear revolves around decertifying the position of librarian. Not requiring a teaching license and certification in library science and educational media is too often seen as a quick fix for finding folks who can staff our school libraries. Along with the rest of the teaching profession, good librarians are in short supply in many areas of the country. An aging teaching profession, low retention rate of beginning educators, opportunities in the business world, and stress-related burnout are all contributing to this problem.

Yet our professional skills in constructivist teaching, authentic assessment, program management, material selection and organization, and information and technology ethics are growing rather than diminishing in importance. We must work with our boards of teaching and other certifying agencies to educate them in what we do, why our skills are vital to schools, and why the total reliance on clerks and technicians will shortchange students.

6. Attracting the best to our field

Each school librarian's work reflects on all other school librarians. Unfortunately, many teachers, principals, and parents have never had the opportunity to work with an excellent librarian. But once they have, they understand and support the position. It's imperative that our profession actively recruits the best and brightest of teachers to our field. Each of us needs to encourage teachers we feel would make good librarians to consider this career path. And we need to encourage our postsecondary institutions to adopt a rigorous selection procedure for admittance into the library certification program.

I am perhaps even more worried about the status of postsecondary library education than anything else. Universities are closing or reducing library schools. Library schools seem to be having a difficult time hiring and retaining those dynamic professors who not only teach the next generation of librarians, but also guide and lead those now practicing. Poor or nonexistent library schools *will* doom the profession.

7. Staying connected

There is one final challenge that may be the most important at all: We need to stay optimistic and mission centered. And the best way to do that is by staying connected with each other and finding ways to renew ourselves when times get tough. Whether through conference attendance, webinar participation, e-mail list conversations, or just meeting with others within our own district for a beer after work, we must support each other.

Despite the challenges that face our profession, I remain wildly optimistic about its future. We are by far the most caring, smartest (and probably best-looking) group of educators now working in schools. Savvy communities are realizing that their best natural resource is a well-educated workforce, and in today's economy well-educated means being not just literate, but information literate. A powerful librarian is indispensable to schools that are dedicated to graduating citizens who can use information in meaningful ways and know how to keep on learning.

Seven ways for librarians to remain relevant in a ubiquitous information environment full of NetGen learners

Thoughtful people are openly questioning the need for libraries—school, public, academic, and special. Why, they ask, when a seemingly endless supply of information can be accessed from the computer on one's desk, on one's lap, or in one's pocket, do we need a separate space filled with books and computers?

OK, true confession time. I don't blame anyone for increasingly using the Internet rather than libraries. I'm doing it myself, despite the fact I am a big fan of libraries of all kinds and my livelihood depends in large part on their continued existence. For example, I recently saved a very short walk from my office to our lovely high school library to obtain a copy of an R. L. Stevenson short story by finding it in about three minutes on the web and printing it out. My own son as a student deemed anything not on the Internet not worth knowing and was a stranger to both his school and public library. According to most studies on the "Net Generation," his attitude toward information is not atypical. People of all ages are simply finding it is really, really handy to have one's information needs met right at their desks or in their homes.

Yet, I have no doubt that many libraries *and* librarians will evolve and survive despite the increasing use of the Internet to fulfill needs those libraries and librarians previously met. The libraries that will continue to thrive will be those which meet *real* needs that *cannot* be met by the Internet (or bookstores or classrooms). Our profession should be defining, discovering, and emphasizing those needs in the current budgetary and political climate.

There are a number of physical businesses and institutions that might have felt just as threatened by the public's increased use of the Internet: bookstores, travel agents, public libraries, and banks, just to name a few. Even virtual schools are now taking the place of brick and mortar buildings for many students. Can we learn from the savvier among these institutions how to escape being replaced by the Internet?

Unfortunately, I've known librarians whose primary goal is to *reduce* the number of students using their programs. The availability of online resources makes accomplishing such a goal quite achievable. But unused libraries don't require staffing. The librarian who truly serves today's students works on interpersonal skills as well as technical skills and designs programs that recognize and honor their NetGen learning preferences. Studies of Net Generation students (Oblinger and Oblinger 2005) suggest ways to increase our value to students.

And even more strategically, can we begin to tailor our programs, policies, and facilities to meet the needs of a new generation of learners? Here are seven ways we can remain relevant to our students and staff.

1. Remaining the information experts

Both the addition of new technology resources and the continuous changes in existing ones makes locating and using information increasingly challenging. The librarian's role as "information expert" for students is more important than ever. Helping today's students select the right search tool, build effective search strategies, and determine the relevance of found information is a primary job of the librarian and probably the most important reason for libraries' continued existence. Helping students take the time to analyze the quality of the information despite their desire for rapid responses and reluctance to reflect is even more important.

Joyce Valenza (Valenza 2004) writes about the complexities in both the attitudes and behaviors of effective searchers including:

- Knowing what he or she is looking for and having a plan
- Realizing he or she has search choices
- Knowing basic strategies for evaluating sources
- Knowing about advanced search screens
- Knowing when quality matters
- Having mind tools for organizing materials
- Recognizing the need for an information professional

Our students may be adept at pushing buttons, but the librarian teaches them to be purposeful and effective while doing so.

2. Supporting an active style of learning

The librarian's work with students on problem-based research assignments is a natural fit for this preferred style of learning. Helping kids learn "how to learn" by finding information and putting it to use is the antithesis of the "rote, restraint, regurgitation" methodology that is the mainstay of too many classrooms. An increased emphasis on primary sources—original surveys, interviews, experiments, and source documents—gives students a chance to use their inductive reasoning skills. And using technology to both find and present information is very much an active, hands-on, applied experience.

3. Valuing information presented visually rather than textually

The acquisition and promotion of both picture books for younger students and graphic novels for older ones is a given in libraries. And while the current generation of educators may learn best verbally and do (rightfully) value print resources, the libraries responding to today's students provide information in a wide variety of formats including both analog and digital video, pictorial and aural resources, and the technologies through which such resources can be viewed or heard. The librarian also recognizes that this generation of Ken Burns–wannabes enjoys communicating visually as well. Librarians must help teach students how to take and edit digital photographs, create digital movies, create multimedia presentations, and serve as the visual literacy experts in our schools, teaching students how to critically examine visual information.

4. Creating personal learning experiences

For many students, research of primarily academic interest (literary criticism, historical research, non-applied science investigation) is seen as irrelevant and unimportant. But it is not just academically oriented kids who need good information and problem-solving skills—all learners need these skills to meet both vocational and personal needs. The library program and its resources have long been a resource for students seeking information for personal, day-to-day needs. The same student reluctant to research an aspect of the Civil War willingly practices information problem-solving skills to figure out the best video game to buy. The librarian finds ways to combine academic assignments and personal interests to reach all students. A student who is interested in hunting may get excited about comparing the firearms used by the North and South in the Civil War if guided by a skillful librarian, hopefully in collaboration with the classroom teacher.

5. Providing a place for collaborative work groups

The librarian fosters student collaboration both online and in the library. The days of the shushing librarian are over. While librarians still work to maintain a physical environment that is conducive to learning, they recognize that conversations are the stuff of genuine involvement and provide the tables, conference rooms, and labs where those conversations can take place. The librarian helps make available and teaches students to use collaborative tools such as wikis, discussion groups, and blogs.

6. Recognizing and honoring students' need for instant gratification

By working both in the virtual and physical world, the librarian helps meet today's students' "any-time learning" needs. Today's students (and an increasing number of adults) tend to be impatient and want to be able to learn outside of school. Librarians are, of course, available during school hours and can help students with questions then, but they can do "virtual" reference as well by providing their e-mail addresses or using social networking tools and responding to questions electronically (perhaps with a disclaimer about an approximate turnaround time). The librarian facilitates timely interlibrary loan of information contained only in physical formats—and teaches the skills needed to access the library collections that contain them.

7. Creating a welcoming and safe environment

Not all students are comfortable in our classrooms and hallways. Bored in classes, intimidated in common areas, these kids need a place where they are welcome, safe, and valued. The library above all else creates a program that serves students who are diverse—socially, economically, culturally, and academically.

A frightful quote was given in a Pew study by a middle school student: "The Internet is like a librarian without the bad attitude or breath" (Arafeh 2002). But if the library provides resources, facilities, and learning opportunities that are uniquely suited to the Net Generation and has a genuine appreciation for their unique attributes and talents, it will be valued in return by this "next greatest" generation. And this in turn is a good thing for the profession as these students become parents, teachers, school board members, and legislators themselves.

Do school librarians have "enduring values"?

On some positions, Cowardice asks the question, "Is it safe?" Expediency asks the question, "Is it politic?" And Vanity comes along and asks the question, "Is it popular?" But Conscience asks the question "Is it right?" And there comes a time when one must take a position that is neither safe, nor politic, nor popular, but he must do it because Conscience tells him it is right.
—Martin Luther King, Jr.

Before you continue reading this book on managing an effective school library program, it's only fair to ask if libraries, library programs, and librarians will be around long enough to make such a reading worth your time. Quite frankly, it's a difficult but extremely important question. And my answer is definitely yes . . .

If.

We already know we need to adapt to changes in technology. We already know we need to be more accountable about the impact of our programs. We already know that we will need to spend time on effective advocacy and developing broad ownership of the library program. We know that our physical facilities will evolve, our areas of expertise are changing, and our libraries' services may be different each year.

So a second question then comes up: Will our libraries be so changed from what we now consider libraries, will they still continue to be called libraries? And my answer is definitely yes . . .

If, we maintain the core values that will transcend the specifics of library programming.

Just as technology was starting to have a major impact on libraries, longtime academic librarian and past ALA president Michael Gorman identified these as enduring central or "core" values of librarianship (Gorman 2000):

1. Stewardship
2. Service
3. Intellectual Freedom
4. Rationalism
5. Literacy and learning
6. Equity of access to recorded knowledge and information
7. Privacy
8. Democracy

Are these core values still held by practicing *school* librarians? Are there other common central beliefs that define us as librarians? When I describe my own professional core values as a librarian, I include:

1. Every child should have access to as diverse a number of opinions as possible and be allowed to draw his or her own personal conclusions about the world. The library program's primary educational role is teaching children to think critically, not simply to memorize or believe.
2. Every child's interests, learning style, and abilities should be respected. Skills are best taught in a personal context.

3. Every child's preference in information format should be respected, both as an information consumer and producer. Information in all formats should be treated equally.
4. Every child's privacy must be honored and protected. It is our role to help children protect their own privacy.
5. The ability to find, evaluate, organize, synthesize, and communicate information is a basic skill for every child.
6. Reading skills are best developed through voluntary free reading on topics of personal interest to students. Students must be intrinsically motivated to read and to learn.
7. Every child should have access to a place in a school where he or she is comfortable, valued, safe, and can learn with other students.
8. Every child must be taught the skills and sensibilities of digital citizenship.
9. The library's primary function is to be of service to children—directly and indirectly through other educational programs and working with other building professionals. Our success is a reflection of how successful we make others.
10. The skills taught and resources provided by the library program are critical to a free society.

As some schools replace librarians with clerks or "technology integration specialists"—or no one at all—my greatest concern is that these values will be lost. Who will fight for information access for all students? Who will fight for intellectual freedom? Who will be concerned about the privacy rights of students and faculty? Who will insist that information literacy is the right of every child?

Now and in the future, the physical room, the title of the person running it, or the kinds of resources provided will not matter. I will know I am in a library by what it values.

Sample professional mission statement and the elevator speech

My mission is to empower all my community's learners by teaching them the skills needed to use information, technology, and ideas to creatively and effectively answer questions and solve problems—both academic and personal, and by providing the resources needed to teach those skills.

> "If all my students are not learning to their potential, I have an ethical responsibility as an educator to create purposeful change."
> —Doug Johnson

The Mankato transition: A case study

In the fall of 1990, a school accreditation team wrote that a serious limitation of Mankato (Minnesota) Public Schools' media program was that "the present structure of separate library and audiovisual departments is not consistent with the current philosophy of providing a unified resource for students and teachers." I was hired a year later and given the charge to address the limitation, and to incorporate the computer program into the library/audiovisual mix as well.

Less than a month after I started the job, a dozen rather anxious librarians came to the newly renamed District Media and Technology Services offices. At that meeting I handed everyone a new computer and explained that it was my goal that each would be the technology "expert" in his or her building, and that technology included computers. "*You* should be the first person your teachers think of for help when they have a question about technology." We then started to learn how to use, hands-on, these scary devices.

"This transformation should take about six months," I thought. At the end of the first computer in-service, one librarian asked quite sincerely if he could please just have the money the computer cost so he could buy more picture books. I revised my timeline—maybe this was going to take more like a full year.

As it turns out, I've been the District Media and Technology Director for twenty years, and I don't know if the district has totally combined its library and technology programs into a "unified resource" or not, but we have come a long way. Here are some things we've done to create a modern library program in the district and some advice for other districts that are attempting to create similar programs.

Actions

Much to the delight of our parents, our building libraries are physically becoming true "learning centers." Wiring and space have been designed to accommodate banks of student research computer stations in all facilities. This has had to be a rather creative endeavor in our smallest libraries that were already cramped and seemingly wired before architects were 100 percent sure that electricity was here to stay. We moved computer labs in or adjacent to the main library area so the librarian can help supervise and teach computer-assisted information skills. The back rooms of our libraries have become wiring closets and equipment rooms that hold the file servers, equipment racks, punchdown blocks, switches, and technician workspaces. When we rolled out wireless Internet connectivity, we started in our libraries.

We of course automated all our library catalogs and circulation systems. These are now completely online, ubiquitously accessible, and remotely hosted to reduce maintenance. Our library systems automatically update patron records from our student information system. Our catalog also allows students to "tag" resources and add reviews.

We've become the go-to place for students and staff for using GoogleApps for Education, which provides e-mail, calendars, productivity programs, and file storage space to everyone in the district. We continue to provide vetted commercial information resources to our schools through online encyclopedias, full-text databases, and streaming video services. Our librarians are committed to keeping the library the informational heart of the school, even as networked classrooms (and networked students) make the entire school a "virtual library."

Our computer resources are used as much to help students produce information as to find it. If you want to make and edit a video, improve the quality of a digital photograph, learn to use our classroom management system (Moodle), record and share a podcast, or use a wiki to organize your research, the library is the place to do so.

Our library classrooms are the first places new classroom technologies are installed, including interactive whiteboards, student response systems, and audio amplification systems, allowing all staff to try these new gadgets out. The library is the home for our carts of laptops and tablets, digital cameras, and other shared technologies.

Buying "things" isn't much of an accomplishment, and the most sophisticated pieces of equipment in the world are just expensive paperweights until teachers and students can use them effectively. This influx of technology into the classroom and library has resulted in Mankato Schools redefining the role of the building librarian.

Before merging the library and technology programs, the librarians in our district had either a traditional print or audiovisual role, and saw little role for themselves in the technology program of the school beyond having an automated circulation system and electronic library catalog. So one of the first (and most continuous) jobs I have undertaken as the library department chair has been to help my librarians see themselves in an expanded role: as a resource for teachers and students who need help with technology and digital resources, as well as print materials. There is an acute, growing need for technology experts in schools. Teachers and students alike need a resource person to help them learn to effectively use and integrate networked resources. The need, in fact, is so great that schools will find this kind of resource person in one way or another. My vision has been to make the librarian that resource in our buildings.

So how did we begin this metamorphosis? Discussion, access, training, role models, and time are all playing a part:

- We have continuous discussions centering around our role in the school—who we are, where we are, and what we want to become. We are creating a common vision of what a Mankato School librarian should be and do. Much of this has happened as a result of librarians playing an essential part in writing the district's media/technology plan. Although the plan has been revised many times by teams of parents, administrators, and teachers, the library's role is clearly articulated in its philosophies and goals.
- Formal in-services for librarians are regularly scheduled. The model we use is a half-day meeting six times a year. Using a "train the trainer" model students and staff come to us for nearly every technology skill training need. Librarians offer regular after-school training on specific tools and resources and participate in district-wide technology staff development efforts. All librarians have an up-to-date portable computer to use when and where they chose.
- Librarians meet in their own Profession Learning Communities on a monthly basis to design and improve our technology skill curriculum at both the elementary and secondary levels. We have some of the best articulated Essential Learner Outcomes and assessments in the district's curriculum.
- Strong technology skills are a requirement when we hire new librarians. (As is a love of reading and knowledge of children's literature, of course.)
- Librarians play a vital role on the district's technology advisory committee, and they meet regularly for conversations and planning with building technicians and district technology managers.
- Librarians regularly attend technology conferences and the technology strands of library conferences.
- Teachers, administrators, and parents are made aware of the changing roles of their librarians through librarian participation on building leadership teams, in-services, presentations at staff and PTA meetings, and articles in building and parent newsletters. Principals and parents are keenly aware of the value of a technologically adept librarian to the educational program.
- We have developed, I believe, an esprit de corps. We have regular socials for all district and building library staff. Our half-day meetings are usually accompanied by an optional meal at a local restaurant. These informal get-togethers help us to develop our group identity as we grow prouder of who we are and what we do.

Hindsight

If your district doesn't already have a combined library/technology program (and it should), I would suggest that the following criteria are vital:

1. Make a single, administrative level person responsible for the change. Make sure that this person has a clear but flexible vision of what the program will eventually look like, and can vividly describe that future to others. Make sure that the person has a background in both libraries and

technology. Ask for at least yearly goals and a report of progress toward those goals, looking for steady progress rather than overnight miracles. Change needs a person in charge and accountable. Librarians must know that that person is their advocate in administrative circles, appreciates their contributions to the schools, shares their feelings about children and books, and genuinely likes and respects them as people.

2. We have found that professional librarians bring critical skills and philosophies to an integrated technology program. They are trained in the selection of materials, including digital resources, and in organizing, evaluating, and promoting those materials. Librarians are the building experts in intellectual freedom and censorship issues that will center increasingly around digital resources. They already know the effectiveness of skill integration into classroom content areas. Librarians take a "school view" of resource allocation, which is especially important in schools where computers and other technologies may have been held hostage by individuals or departments. Strong leadership by a school librarian can keep technology use from being only drill and practice or passive viewing. And remember that the traditional librarian brings a love and understanding of literature in various media and knows how it can address the affective side of the learning process. It is for these reasons that the head of library/technology services should be a librarian as well.

3. Do not underestimate the time and energy needed for librarian training in technology skills. Do not expect librarians (or anyone else for that matter) to learn on their own. Administrators must be informed that our profession is changing more rapidly than any other in the school, and therefore has exceptional in-service needs.

4. The effect of change on people and institutions needs to be studied by the administrator in charge. The losses and gains that go with change need to be discussed and understood by those being affected by it. We needed to both celebrate getting the new electronic catalog running, and take time to mourn a bit the passing of the wooden box of drawers and rods. Getting a full-text magazine database meant giving up favorite *Readers' Guide* lessons carefully constructed over the years. A new skill in the curriculum might mean a favorite story taken out. I personally wish I had taken more time to acknowledge and honor the good of the past traditional library program in our district.

5. Individuals and their contributions to the program need to be recognized throughout the transition process. In no other school program does success or failure, effectiveness or ineffectiveness, depend so completely on personnel as it does in the library program. Because of this, change must be transformational rather than transactional. In other words, the difference in people and program cannot be in actions and activities alone; the difference must be rooted in self-perception, philosophy, and mission. I like to believe that increased feelings of worth and importance and job satisfaction are the prime motivation for all librarians changing not just what they do, but who they are. The best changes are those that benefit both the institution and the librarian. They are the ones that will be of long-term benefit to our children.

I am not always a patient person. I know that my librarians and I both become frustrated and maybe a little frightened when I ask them to accept new roles and responsibilities, and they are not immediately en-thusiastic. And even I admit, my ideas usually mean more work for all of us. But my impatience comes from knowing that the mission of a true library program—to ensure that students and staff are effective users of ideas and information—cannot be carried out effectively if it is divided into separate library and technology programs. And we continue to evolve.

For reflection: Why are you in the profession?

At the turn of the century, this country had lots of blacksmiths. Some stayed employed and some didn't. Why? If you asked the soon-to-be-unemployed blacksmiths why they were in the business, they'd have said, "Because I like horses." If you asked the other blacksmiths, those who stayed viable in their changing environment, the same question, they probably said, "Because I like helping people get from place to place."

When the first "horseless carriage" came along, those with the transportation mission fixed wheels, banged out fenders, and even tinkered under the hood. They remained transportation specialists.

Ask yourself the same question: Why am I in the business? "Because I like books and quiet places" is the wrong answer. I hope you said, "Because I like teaching people how to find, evaluate, use, and communicate information."

As technology fills our schools, you're probably helping kids do targeted searches, bang out reports with wikis, and even work collaboratively online. The tools we use have changed; our mission has not.

References

Arafeh, Sousan, Doug Levin, Lee Rainie, and Amanda Lenhart. "The Digital Disconnect: The Widening Gap between Internet-Savvy Students and Their Schools." Pew Internet and American Life Project, 2002.

Gorman, Michael. *Our Enduring Values: Librarianship in the 21st Century*. Chicago: American Library Association, 2000.

Oblinger, Diane, and James Oblinger. *Educating the Net Generation*. Boulder, CO: EDUCAUSE, 2005.

Valenza, Joyce. "Substantive Searching: Thinking and Behaving Info-Fluently." *Leading & Learning with Technology*, November 2004.

Valenza, Joyce, and Doug Johnson. "Things That Keep Us Awake at Night." *School Library Journal*, October 2009.

Chapter Two

Program Assessment

Creating long-term change

Will you be facing the same problems—lack of funding, understaffing, job insecurity, poor physical facilities—five years from now that you do today? It's a depressing thought.

When working in the trenches, some situations seem insurmountable. Dismal educational funding, teach-to-the-test curricula, programs that show small regard for the intrinsic value of reading, and insular classrooms look like immovable objects in many schools—perhaps yours.

You can be the irresistible force that can make permanent, positive change in both your library program and your school. Wishful thinking, deus ex machina state program or staffing mandates, or simply doing what you've always done and expecting different results (Einstein's definition of insanity) won't create these changes, however.

Actively engaging in ongoing evaluations, collaborative goal setting, and deliberate reporting can. Long-term change has three essential elements:

- Assessing your program
- Developing long-term goals and annual objectives
- Reporting how well your goals and objectives have been met

We'll look at each element in the next chapters, but before we do, I am going to stop here and offer a warning. The tasks in these next chapters: Program Assessment, Planning, and Communications and Advocacy will be a challenge for every librarian. Why?

The table below is my adaptation of Steven Covey's time management matrix in his book *The 7 Habits of Highly Effective People* (Covey 1989) that helps me understand why creating long-term change is difficult.

Table 2-1
Covey's time management matrix

	Urgent	Not Urgent
Important	Quadrant I • Dealing with crises • Solving pressing problems • Completing deadline driven tasks	Quadrant II • Preventing • Assessing/planning/reporting • Building relationships
Not Important	Quadrant III • Handling interruptions • Answering some mail and completing some reports • Attending some meetings	Quadrant IV • Working on trivia or doing busy work • Wasting time on non-job tasks • Procrastinating

None of the specific things people need to do to create change are very difficult. But what *is* difficult is finding the time to do them—planning, reporting, assessing, and relationship building.

Covey advises that the only way to make more time for Quadrant II activities—those that lead to long-term change and a reduction of Quadrant I tasks—is to find Quadrant III and Quadrant IV activities to eliminate. He also states that the more time one spends on things like planning and relationship building, the number of emergency, unscheduled tasks in Quadrant I goes down. (Might planning with teachers on units result in fewer surprise library visits by classes?)

This is the only time management strategy I've found that makes much sense. Try listing the Quadrant III and IV things *you* do. Yes, you have them. Everyone does. These are tasks that someone else could do, that can be automated, that may matter only to you and no one else. Now trying cutting back on them and use the time for the important, but not urgent, tasks you'll encounter in these next three chapters. Schedule even thirty minutes a day to complete activities that are "important but not urgent." You *will* see the results.

How will you show your program is impacting student achievement?

At an interview for a new high school librarian in our district, the stumper question was: How will you demonstrate that the library program is having a positive impact on student achievement in our school?

How did that tricky little question get in there with "Tell us a little about yourself" and "Describe a successful lesson you've taught"? Now *those* questions most of us could answer with one frontal lobe tied behind our cerebellum.

Given the increased emphasis on accountability and data-driven practices, it's a question all of us in education need to be ready to answer—even if we are not looking for a new job or don't want to be in the position of needing to look for one.

While I would never have been quick enough to have said this without knowing the question was coming, the best response to the question might have been another question: "How does your school measure student achievement now?"

If the answer was simply, "Our school measures student achievement by standardized or state test scores," I would then reply, "There *is* an empirical way of determining whether the library program is having an impact on such scores, but I don't think you'd really want to run such a study. Here's why:

- Are you willing to have a significant portion of your students and teachers go without library services and resources as part of a control group?
- Are you willing to wait three to four years for reliable longitudinal data?
- Are you willing to measure only those students who are here their entire educational careers?
- Are you willing to change nothing else in the school to eliminate all other factors that might influence test scores?
- Will the groups we analyze be large enough to be considered statistically significant?
- Are you willing to provide the statistical and research expertise needed to make the study valid?

No school I know of has the will to run such a study.

If the interviewer's answer to the question "How does your school measure student achievement?" was more complex ("Our school looks at a variety of variables that indicate learning and student success such as the successful completion of rigorous course work, authentically assessed mastery of problem-solving skills, reports of postsecondary success by graduates, successful participation in extracurricular activities, high graduation rates, and alumni and employer satisfaction surveys."), then my response could not have been so flip.

But the question, although tricky, is a fair one to ask. Administrators, teachers, parents, and taxpayers deserve accountability from every program that uses the finite resources available to their schools. And good library programs aren't inexpensive. Every thoughtful person should want to be getting the most bang for his or her educational buck.

Why assess your program?

It is difficult if not impossible to statistically casually link library programs to student test score performance, but that doesn't let us off the hook for accountability. We owe it to our students, fellow professional educators, parents, and taxpayers to in some ways measure the impact of the library program.

The primary means of doing this is through meaningful assessment, taking a hard look at what we are doing.

Yet, traditional program assessments generally cause far too much stress for school librarians. Formal evaluations nearly always mean hours of work, sometimes result in undeserved criticism publicly stated and, far too often, do not result in any positive change. Is it any wonder many of us shudder when we hear, "Your program is under review this year"? And it often seems we just don't know how to do meaningful ongoing assessments or have the time and resources to do them.

After having participated as both the victim and perpetrator of about a dozen library and technology program evaluations, I strongly believe these things:

1. Program evaluations do not need to be long, tortuous, stultifying ordeals. By collecting and interpreting only meaningful data, the process can be not just painless, but interesting and possibly even fun.
2. Program evaluations should only exist as tools that will help us increase our budgets, improve our working conditions, and make our programs essential to our students' learning. An effective program evaluation used as a starting point for long-range planning is the *only* thing that can improve a school's library program significantly and permanently.
3. Program assessments can be used to help establish a link between the library program and school success if the assessment is directly related to whole-school goals.

The traditional method of library program assessment follows a pattern set by many school accreditation organizations. And while I hope many of us conduct comprehensive efforts like this, given the rate of change in education, ongoing assessments are now critical and just as meaningful.

Here are some ideas about doing both effective formal and ongoing library program assessments.

The formal library assessment

The purpose of a formal program evaluation is to help improve the school library and technology program, resulting in a more effective total school program. Like it or not, school library programs have changed since most community members, parents, and school staff were in school themselves. The addition of new technologies, the increased importance of information literacy skills, and the demand that all students show proficiency in basic skills through standardized testing have changed the role of the library from a quiet place for study run by a teacher who was unable to cope in a classroom to a dynamic combination of programs and resources that can genuinely improve educational opportunities for all students directed by a team of cutting-edge educators.

The end results of a program review should include:

- Assessment of the current status of district library program
- Agreement on long-term goals based on recognized standards and building/district needs
- Establishment of short-term objectives that help meet those goals
- Development of a formal method for reporting the attainment of those goals and objectives
- Assessment of the program as a part of the library librarian's professional evaluation

A team approach to evaluation

Library program assessment is most effective when the librarians, building principals, and district personnel all share the responsibility for it. The team needs to recognize and approve of all elements of the evaluation process if that process is to lead to genuine improvement. The team should include not just librarians, but administrators, teachers, technology specialists, parents, and possibly students as well. All members of the assessment team need to be identified and their roles and responsibilities clearly identified. As part of the assessment process, an outside consultant may be brought in to help determine the validity of the findings and recommendations of the community-based committee.

The team leader is ideally the administrator in the district in charge of library and technology programs. It is this individual's job to organize the team, help it identify its goals, facilitate the visit of the outside evaluator, and see that the final report is completed. If the district does not have an administrator in such a position, an experienced librarian given release time or additional compensation makes an excellent team leader.

Timeline

A complete study of a district's library program should allow time for planning, distribution, return and analysis of surveys; compilation of the written self-study; a visit by an outside evaluator; a report to the school board; and a follow-up action plan. My experience is that the process can take up to a full year. Here is a timeline I have used in the past:

September	Selection of study committee and its leader
October	Organization of meetings to determination of goals of study review and to review professional library standards
	Design or modification of surveys
November	Distribution of surveys
	Meetings of librarians to complete standards rubrics
	Collection of inventory information
December	Collection of surveys and compilation of findings
January	Analysis of data from surveys and draft of program strengths, concerns, and actions
	Writing a draft of the self-study
February	Review of self-study draft by stakeholders

March	Site visit by outside evaluator
April	Report from evaluator reviewed and accepted
May	Presentation of consultant report and self-study plan to board and administrative team
Summer	Writing of action plan or goals and objectives written based on assessment

Data gathering

Multiple data sets will improve the reliability of the assessment, as well as its credibility in the eyes of others who read it. Here are some tools that can be used to obtain reliable data about the library program.

Evaluation rubrics tied to external standards

Happily, there are a number of tools based on state and national standards that provide a guide for assessing school library programs. These guides, checklists, and rubrics offer a description of the services of an effective library. The rubric-like organization of some of these guides can provide a growth path for all libraries regardless of their current level. Check to see if your state has specific guidelines for school library programs. The American Association of School Librarians (AASL) publishes program standards that are regularly updated if your state does not have such a document. If your school is a member of an accreditation organization, see what that organization has for library evaluation tools.

An important use of such an assessment tool is to determine the current state of a building or district's library program compared to what experts agree an effective library program looks like. The assessment team should have the opportunity to discuss the assessment tools prior to completing them for their own buildings so that common understandings of terms can be agreed upon and any questions clarified. For example, when the tool asks for the number of books in the collection, is that the number of individual titles or the number of individual volumes?

Most of these assessment tools have more areas that can be measured than are practical to deal with in a single year or even longer improvement cycle. It's extremely important that the librarian, principal, and building staff use their own building goals to help them select a few key areas for focused improvements. One way to determine which areas should be the focus of the evaluation is to consider specific content area, building, and district educational goals. This approach helps make the library program a vital part of the entire school program—and makes us accountable for adding educational value.

Surveys and focus groups

An important source of information about the library program comes from the patrons it serves. Short, easily understood surveys specially designed for parents, students, teachers, and principals should be given to a random sample of these groups in every building. Online surveys are easy to distribute and result in a higher percentage of survey returns from parents, and return data in easily interpreted digital forms. Student surveys can be completed during visits to the library. All survey responses should be anonymous in order to get more accurate findings.

Here is an example of a short library program survey. A 1 to 5 Likert scale rating is used for items 1–12. Consider adding an "I don't know" response to each question that may indicate a need for better communication efforts.

Parents Survey Questions

1. I have a means of helping determine what activities, policies, and materials are parts of the library program.

Strongly Disagree	Disagree	Neither	Agree	Strongly agree
1	2	3	4	5

2. The librarian regularly communicates with parents about activities and resources using a variety of methods.

Strongly Disagree	Disagree	Neither	Agree	Strongly agree
1	2	3	4	5

3. The collection of books, audiovisual materials, computer software, online resources, and equipment is adequate to meet my child's needs.

Strongly Disagree	Disagree	Neither	Agree	Strongly agree
1	2	3	4	5

4. Resources for the library are carefully chosen to reflect curriculum and student needs, and the resources are of high quality.

Strongly Disagree	Disagree	Neither	Agree	Strongly agree
1	2	3	4	5

5. The resources in the library are easy to locate, readily accessible, well-maintained, and up-to-date.

Strongly Disagree	Disagree	Neither	Agree	Strongly agree
1	2	3	4	5

6. The skills being taught in the library are important and are an integrated part of the total school program.

Strongly Disagree	Disagree	Neither	Agree	Strongly agree
1	2	3	4	5

7. The library is adequately available for my child's use.

Strongly Disagree	Disagree	Neither	Agree	Strongly agree
1	2	3	4	5

8. The librarian provides help and answers questions when my child or I request them.

Strongly Disagree	Disagree	Neither	Agree	Strongly agree
1	2	3	4	5

9. The library is staffed so that its resources can be fully utilized by my child.

Strongly Disagree	Disagree	Neither	Agree	Strongly agree
1	2	3	4	5

10. My child and I feel welcome and comfortable in the library.

Strongly Disagree	Disagree	Neither	Agree	Strongly agree
1	2	3	4	5

11. The library is orderly and purposeful, allowing my child to accomplish his/her learning tasks.

Strongly Disagree	Disagree	Neither	Agree	Strongly agree
1	2	3	4	5

12. Technology is being taught and used in the library to improve student access to information.

Strongly Disagree	Disagree	Neither	Agree	Strongly agree
1	2	3	4	5

13. Please list the best characteristic(s) of your school's library program.

14. Please list the way(s) the library program could be improved to better serve you and your students.

15. Other comments or observations.

While this is a generic survey, targeted surveys asking more specific questions can be used. The same questions, properly written, should be designed for students, teachers, administrators, and parents for a more complete picture.

Focus groups

Focus groups of students, teachers, and/or parents can also provide good data. Discussions using a survey as a means of guiding the discussion along with a good recorder taking notes can result in richer, more complete observations and comments than written surveys alone. Holding such meetings on a regular basis is also a way to meaningfully engage with parents and teachers—and get them into the library.

Counting things

It is important to have a good inventory of the resources that make up the library program. These resources include personnel, print materials, budgets, and technology. Simple spreadsheets that allow quick analysis of data such as professionals per student are a good way to report such data.

One of the more difficult parts of completing an inventory is agreeing on what and how things should be counted. Should all computers be counted or just the ones that are less than five years old? A building that counts all its old computers that may be running keyboarding programs may show a significantly higher computer to student ratio than one that only counts the multimedia, networked computers. A library collection that counts each copy of a book will show a higher book to student ratio than one that only counts each title of its collection. The study team can choose whatever criteria it would like to count items, but the criteria should be as consistent as possible throughout the study and clearly identified in the findings.

You may have noticed that some tools may count technologies throughout the building rather than just those found in libraries. Our district has a combined library and technology department, and so when evaluating one we evaluate both. Use the counting tools that best suit your own organizational structure.

Data analysis

The purpose of gathering data, of course, is to help identify both the strong and weak areas of the library program. While we usually dwell on the areas we know need work, it's also important that we use program evaluation to highlight our strengths and successes. My experience has been that a district will fund programs it knows to be successful and popular.

Weaknesses (or concerns) should be used to help develop a long-range plan for improvement. Identifying recommendations for improving stated areas of weakness are the final step in the data analysis process.

The data gathered by the surveys, inventories, and rubrics should be carefully tabulated and examined for patterns that indicate a high degree of agreement in particular areas. Anecdotal comments from surveys and focus groups can powerfully illustrate points that cold numbers only suggest.

The kernel of the program evaluation report is the identification of the strengths, weakness, and recommendations for improvement with each of these areas supported by empirical or anecdotal evidence found elsewhere in the report.

Data analysis, at least to me, is as much an art as it is a science. For most of us, good empirical or anecdotal evidence will support the gut-level knowledge that we already have about our programs. We may sense that our libraries are too small. We may feel that there is better student technology access at the secondary level than at the elementary level. We may believe that our collections have aged as a result of inadequate funding. These are all things we can *demonstrate* to decision makers through strong evidence.

But I also hope that by keeping open minds and a spirit of genuine inquiry, the self-study team members will also look for trends, patterns, and problems that may be less apparent. For example if students, parents, and teachers consistently rate library climate as a concern, we should be willing to consider the reasons for those ratings even if they may seem critical or opposite the view of the library professionals. Such evidence can help make genuine improvements to the quality of the library program and the entire school.

The outside consultant

Should a district hire a consultant from outside the district to help evaluate its library program? Since I have at times served as a consultant myself, you need to know that my advice may be somewhat self-serving. But here it is anyway . . .

There are a number of good reasons *not* to hire a consultant to help in the evaluation process:

- Good consultants may be expensive. *(An alternative to a hired gun is to have a reciprocal agreement with another district to trade external evaluators. The North Central Association uses volunteer evaluators from member schools. These folks know they in turn will get volunteers when they are evaluated.)*
- Consultants may not understand the culture, philosophy, and goals of the district.
- Consultants may come to the evaluation with a set of prejudices not in keeping with district philosophy.
- Consultants may not come from recent practice in the field.
- Consultants can only discover a limited amount of information during a site visit. One or two conversations or experiences may play too important a factor in the consultant's final recommendations.

Other than that, we are charming and lovable people and can add value to the evaluation process:

- Consultants can bring a sense of objectivity to the evaluation.
- Consultants can bring expertise in building good programs to the district.
- Consultants can lend credibility and validity to the work done by the district evaluation team if the administrative team and school board regard them as impartial and expert.

- Consultants can bring knowledge of current best practice and future trends in the field, and may have knowledge of what other schools are doing that is innovative and effective.

If you want to get the most value from a consultant:

- Spell out exactly what result you expect from his/her involvement. (What questions do you want the consultant to help you answer? Do you want a site visit, written report, follow-up, etc.? What is the agreed-upon timeline for completion of the work?)
- Have good information for the consultant to use. Inventories, survey results, etc., should be done prior to his/her involvement. (A good consultant should be able to provide sources for good evaluative tools.) The consultant should only be analyzing the data and making recommendations, not gathering it.
- Get recommendations from others who have used the consultant. Ask about his or her communication skills, timeliness, reliability, and the usability of the consultant's product.
- Hire someone with credibility and recent experience in the library field.

When I visit a district as a program evaluator, my main objective is to help the head of the library/technology department get across whatever message he or she needs to have the administration and school board hear. Most people for whom I have worked have a very realistic picture of the strengths and weaknesses of their programs, but as the "expert from over 75 miles away," I have credibility that may be more carefully regarded.

I also attempt to answer genuine questions these folks might have: Why are more classes not using technology for research purposes? To what extent do our physical facilities help or hinder our library programs? How might we better use the computers we have in our elementary schools? Do our resources, print and electronic, meet the needs of our students and staff? How can we better allocate our library and technology dollars?

The main point here is that the better the district knows what it wants from an outside consultant evaluator, the better that person is able to provide it. And this leaves everyone satisfied and the district with useful information that can be used to improve.

The written report

The written report as indicated earlier has at its heart the findings of strengths and weakness of the program, recommendations for improvement, and the data used to draw those conclusions.

In order to place the recommendations and data in context for an audience who may not be familiar with the school district, an effective report may need additional information. This information may include demographic information about the district and copies of the district's technology plan, library curriculum, organization chart, and library policy manual.

This document can make the difference between getting a meaningful evaluation by an outside consultant and wasting your district's money. Most outside evaluators can visit a district for a short time and spend very little time in individual buildings. When I visit a district for the purpose of helping evaluate its library/technology program, I rely heavily on documents, especially the self-study, for specific things I want to look at.

The final report will consist of the self-study and, if used, the consultant's report that validates the self-study and may add additional observations, comments, and recommendations.

Can a report be too long? Absolutely. The body of the report should be short with as much data as possible placed in a separate document of attachments.

Sharing the findings

There isn't much sense in spending time, money, and effort on doing a program evaluation only to have its results sit in a drawer of the superintendent's desk. The results of any program evaluation effort should be disseminated as widely as possible.

Copies of the **full written report** should be given to the administrative team, school board, district library/technology advisory committee members, and members of any building-level library/technology advisory team. A copy of the report available on the district's website allows any interested individual access to it.

An **oral presentation summarizing the findings** of the evaluation should be presented at a regular school board meeting, at the district library/technology advisory committee, and at building staff meetings.

A **one-page executive summary** should be shared with all district staff members. Many administrators and teachers who might ignore the longer document may well read this.

The head of the evaluation committee or the school's public relations department should write a **news release** about the study. This release should be written so that buildings can customize it for publication in their parent newsletters.

As library/technology director, I would also offer to present the findings at the meetings of local service organizations such as Rotary, Kiwanis, or Lions. Members of these organizations are often powerful opinion leaders in the community and they appreciate interesting programs for their meetings.

Follow-up

Good assessment tools are not used to simply evaluate work at the end of a given time period. They should serve as a guide and reminder for day-to-day activities. Regular conferences with the principal and/ or building library committee have always helped force me into working on objectives throughout the year rather letting my natural sense of procrastination convince me to set them aside until May. Progress toward long-term goals based on the needs outlined through a formal program assessment can guide the discussion at such conferences.

If library goals truly support the building goals, then everyone who has responsibility for achieving building goals should be apprised of if and how well they have been met. As a part of a staff meeting or as a distributed written report, the librarian needs to say, "Yes, this, this, and this were accomplished; this is nearly done; and this did not happen because . . ." It's called accountability.

Once general goals are established and recommendations made, the hard work of identifying specific objectives that will help meet those goals must be articulated (see chapter three for more details).

The cumulative effect of developing long-range goals and yearly objectives then is that by the time another formal program evaluation is conducted, the weaknesses identified in the previous study have been effectively addressed.

Ongoing assessments

One of my favorite quotes comes from George Bernard Shaw: "We should all be obliged to appear before a board every five years and justify our existence . . . on pain of liquidation." While Shaw was commenting on one's social worth, his words today could come from any number of administrators, school boards, and legislatures and be aimed directly at school library librarians. Finding a persuasive answer to the question "How do we demonstrate our impact on student achievement?" is increasingly important for every librarian in the country, and increasingly formal assessments are not timely enough to be helpful in times of rapid change.

Let's look at a number of ways, none perfect but powerful when used in combination, that can be used every year on an ongoing basis.

1. Standards and checklists

As discussed above a common means of assessing a school library program (and by inference assessing its impact on student learning) is by comparing an individual library program to a state or national set of program standards. Rather than tackle an entire program review, specific areas can be targeted each year using parts of these standards.

For example, MEMO's "Standard One" under the Learning and Teaching section reads: "Is the program fully integrated?" and gives these levels (Minnesota Educational Media Organization 2000):

Minimum
25%–50% of classes use the library's materials and services the equivalent of at least once each semester.

Standard
50%–100% of classes use the library's materials and services the equivalent of at least once each semester. The librarian is a regular member of curriculum teams. All library skills are taught through content-based projects.

Exemplary
50%–100% of classes use the library's materials and services the equivalent of at least twice each semester. Information literacy skills are an articulated component of a majority of content area curricula.

2. Counting things

Year-end reports that include circulation statistics, library usage, and collection size data are a common way for building library programs to demonstrate the degree to which they are being used, and by inference, having an impact on the educational program in the school.

Our district's very basic "Year End Report" asks librarians to enumerate the following:

Circulation statistics:
- Number of print materials circulated
- AV materials circulated
- In-library use of print
- In-library use of AV materials
- Equipment circulated
- Commercial online resource subscription use data

Use of space:
- Classes held/hosted
- Drop-in users

- Computer lab use
- After-hours use
- Other uses

Collections:
- Number of books acquired and deleted
- Number of AV materials acquired and deleted
- Number of software programs acquired and deleted
- Number of commercial online resources added and deleted

Leadership team activities: (List any building/district committees on which you have served and your role on them.)

Instructional activities:
- For primary, please list for each grade level library units taught that support classroom units and major skills taught
- For secondary, please list all units taught collaboratively and skills for which you had major responsibility for teaching
- Number of resource guides created (pathfinders, bibliographies, "how-to" instruction sheets for digital resources)
- Number of in-services given to staff and topics

Special programs or activities: (in-services, reading promotions, authors, events)

Please share a minimum of three instructional highlights for the past year: This is very helpful when concrete examples of library/tech services are needed.

Communications: (Please list how you have communicated with parents, staff, and students this year.)

There is a movement away from counting things—materials, circulation, online resource uses, website hits, individual student visits, whole class visits, and special activities conducted (tech fairs, author visits, reading promotions, etc.)—to enumerating how many instructional activities were accomplished—book talks given, skill lessons taught, teacher in-services provided, pathfinders/bibliographies created, and collaborative units conducted. Administrators are less concerned about how many materials are available and more concerned about how they are being used.

Information and technology literacy skill attainment, if assessed and reported, is another means of "counting" one's impact. Our elementary librarians have primary responsibility for teaching these skills and completing sections of student progress reports similar to those done in math and reading. At the building level, it is possible for the librarian to make a statement like: "89 percent of 6th grade students have demonstrated mastery of the district's information literacy benchmarked Essential Learner Outcomes."

3. Asking people

Asking library users to complete surveys and participate in focus groups is also an effective means of collecting information about the impact of the library programs on an ongoing basis. A more focused set of survey questions than the one used in formal program assessments is better, but the concept is the same.

Remember that surveys and focus groups can be conducted with students, teachers, administrators, and parents, each yielding good information.

Some librarians have conducted video "exit interviews" of graduating seniors at their high school that help them determine the effectiveness of the library programs over the academic careers of their students. Surveys given at the end of individual research projects can help determine the adequacy of resources for specific areas of the curriculum. Short surveys following any teacher trainings are useful.

4. Anecdotal data

Is there value to anecdotal evidence and stories? Despite my favorite statistics teacher's dictum that the plural of anecdote is not data, I contend that empirical evidence without stories about the numbers is ineffective. One skill all great salespeople have is the ability to tell compelling personal tales that illustrate the points they wish to make. It's one thing for the guy down at the car dealership to show a potential buyer a *Consumer Reports* study. But the real closer is his story of how Ms. Jones buys this exact model every other year and swears each one is the best car she has ever owned. When "selling" our programs, our visions, and ourselves to those we wish to influence, we need to tell our stories.

Don't discount how powerful "digital storytelling" can be as well. A short video or even photographs of students using the library for a variety of activities can be persuasive. How many times have you said, "If only the parents could see this, they would support the library 100 percent"? Though digital photography and a presentation to the PTA or Kiwanis organization, they can *see* your program.

Context and focus

Numbers alone, of course, mean little. They need to be interpreted and placed in some type of meaningful context. Context can be achieved by setting and meeting goals and by looking at numbers in a historical context. Look, for example, at how each statement gets more powerful:

- 28 teachers participated in collaborative units (Is this good or bad?)
- 78 percent of teachers in the building participated in collaborative units (This tells me more.)
- 78 percent of teachers, up from 62 percent of teachers last year, participated in collaborative teaching units (This shows a program that is getting stronger.)

In light of No Child Left Behind's focus on the achievement of subgroups within a school, data that relate specifically to target populations may be more powerful than that which applies to the entire school population. While numbers showing that book circulation has grown by x percent this year are good to report, numbers that show book checkout by the building's English-language learners has increased by x percent are probably of more interest to your administration.

David Loertscher's *Project Achievement* (Loertscher 2003) suggests that data collection should be done at three levels in order to triangulate evidence: at the Learner Level; at the Teaching Unit Level; and at the Organization Level and he provides tools to do just that. He also suggests evaluating the impact of the library program on four areas: Reading, Collaborative Planning, Information Literacy, and Technology.

My suggestion is to pay careful attention to your building and district goals and annual objectives. If reading is a focus, then look at reading activities, promotions, collection development, and circulation. If there is a focus on a particular demographic within your school, focus on it. Your own goals, and the accomplishment of them, can also provide an effective means of assessment.

Check to see if your district is using some form of formal continuous improvement model. Use your own district's means of assessment when you can.

For the school library program, some form of assessment should be conducted, analyzed, and reported several times during the school year. A simple survey, a compilation and analysis of usage numbers of a particular resource, or reporting of units planned and taught become integral parts of regular communication efforts with staff and parents, and then can be easily aggregated for a final year-end report. Results of ongoing assessments should be shared on the library's website throughout the school year.

We can no longer afford to complete a program evaluation once every five years and have the results thrown in a drawer and never looked at until the next formal assessment. Our assessments need to help us improve our practice, to serve as indicators for our planning efforts, and to be an integral part of our communication efforts with our teachers, administrators, parents, and communities. Assessment takes time, of course, but less time than finding another job.

How are you "demonstrating your library's impact on student achievement"?

A 12-point library program checklist for principals

The simple checklist below can be used to quickly evaluate your building's program with your building principal's collaboration. It is not a good substitute for some of the ideas mentioned previously in this chapter, but it can provide a discussion starter for additional assessment efforts . . .

Rapid changes in technology, learning research, and the library profession in the past 20 years have created a wide disparity in the effectiveness of school library programs. Is your school's library keeping current? The checklist below can be used to quickly evaluate your program.

1. **Professional staff and duties**
   - Does your library have the services of a fully licensed school librarian?
   - Is that person fully engaged in professional duties? Is there a written job description for all library personnel: clerical, technical, and professional?
   - Does the librarian understand the changing roles of the librarian as described in current professional publications by state and national library organizations?
   - Does the librarian offer regular staff development opportunities in information literacy, information technologies, and integration of these skills into the content area?
   - Is the librarian an active member of a professional organization?
   - Is the librarian considered a full member of the teaching faculty?

2. **Professional support**
   - Is sufficient clerical help available to the librarian so that she/he can perform professional duties rather than clerical tasks?
   - Is sufficient technical help available to the librarian so that she/he can perform professional duties rather than technical tasks?
   - Is there a district library supervisor, leadership team, or department chair who is responsible for planning and leadership?
   - Does the building principal, site leadership committee, and staff development team encourage library personnel to attend workshops, professional meetings, and conferences that will update their skills and knowledge?

- Does the librarian participate in your district's Professional Learning Communities and in informal Personal Learning Networks?

3. **Collection size and development**
   - Does the library's book and audiovisual collection meet the needs of the curriculum? Has a baseline print collection size been established? Is the collection well weeded?
   - Is a variety of media available that will address different learning styles?
   - Have online resources been added to the collection when appropriate? Are there sufficient computers and Internet bandwidth for groups of students to take advantage of these resources?
   - Has a recent assessment been done that balances print collection size and digital resources? Have some print materials been supplanted by online subscriptions? Has space formerly used to house print materials been effectively repurposed?
   - Are new materials chosen from professional selection sources and tied to the curriculum through collection mapping?

4. **Facilities**
   - Is the library located so it is readily accessible from all classrooms? Does it have an outside entrance so it can be used for community functions evenings and weekends?
   - Does the library have an atmosphere conducive to learning with serviceable furnishings, instructional displays, and informational posters? Is the library carpeted with static-free carpet to reduce noise and protect electronic devices? Is the library climate-controlled so that materials and equipment will not be damaged by high heat and humidity, and so that it can be used for activities during the summer?
   - Does the library contain general instructional areas, a story area (in elementary schools), a presentation area (in secondary schools), and spaces for individuals, small groups, and entire classes to work?
   - Does the library contain a computer lab or wireless laptops/netbooks/tablets for students and teachers working with a class or independently in the library and for the librarian to use to teach? Does the library contain and support multimedia workstations and digital video production facilities?
   - Is the library fully networked with voice, video, and data lines in adequate quantities? Does the library serve as the "hub" of these information networks with routers, file servers, video head ends, and technical staff housed there?
   - Does the library maintain a useful, up-to-date web presence with linked resources for students, staff, and families?

5. **Curriculum and integration**
   - Is the librarian an active member of grade-level and/or team planning groups?
   - Is the librarian an active member of content curriculum writing committees?
   - Is the librarian a part of grade-level or content area Professional Learning Communities?
   - Are library resources examined as a part of the content areas' curriculum review cycle?
   - Is there an information literacy curriculum—either stand-alone or embedded with content areas? If it does exist, is it based on national or local standards?
   - Are library and information technology skills taught as part of content areas rather than in isolation? Are the information literacy skills of evaluating, processing, and communicating information being taught as well as accessing skills?
   - Is the safe and appropriate use of online resources a part of the information and technology literacy curriculum?

6. **Resource-based teaching**
   - Does the librarian with assistance from building and district leadership promote teaching activities that go beyond the textbook and provide materials to help differentiate instruction?
   - Do teachers and administrators view the librarian as an instructional design and authentic assessment resource? Does the library program support inquiry-based and student-centered learning activities throughout all curricular areas? Does the librarian collaborate with students and teachers to create a wide range of opportunities that enable the development and practice critical thinking skills and responsible digital citizenship?
   - Does some flexible scheduling in the building permit the librarian to be a part of teaching teams with classroom teachers, rather than only covering teacher preparation time?
   - Is a clear set of information literacy and technology benchmarks written for all grade levels available? Are these benchmarks assessed in a joint effort of the librarian and classroom teacher? Are the results of these assessments shared with stakeholders?
7. **Information technology**
   - Does the library give its users access to recent information technologies such as:
     - an online library catalog and circulation system for the building collection
     - access to an online union catalog of district holdings as well as access to the catalogs of public, academic, and special libraries from which interlibrary loans can be made
     - full online access to the Internet
     - a wide variety of online reference tools like full-text periodical indexes, encyclopedias, atlases, concordances, dictionaries, thesauruses, reader's advisors, and almanacs
     - a wide variety of computerized productivity programs appropriate to student ability level such as word processors, multimedia and presentation programs, spreadsheets, databases, desktop publishing programs, graphic creation programs, still and motion digital image editing software
     - access to collaborative learning/networking tools such as wikis, blogs, and other online sharing programs and cloud computing resources such as online productivity tools and file storage
     - production hardware such as multimedia computers, still and video digital cameras, scanners, and LCD projection devices
     - access to desktop conferencing equipment and software
     - educational computer programs including practices, simulations, and tutorials that support the curriculum
   - Are the skills needed to use these resources being taught to and with teachers by the librarian?
8. **Reference, networking, and interlibrary loan**
   - Does your librarian have the expertise needed to provide effective and timely reference services to the building students and staff?
   - Is your school a member of a regional library multi-type system or consortium?
   - Does the librarian use interlibrary loan to fill student and staff requests that cannot be met by building collections?
   - Does the librarian participate in cooperative planning and purchasing opportunities with other schools, both locally and regional?
9. **Planning/yearly goals**
   - Does the library program have a district-wide set of long-range goals?
   - Does the librarian set yearly goals based on the long-term goals that are tied directly to building and curriculum goals in collaboration with building leadership?

- Is a portion of the librarian's evaluation based on the achievement of the yearly goals?
- Is the library program represented on the building planning committees? On the district technology planning committee?

10. **Budgeting**
    - Is the library program budget zero or objective based? Is the budget tied to program goals?
    - Does the librarian write clear rationales for the materials, equipment, and supplies requested?
    - Does the budget reflect both a maintenance and growth component for the program?
    - Does the librarian keep clear and accurate records of expenditures?
    - Does the librarian write grant applications when available?

11. **Policies/communications**
    - Are board policies concerning selection and reconsideration polices current and enforced? Is the staff aware of the doctrines of intellectual freedom and library user privacy? Do these policies extend to digital resources?
    - Does the district have a Children's Internet Protection Act–compliant safe and acceptable use policy (or responsible use policy) for Internet and technology use?
    - Does the librarian serve as an interpreter of copyright laws? Does the librarian help others determine the rights they wish to assign to their own intellectual property?
    - Does the librarian have a formal means of communicating the goals and services of the program to the students, staff, administration, and community? Is the library's web presence professional, easy-to-navigate, current, and useful? Does the librarian use social networking tools to communicate with stakeholders?

12. **Evaluation**
    - Does the librarian determine and report ways that show the goals and objectives of the program are being met and are helping meet the building and district goals? Does the librarian create an annual library report for administrators, staff, and parents that includes qualitative and quantitative measurements?
    - Do all new initiatives involving the library and technology program have an evaluation component?
    - Does the district regularly evaluate the library program using external teams of evaluators as part of any accreditation process?
    - Does the librarian participate in formal studies conducted by academic researchers when requested?

The purpose of this tool is not to serve as formal evaluation of either the librarian or library program, but to help the building administrator become aware of areas where you may need additional resources and assistance in order to make a major impact on you school's overall program.

For reflection: Linking libraries and reading achievement

My lovely wife Anne is a superb elementary librarian. To her craft she brings intelligence, passion, and creativity. She has sufficient confidence in her abilities to share her practice with others at our state library conferences by giving workshops on interactive storytelling and puppetry. I've participated in a number of these (as reward, I believe, for humping the some 400 pounds of props to the room) and am always amazed at how she can get reticent old people singing, acting, and interacting with the stories. She makes the literature she uses come alive and just plain fun.

My only concern, I tell her, is that we are living in an educational environment that seems to place very little emphasis on the pleasurable side of learning. In so many words, our building goals say that student reading test scores will improve, not that more students will read, enjoy reading, and come to love literature. She never makes the implicit connection between what she is doing—getting kids turned on to reading—with the stated objectives of the educational system to her principal or fellow teachers.

Both through long experience and professional intuition, Anne knows, as do all of us who work with children in libraries, that our storytelling, our puppet shows, our book talks, our reading promotions, our book displays, our one-on-one book recommendations, and our careful building of high-interest collections do get kids reading and, for many, many kids, into the reading habit. But experience and intuition may no longer be enough for our "data-driven" administrators and state policy makers.

Fortunately, *The Power of Reading* (Krashen 2004) provides the research that connects what we do—getting kids to read—with what the bean counters want—data that shows reading itself improves reading ability. Long a thorn in the side of advocates of direct reading instruction, Krashen has updated his 1993 classic with timely, comprehensive, and compelling research, dividing his book into three major sections: The Research, The Cure, and Other Issues and Conclusions.

The first section makes the case that Free Voluntary Reading (FVR) is as, if not more, effective than direct instruction for both children and adults and for both native English speakers and for those for whom English is a second language. Krashen uses a wide variety of academic research along with anecdotal reports to conclude: "Studies showing that reading enhances literacy development lead to what should be an uncontroversial conclusion: Reading is good for you. The research, however supports a stronger conclusion: Reading is the only way, the only way we become good readers, develop good writing style, an adequate vocabulary, advanced grammatical competence, and the only way we become good spellers" (p. 37).

It is the second part of the book that we as librarians need to share with others. The best way to support FVR is to make sure readers have access to engaging reading materials—access to which is best provided by home, classroom, school, and public libraries—and that educators encourage reading for its intrinsic rather than extrinsic value. Krashen cites data from studies showing a correlation between good school libraries and improved performance on reading tests. Access to good libraries is even more important to economically disadvantaged students: "schools can counter the effects of poverty in at least one area: access to books" (p. 70). Comic books, graphic novels, and "light" reading materials such as teen romances and magazines are examined and shown to be a "conduit" that "provides both the motivation for more reading and linguistic competence that makes harder reading possible" (p. 116). The section concludes with research on using extrinsic motivation to encourage reading (gold stars, cash awards, etc.) and reading management programs such as Accelerated Reader, concluding that there is no evidence they improve reading achievement or attitudes toward reading. As librarians, this section should be studied and shared not just as an advocacy tool for our programs, but as a guide for how we can make our programs themselves more effective.

In the final section of the book, Krashen tackles some sticky issues: Are there areas of literacy FVR does not effectively address? (Yes.) How are writing skills best learned? (Through more reading, not more writing.) What impact does television have on reading? (It is not the presence of television, but the absence of good reading materials that keeps kids from reading.) And what strategies for reading and language acquisition should be used with second-language learners? (Learning to read in the primary language makes learning to read in the second language easier.)

I have to admit that I am a reluctant reader—when it comes to reading research anyway. My MEGO (My Eyes Glaze Over) tolerance is very low, and I generally skip all that procedure and statistics boo-rah and cut right to the chase—summary and recommendations. *The Power of Reading*'s readable text, clear organization, and especially its clear layout with wide margins in which "sound bites" and summaries from the text appear, all greatly reduce the MEGO factor. This is research made, if not totally enjoyable, at least accessible.

I am not exactly sure when reading became political. But without a doubt it has. Federal funds can only be expended on materials that have been validated though "empirical" research. (Read: Only those materials from companies that make large campaign donations?) These "approved" reading programs are often highly directive to the point of being "teacher-proof," stressing skill acquisition one small bit at a time, and rely heavily on drill and kill, worksheets, and testing, testing, testing. I, for one, might stop reading altogether, if I knew each paragraph would be followed by a worksheet. Krashen offers an "empirically-supported" anti-dote to such methods, supporting his conclusion that "While it may not be true that everything that is good for you is pleasant, the most effective way of building literacy happens to be the most pleasant" (p. 151). School libraries can and should take a primary role in planning, encouraging, and supporting pleasantly effective practices of building reading skills. Keep doing those activities that get kids excited about books with the little ones, Anne—and the thousands of other committed librarians out there!

This is a book that all school librarians should purchase, read, highlight, and share with their principals, reading specialists, teachers, and parent organizations. Its readability, relatively short length, and universal applicability throughout the school make it a prime candidate for the type of school-wide book discussions advocated by "professional learning communities" proponents. In short, this is a book every person who cares about literacy improvement *and* truly cares about children needs to read.

Romantic that I am, I got Anne a copy for our anniversary.

References

Covey, Stephen. *The 7 Habits of Highly Effective People.* New York: Free Press, 1989.

Krashen, Stephen. *The Power of Reading.* 2nd edition. Santa Barbara, CA: Libraries Unlimited, 2004

Loertscher, David. "Project Achievement." 2003. http://www.davidvl.org/achieve.html (accessed Jan. 20, 2013).

Minnesota Educational Media Organization. "Minnesota Standards for Effective School Library Programs." 2000. http://api.ning.com/files/*kdeHxbh3EOrzN*U5fujpvRrsnOMZq3AyGTfXAGobOFvYRFSKioEbdbxR3VYCL w1QviFaYGE2gG-Jq9x8tbc4RnGpbf6IDOx/MN_Media_Program_Standards.pdf (accessed Jan. 20, 2013).

"School Libraries Work." Scholastic website, 2008. http://listbuilder.scholastic.com/content/stores/LibraryStore/pages/ images/SLW3.pdf (accessed Feb. 12, 2013).

Chapter Three

Planning

The library program at Lincoln Elementary School prides itself on its impact on the rising reading scores in the building. Paul, the librarian, works hard with teachers to see that all students have books to read that reflect their ability and interests, runs regular reading promotion programs, and uses the material budget to purchase extra materials he knows reluctant readers will enjoy.

The library at North Middle School seems to always be full of students working on projects that use technology to help communicate a message. When kids and teachers need help with a video production, webpage, wiki, or brochure full of digital photographs, they know they can turn to Judy their librarian for help.

Mary is close to accomplishing her goal of working with all her City High School teachers to team teach at least one major research project each year. She and the teachers are excited about how motivating the projects are to most of the students. By stressing higher-level thinking skills and being tied to personal interests, these projects are not just interesting, but are equipping students with skills they will need to know both at school and on the job.

As the examples above suggest, no two effective school library programs are alike. Each usually has areas that are strong and other areas that need improvement. As we discussed in the last chapter, the assessment of a building's school library program is a vital task that can lead to improvements not just in the delivery of library and technology services, but in improvements of the effectiveness of the total school.

But unless the data obtained from an assessment is used purposely, all efforts expended will be worthless. Remember that we don't want our reports just gathering dust in the superintendent's desk. That's why the next critical component to making long-term change is creating a shared vision for the library program by the construction and use of a library plan.

Seneca wrote, "Our plans miscarry because they have no aim. When a person does not know what harbor he is making for, no wind is the right wind." I have found that writing a simple planning document that is modified and approved by the building principal and the library/technology advisory committee gives librarians direction throughout the year. And importantly, builds broad library support.

Critical elements of a library/technology plan

Effective library plans (and now library/technology plans) have these important elements:

1. Purposes and Directive
2. Planning Team and Procedures
3. Mission and Beliefs

4. Library/Technology Long-term Goals
5. Library/Technology Short-term Objectives
6. Budget
7. Implementation Timeline

Let's look at each in more detail.

1. Purposes and directive

This short section simply states why the plan exists and if it was created under a specific directive. It can simply read something like this:

The purpose of this document is to guide the short and long-term efforts of the library/technology program, to assure its goals are aligned with building and curriculum goals, and to provide a means of assessing the progress made creating a vital library/technology program. The plan is created at the directive of the library supervisor and district administrative leadership on the recommendation of a formal library assessment.

2. Planning team and procedures

This section should tell who helped formulate this plan and how it was done.

A library/technology plan is most effective when the librarian, the building principal, and a library/technology advisory committee share the responsibility for it. Collaborative planning gives the document a broad base of support and a more balanced view of what the priorities of the plan should be.

By using a library/technology advisory committee (see some guidelines for this in the reflection at the end of this chapter), the plan has credibility and more weight than if constructed by the librarian alone. This is especially important if the building administration may not be knowledgeable about or especially supportive of libraries in general. Such a plan can also tie the efforts of the program to curriculum areas, grade levels, and the technology uses.

If your building is too small or there is a lack of interest by staff members in creating a separate library/technology advisory committee, ask that the building leadership committee or building improvement committee provide input into the plan as a part of its responsibilities.

This section might look like this:

The 2013–2014 library/technology plan was written and endorsed by the librarian and library/technology advisory committee with input from the building principal. The library/technology committee's membership for the 2012–2013 school year was:

> *Jane Smith, kindergarten teacher*
> *Robert Garcia, third grade teacher*
> *Mary Anderson, sixth grade teacher*
> *Philip Ubezwe, reading specialist*
> *Linda Alvorez, building technology integration specialist*
> *Akesha Lawrence, sixth grade student*
> *Don Clooney, parent*
> *Cindy Barnes, librarian*

3. Mission and beliefs

Record here any agreed-upon mission statements for the library/technology program and any strongly held beliefs held by the planning committee. A meaningful mission statement with wide ownership can be a guide for the advisory committee in preparing the rest of the document.

Library Program Mission Statement
The Mission of the library/technology program is to ensure all individuals in the school district are lifelong learners; effective and critical users of information; intrinsically motivated readers; effective users of technology; and good digital citizens.

Our basic beliefs concerning the use of libraries and technology by students, staff, parents, business, and community include:
- *The primary role of good library service and educational technology is to improve student achievement through meeting building and curricular goals.*
- *Library and technology efforts must be designed to meet measurable learning outcomes and must be continuously assessed.*
- *The ability to access, process, and communicate information in both print and digital formats is an essential skill that must be acquired by students and modeled by staff.*
- *Constructivist, student-centered learning has a strong, positive influence on achievement and lifelong learning attitudes.*
- *Digital citizenship skills including online safe and appropriate use are critical for both students and staff.*
- *Library resources must be networked throughout the district and to the home when possible.*
- *Information and technology skills should be integrated throughout the curriculum and at all grade levels.*
- *An effective library/technology program requires adequate resources: equipment, digital and print resources, physical facility, staffing, and training.*
- *Library/technology planning must be a coordinated effort among all stakeholders.*

4. Library/technology long-term goals

The AASL (American Association of School Librarians 1988) defines goals as "broad statements describing a desired condition." In other words, what should the library/technology ideally be providing? I believe these are best stated in terms of aspirational qualities that have lasting value. Once created, these need to be revisited each year but not rewritten.

Library/technology program goals must be linked to any state standards; district and building objectives; the library/technology curriculum; and content-area and grade-level department goals. Goals, while attainable, should expand the role of the library/technology program and make those responsible for attainment think creatively and work purposely. It is better that goals be overambitious than under-ambitious.

Building program goals should be divided into broad categories like the ones below. Your goals might look like this:

Johnson School Library/Technology Program Goals
- Student and faculty information literacy and technology competencies:
  A combined library and technology curriculum for all grades will be articulated, integrated into all content areas, and taught in collaboration with all classroom teachers. Student competency in these areas will be assessed and reported to parents and guardians.

- Student reading abilities and attitude:
  The library will contribute to student reading by providing access to current quality reading materials on a wide range of reading interests and abilities. The program will use incentives to make reading a lifelong, intrinsically motivating activity for all students.

- Collaboration:
  The librarian will co-teach units with every classroom teacher at least two times a year. The librarian serves on content area curriculum committees, the technology committee, and the building leadership team.

- Learning opportunities for building staff:
  The librarian will give or facilitate in-services for teachers on technology use and resource-based teaching based on a formal plan. The library will provide a wide range of professional resources to all district staff.

- Resources and collection development:
  Students, staff, and families will have access to library resources that support curricular objectives and meet personal interests at an exemplary level both in school and at home.

- Library facility and staffing:
  All students and staff will have access to library and technology facilities and library help that are adequate to meet their needs. The librarians will have the time and flexibility to team-teach with classroom teachers. Students and staff will have the services of a clerk in each library and a computer assistant and technician under the supervision of the librarian.

- Technology use and adequacy:
  Students and staff will have access to computers and other technologies in sufficient amount to have a significant positive impact on the educational process, enabling teachers to create student-centered, constructivist-based learning experiences and support effective teaching practices. These include cooperative learning activities, multidisciplinary teaching, whole-language instruction, and differentiated instruction.

- Communications and advocacy:
  Staff, administrators, and parents will be kept informed about the library/technology program, its services, and resources through a formal communications plan that includes a variety of communication channels. The library will maintain a high profile in the community and state through a formal public relations program, cooperating with area newspapers, television stations, the school board, service clubs, statewide professional organizations and the district newsletter.

- Professional development:
  The librarian will attend a minimum of one professional conference, seminar, or workshop each year in order to keep current on developments in education, technology, and libraries.

These are categories that have fit my goals as a building librarian; others will have divisions that may better suit their own programs. There are probably more goal areas here than are practical to deal with in a single year or even improvement cycle. Therefore a subset of improvement areas needs to be identified and the long-range goals written to just those areas. It's extremely important that librarians use their own building goals to help them select those areas for focused improvements. A close correlation to building goals helps make the library program a vital part of the entire school program.

5. Library/technology short-term objectives

Once general goals are established, specific objectives that will help meet those goals must be articulated. While the goal-setting process needs only to be written every few years and then revised as needed, writing objectives is an annual event.

Objectives are the specific things that the librarian should do within a stated time frame (ideally during one school year) that can be measured, can be observed, or can be produced. The AASL (American Association of School Librarians 1988) defines an objective as "a short term statement describing the result of specific actions." I like to use the old SMART guidelines: objectives must be **S**pecific, **M**easurable, **A**ttainable, **R**esults-centered, and **T**ime bound. (There is a good Wikipedia entry under SMART criteria for more information.)

Each objective written can be done—it's realistic. The number of objectives should be purposely ambitious, realizing that it is possible not every objective will be met during the planning year. I believe this "overplanning" is important. Why? It is more psychologically beneficial to diligently work to one's ability and fall a bit short than to do everything and have others wonder what more I could have done. It's also better for the administration and faculty to perceive one as being overextended than underutilized. Machiavellian? It works.

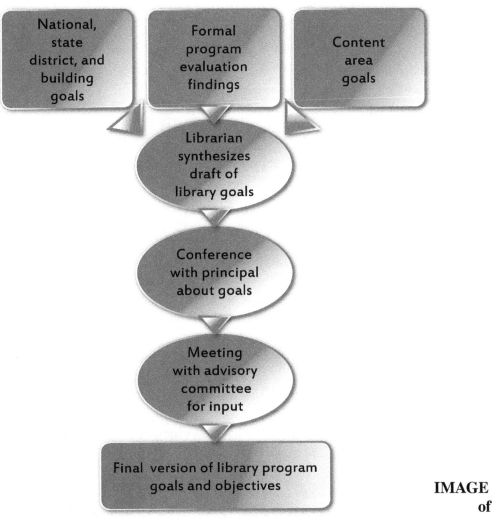

IMAGE 3.1   Developing ownership of the planning process

Here's an example of how a goal is supported by objectives:

Long-term goal:
A combined library and technology curriculum for all grades will be articulated, integrated into all content areas, and taught in collaboration with all classroom teachers. Student competency in these areas will be assessed and reported to parents and guardians.

This year's annual objectives:
- *By the end of the first semester, the librarian and members of the social studies department will design activities assessments for the Global Citizenship unit in ninth grade.*
- *The librarian will facilitate the use of a classroom blog for use in the Advanced Composition class that supports the collaborative writing objectives in the English curriculum during the second semester. Skillful and appropriate use of digital collaboration tools will be a part of the unit assessment.*

- *The librarian will participate on the science curriculum revision committee during the school year.*

Not every goal will have objectives in any given year. But those goals that are written should be demonstrably completed.

6. Budget

Include or relate your library/technology program's proposed budget to the goals and objectives. Budgeting will be discussed in detail in chapter eight, but a summary of the proposed budget should be included in the library/technology plan to help align the budget with specific objectives.

7. Implementation timeline

If some of your goals will be met by objectives that will span multiple years, spell this out.

The planning process

The planning process needs to be done annually and purposefully. It begins with the librarian reviewing the library/technology program goals and gathering information needed to construct annual objectives. This means summarizing data from any assessments done of the library program, reviewing building improvement plans, and soliciting input about curricular goals from other teachers. Once this information is synthesized, the librarian writes a draft version of the following year's objectives, each categorized by the goal it supports. This needs to be done in the spring preceding the school year the plan is to take effect.

Share this draft well before school is out with the principal and the library/technology advisory committee. The draft should be accompanied by a request for comments and suggestions needed before approval. Before the year ends, the draft needs to be discussed and approved by the principal during a face-to-face conference and by the advisory committee at its last regular meeting of the school year. The draft should go out at least a couple of weeks before these meetings so it can be reviewed and reflected upon by those whose endorsement you seek. In these meetings, make sure everyone understands each goal and objective, knows how it affects the entire school program, and recognizes the cost of each goal in money and/or labor. It's also a good time to suggest to the principal that this document can help him or her write the librarian's yearly job evaluation (see "Using goal setting to help in professional evaluations" in this chapter).

Use the input from these meetings to modify, reprioritize, and/or add to the annual objectives.

If your school is not one that has had an active, vital library/technology program, both the principal and advisory committee may do little more than "rubber stamp" what you have written for the first year or longer. As your program becomes more visible and the principal and committee members more knowledgeable about what you and your program can accomplish, expect more suggestions at your planning sessions.

Early in the fall of the school year, share this plan—or a summary of it—as widely as possible with your staff and parents. Put it on your library webpage. Let as many people as possible know what exciting things you have planned for the coming year.

I regard this planning process as the most important thing a librarian can do every year. Not only does it give you, the librarian, a focus for your daily activities, it also gives your library program a broad base of support. It's not just you who wants the library to function effectively; a dozen other professionals and parents also have an interest in its success. The principal has changed from an agent of malevolent criticism, apathetic ignorance, or benevolent neglect to a committed supporter of a program of acknowledged value that he or she has helped create. Budget and staff requests can be directly related to "approved" program goals. And should budget or staff cuts threaten the library program, you can at least say, "But look, here are some goals and objectives to which you, faculty members, and parents have agreed. How am I going to meet these objectives without support?" The burden of making the program succeed is shared.

By getting input from other professionals in the school, you give yourself a yearly "reality check." Areas that you think are important may not seem as important to the faculty. For example, an in-service on using social networking tools to communicate may be of higher priority to teachers than learning about the digital editing software that excites you. Teachers might report that certain groups of students are having difficulty finding good fiction in the collection and you may need to reprioritize you budget. Listening to this formal committee's comments can alert you to problems you may be too near to recognize, and to the special needs of your individual building.

I personally believe there is no such thing as a perfect library program based on state or national standards. But I do believe there are library programs perfectly suited to the specific needs of individual schools. Take this to heart.

Keep the finalized planning document handy and refer to it at least once a month. It serves to help prioritize your purchasing and use of discretionary time. And you will be able to use it as a guide for your communication plan, as we will examine in chapter four.

Using goal setting to help in professional evaluations

Asking the librarian to be accountable for specific objectives creates a natural bridge to the evaluation of the librarian as well as the assessment of the library program.

An often-heard complaint among librarians is that principals use the same forms and methods to evaluate them as they use to evaluate classroom teachers. While such evaluation methods can and should be used to help evaluate the librarian's teaching abilities, principals need to recognize that a large part of the librarian's job falls outside what such methods evaluate. Librarians have administrative duties such as budgeting, supervision of paraprofessionals, public relations, collection development, and policy making. The degree of effectiveness of the individual in these areas is directly reflected in the degree to which the program's yearly goals have been met.

For reflection: Twenty-plus years of working with advisory groups—what I've learned

My first library advisory committee was born out of pure frustration. I had been hired by a small high school in 1989 to replace a librarian who had been in the same position for thirty-five years. By the end of Bertha's term (names have been changed to protect the innocent), this poor tired soul had two main goals: to never, ever throw anything away and to keep as many people out of the library as possible so she could have some peace and quiet. OK, those probably weren't her real goals, but it seemed like it given the state of the program and collection.

So, I weeded and weeded. I added some new and exciting resources, including, as I remember, one of the first Grolier electronic encyclopedias on a stand-alone workstation. I spruced the place up. I put out the word that students and teachers—alone, in groups, or as classes—were welcome and appreciated. I did about everything I could except pay people to come to the library.

But at the beginning of the second semester of my first year, I still felt like the lonely Maytag repairman.

As anyone will tell you, I am not a patient soul and I was desperate. I decided to invite a few of my fellow high school teachers over to my house one evening for a little wine and cheese party. Sensing free booze and food, some even showed up. After getting them a little tipsy and feeling guilty for eating all my crackers, I pulled a fast one on them. "You are," I announced, "my newly formed library advisory committee. I don't know what the devil the teachers and students of this school want in a library program, so you're going to tell me." And happily, they did.

For just a little wine and cheese, these wise folks would leave their families and far more interesting activities to come to my house a few times a year and talk about libraries and computers and how adolescents learn best. We hammered out an articulated vision of what a library and technology program should do. They helped me set my professional goals, and then listened when I reported my trials and triumphs. It was the best deal I ever made.

Their suggestions turned into my first library plan with goals and objectives. The principal was delighted. I felt I had others now helping move the program forward and, in return, making me successful.

While this first group I formed was just a few teachers and a couple of parents, my advisory committees have become district-wide, larger, and more formal since that time, but they still serve very much the same purpose: to help me make better decisions. Every year advisory committees have given me terrific ideas, huge challenges, and timely warnings.

After having been served by and having served on a number of these advisory groups, I offer some advisory advice.

Keep your group small. Any committee much larger than a dozen is difficult to get together and difficult to bring to consensus. If you need a much larger representation, keep your full meetings few and do most of your work in subcommittees.

Work for a wide representation of stakeholders who serve limited terms. My current committee is comprised of teachers, librarians, students, and administrators, of course. But parents, business people, a multi-type library representative, and postsecondary educators also serve. Our computer coordinator, student information system manager, network manager, and a building technician are permanent members. We don't have a set selection process for membership, but no one usually serves for more than three years. Remember when selecting your members, that communication is a two-way street. What your representatives learn at your meetings will be taken back and shared with that person's colleagues.

Have few, but important, meetings. Advisory committees only need to meet three or four times a year. A fall meeting is a good time to establish working subcommittees and refine the year's goals. One or two meetings to work on budget or policy issues in the winter and a final spring meeting to review the year's work and set objectives for the coming school year are enough. Setting our meeting dates for the year at our first meeting makes them a priority for many members. Take attendance, and include who is there in your minutes.

Only hold meetings when there is needed input by the committee membership. If the communication at meetings is only one-way, members will begin to wonder why this business could not have been done simply through e-mail.

Send out good agendas and write clear, concise minutes that are quickly distributed. If members see agenda items that they think are important (how the budget is to be used this year for example), they'll be more likely to attend. All my advisory group members use e-mail, and we rarely send hard copies of anything through the mail. I e-mail myself a copy of all agendas and minutes for easy filing and retrieval. Our meetings themselves are mostly paperless.

Give your group well-defined responsibilities. Yes, sometimes these committees can try to micromanage a program. I heard a story once of a parent member wanting the library rearranged based on feng shui principles, much to the librarian's discomfort. A committee should not be making your professional decisions for you, but it should have the power to shape the direction of the library/technology program. And well it should, since these folks, as well as you, will be held responsible for the program's weaknesses as well as its strengths. My advisory committee works on:

- long-range planning and goals and my department's yearly objectives
- program assessments
- budgets
- policy making

And that's about all the work we can do. And remember, it's an *advisory* committee. If they offer advice that you believe is not in the best interest of your students, you may respectfully not take it.

Expect and accept the "ugly baby" comments. Ask any group of people if they themselves are the parents of an ugly baby. No one is. Ask the same group of people if they have ever seen an ugly baby. Nearly all the hands go up. This phenomenon is why all of us need reality checks of our programs, our policies, and our priorities. The things we hold dear and have ownership of always look pretty darned good to us. Our advisory committee can tell us if we have some "ugly baby" qualities of which we may not be aware. It's not always easy to accept these criticisms, but it's in our students' best interest to get an objective opinion on our programs—even when they are our "babies."

Ours can be a professionally lonely profession. In all but the largest schools, there is rarely more than a single librarian. Kindergarten teachers, custodians, coaches, special education aides, and administrators outnumber us. An advisory committee is one way of giving ownership of the library program to everyone in the building. If the goals, the budget, the assessments, the long-range plan are known to be important to more than just a single person, when they are presented to decision makers they will carry more weight. And if your advisory group includes parents, community members, and students, it will be seen as a very important body indeed.

Reference

American Library Association. *A Planning Guide for Information Power: Guidelines for School Library Media Programs*. Chicago: American Library Association, 1988.

Chapter Four

Communications and Advocacy

My first relationship with a school principal was adversarial and goes back to about the second grade when I was sent to "The Office" for rendering a rather rude pencil sketch of my classroom teacher. In Iowa schools of the late 1950s, corporal punishment was not only allowed, it was encouraged.

Over the next 30 years, my view of school administrators did not improve a great deal as I moved from being a student to being a teacher to being a librarian. The worst principal I worked for often bragged that he managed to obtain his college degrees without ever setting foot in a library. I told him I could tell.

The best principal I had, I considered an agent of benevolent neglect. There was an unspoken agreement that if I left him alone, he would leave me alone.

Then I met Gil Carlson from St. Peter, Minnesota, who was convinced that a good library program would be in the best educational interests of his students. He didn't know what all that entailed so it was up to me, he said, to educate him about what a good library program did. I did my best, and found that a principal could be a staunch ally against ignorance and textbook learning—and a firm library supporter.

But I also found that I had to do the educating. And not just of him, but of other stakeholders in the district, including the staff and parents. I had to figure out how to communicate what good library programs, and especially my library program, were doing to help both schools and the individuals in them to succeed.

I also found that by keeping stakeholders apprised of what the library program was doing, I could build true advocates for the program. Self-advocacy is not particularly effective since it is also self-serving. But others can't advocate on your behalf if they don't know about what you do. Good communication is the key element in any successful advocacy story.

And leaving such education to chance wasn't possible. I needed to create a real communication plan—and commit to it.

What are the components of an effective communications program?

Good communications efforts don't just happen. They are carefully designed, implemented, and evaluated for effectiveness. Communications, like assessment and planning, fall into Covey's Quadrant II (discussed in chapter two) of things that are important, but not urgent, and therefore easy to never get around to doing. A good plan, however, will structure your communication efforts, give you a timeline, and increase the chances of getting them done.

Here are six steps you can take in creating a communications plan with impact.

1. Identify your audiences

Who needs to know about what your program does? What you do? Why good library programs are important to students? I suggest three main groups to which you should target communications: your principal, your staff, and your parents.

Why not students? Yes, they also need to know what's happening in the library, but we tend to have a lot of opportunities to inform them of what's happening and, as a part of the school, they should already have firsthand knowledge of the library and how it serves them. And unfortunately, students are rarely consulted on matters of budgets, staffing, and curriculum, if ever.

One advantage of having a planning document as discussed in the last chapter is that it can serve as a basis for what you communicate. Progress on the completion of your annual objectives should be of interest to all parties since input on its content came from members of each group. While you should formally report at the end of the year to the principal and advisory committee using the planning document to give an honest appraisal of how well the goals and objectives for the year were met, keeping everyone updated on progress through the year also keeps everyone mindful of the library program and the wonders it performs. You need to target your communications specifically to each group.

The principal

The principal is the single most important person you need to keep informed. He or she is your supervisor. He or she has control over budgets, staffing, policies, and facility use. The success or failure—even existence—of your library may depend on your principal's view of it.

Remember that all administrators *hate* surprises. Your principal does not like to be surprised by either good or bad news about your library delivered by someone else. (As a true administrator myself, I like knowing of bad things in advance so I can figure out someone else to blame. I like knowing about good things in advance so I can figure out how to take the credit.) Your principal should *never* first hear about something happening in your library from a teacher, a student, or, especially, a parent. Principals want to know everything that is going on in their buildings—both problems *and* successes.

A bimonthly principal's report should cover all activities in which you are involved over a two-month period, succinctly described. These activities may include:

- Teachers whose classes are using the library and with whom you have been cooperatively teaching (Mr. Gomez's students worked with the new database of countries from March 12th through the 15th.)
- New resources and how they are being used (I am helping students use GoogleDocs to write their career plans.)
- In-services given or facilitated by the library staff (My after school "Techie Tuesday" in-service on how to edit and add graphics to teachers' websites was attended by twelve staff members.)
- Special administrative tasks performed (I've updated the job description for our library paraprofessional to reflect new technology support responsibilities.)
- Problems encountered and how they are being dealt with (Library overcrowding during the lunch hour is being discussed at the next building leadership team meeting.)
- Circulation and library usage figures (Over the last two months, an average of twenty books per student were circulated and the library had an average of thirty-seven students per hour using it.)
- Professional activities including workshop and conference attendance (At the recent tech conference, I learned about some online resources for the astronomy class that I've shared with the teachers.)

Use your library calendar and to-do list to help remind you of your previous months' activities. Keep the reports upbeat, complimentary, and as short as possible. A good proofreading before sending them out is always necessary.

There are two things to avoid in these reports. First, do not criticize teachers or students in them. Some principals may share the reports with staff. If you have problems with individuals or policies, and we all do, schedule a face-to-face meeting with your principal to discuss them. Second, do not whine. Whining is going to your supervisor with a problem about which nothing can be done. It feels good to just let it all out sometimes about things that really can't be changed. But listening to that sort of venting is what your spouse, your mom, or your cat is there for—not your principal.

Oh, it's a good idea to schedule a time to review these reports face-to-face after you've sent them out to clarify and address any questions or concerns.

The staff

A staff newsletter should be distributed monthly that contains information teachers will find useful and important.

- New materials and equipment your library may have acquired since the last newsletter (Come to the library and see our latest books purchased just for our English-language learners.)
- Reminders to teachers of library services (Don't forget that the library staff will do laminating for you.)
- Units teachers and you have collaboratively taught (Ms. Tong's first grade class used an online drawing tool to create their eye diagrams. I am happy to help other teachers who want to try similar activities.)
- Links to interesting articles or blog posts (Here's a link to an article that predicts schools will be "paperless" by 2025. What do you think?)
- Appropriate quotes, jokes, or cartoons to add interest (A T-shirt that reads *"Yes, I know they pick on you at school and call you names, but you still have to go. YOU'RE THE TEACHER!"*)

This newsletter should never be more than two pages in length and use lots of white space, cartoons, and photos. It can be delivered in print or electronically. Again, always stress the positive.

The parents and guardians

While reaching students' homes may be the most challenging communications effort you can undertake, as you will see when we discuss advocacy below, it is vitally important. Parents cannot support programs they don't value, and they don't value programs about which they know little or nothing.

A monthly article in your school building's newsletter, website, or blog may be the most effective way of reaching students' families. While many of the same topics that are of interest to principals and staff are also of interest to parents, a single, broad-based topic that is discussed in more detail is also helpful to parents. Such topics might include:

- How technology is being used in your school and library
- Important information and technology literacy skills students need to have
- Efforts the library is undertaking to make sure students are safe and ethical when online
- How library resources support differentiated instruction
- New technologies that the school and library may be piloting or adopting

- The difference between intrinsic and extrinsic motivation and how such motivation applies to reading skills

The purpose of the column is to explain, in lay terms, how the library program, directly and indirectly, benefits the reader's children: creating lifelong learners, making informed decision makers, allowing wide use of technology, providing individualized learning opportunities for all students, and creating a learning space in the school for collaboration and acceptance.

Write in a readable, informal prose, avoiding (or explaining) "education-ese." Keep in mind that while the column is written for parents, the school staff and students also read the newsletter.

This can be a joint effort among all librarians in your district. One column of interest to all district families can be written and then published in all buildings' newsletters.

Here is a sample column for parents:

Dear Parents and Guardians of Johnson Elementary School:

This fall, all students in grades 3–12 were supplied with a new resource, GoogleApps for Education.

GoogleApps for Education is a set of online tools for communication, collaboration, time management, and document storage. Provided by Google to the district at no cost, these tools include:

- *Gmail: a full-functioning e-mail program (grades 6–12)*
- *Calendar: a customizable calendar and to-do list*
- *Contacts: an address book*
- *GoogleDocs: a word processing, spreadsheet, presentation, and drawing program that allows multiuser access and editing*
- *Google continues to add new tools and the district will evaluate each for its educational potential*

All of these tools are housed on the Internet and can be accessed from any Internet-connected computer with a web browser. No special software is required.

Our primary reasons for supplying these tools to students are:

- *To give our students practice in using current technology applications and tools*
- *To give students the ability to work on common, no-cost tools on their own documents both at school and outside of school*
- *To facilitate "paperless" transfer of work between students and teachers*
- *To provide adequate long-term storage space for student work*
- *To help students work collaboratively, engage in peer-editing of documents, and publish for a wider audience*

There is also a cost savings to the district since fewer licenses for commercial copies of programs will need to be purchased and less file storage space will need to be maintained.

To ensure the safety of our students, GoogleApps for Education student domains are "closed." This means that students can only e-mail and share documents with their teachers and other students within the district or to those individuals to whom they give specific permission (like parents). The applications also have spam filtering enabled and do not contain advertising.

I, along with the other librarians in the district, will be reviewing our district's acceptable use policy and Internet safety guidelines when we introduce these tools to students when teaching your students to use them. Using online tools responsibly will be an important part of the learning experience.

Please ask your children about this new resource and have them demonstrate how it works to you. And please contact me if you have questions about GoogleApps for Education and how this exciting new resource is being used in our school.

Sincerely,

Your librarian

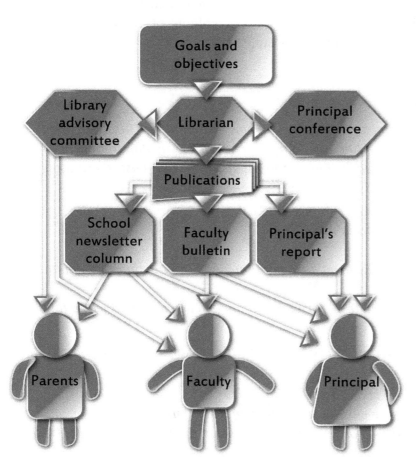

IMAGE 4-1   Reporting flowchart

2. Determine your format and use good communication principles

How does your school already communicate? The paper "bulletin" is dead or dying, being replaced by e-mail, websites, and other digital communication methods, both internally and externally (see below). In many schools, the paper newsletter to parents, stuffed in student backpacks—along with a prayer that it will make it home—has been replaced by regular e-mails sent using the student information system. The school website has become a genuine resource for families, providing schedules, links to teacher webpages, supply lists, permission forms, and links to learning resources for home use. Use the means of communication to which your audiences are accustomed to receiving other school information. (If you want to try new methods of communication, do, but continue with the traditional method until you know the new one works.)

Regardless of the format, there are some good communication principles you should use:

- Write in clear, understandable, error-free language
- Format your document using good design including white space, headings and subheadings, graphics, and clear fonts
- Be as brief as possible

One undervalued method of communication that appeals to all audiences is the use of photographs of HPLUKs: **H**appy **P**roductive **L**ibrary-**U**sing **K**ids. It's too seldom that others are present when the really magical moments happen in our libraries. Who hasn't said, "If only _____ (parents, the principal, the school board, legislators, etc.) could see this, they would support my library program." With a digital camera and a little foresight, those important decision-making people *can* see how students benefit from having a good library program when we include such pictures in all our reports, newsletters, and columns. When using pictures of students, we should, of course, consider their privacy rights. Make sure you have a parental consent forms on file for the students whose pictures you use or run the pictures through an artistic filter in a photo-editing program so that students are unrecognizable.

IMAGE 4-2   Students at computers in the library

Soliciting feedback and asking questions about the library program can also be an important part of your communication effort. Create "Thirty-Second Surveys" of two or three questions using an online polling tool about something in your program and then share the results in the next newsletter. ("Should library policy allow students to use their MP3 players or iPods while working in the library?") Most people like to be asked their opinions and know they've been heard.

3. Commit to a regular schedule

One of the basic rules of effective communication is to keep your message simple and repeat it often. Your goal should be to communicate with your target groups regularly, not just when the spirit moves you. By committing to regular communication efforts, you again move a task that falls in Covey's Quadrant II to Quadrant I—Important *and* Urgent.

While schedules are recommended above, your time and resources will dictate a schedule that works for you and your program. You will need to determine if shorter communication efforts sent more frequently or longer messages sent less often suit the needs of your staff. When I polled our district staff on whether they would like frequent e-mails or monthly newsletters from our department, over 80 percent of respondents indicated a preference for a monthly newsletter summarizing the information, delivered by e-mail.

4. Create a formal report at the end of the year

Every librarian, regardless of any other communication effort, needs to write and distribute a year-end summary of the library/technology programs and activities that happened during the school year. This should include, at minimum:

- A report on the attainment of the annual program objectives.
- Data on library circulation, changes in collection size, new resources added, numbers of students using the library, number of classes collaboratively taught by the librarian, and number of in-services given and any special events held. (See sample "Year End Report" in chapter two.)
- Any major events or projects not accounted for in the program objectives.

While this document is written and should be shared on the library website, clever librarians are also creating summaries of such documents using multimedia tools—short videos or animation tools such as Animoto—that appeal to visual learners and the time-challenged.

5. The community

Communicating to the general public is important but takes real initiative. I found that these means of communications can build community awareness of the role of library/technology programs:

- Reports at school board meetings. A ten-minute report on the library/technology program at a school board meeting is heard not only by those in attendance (all important school board members and administrators) but also the community as a whole when the meeting is recorded and broadcast over the community access channel or via the web.
- Articles and stories in the mass media. If something special is happening in your library—a special reading promotion for I Love to Read month, an author visit, a new technology being implemented—invite local newspapers and television stations to cover the event. Get to know your newspaper's education reporter, who will appreciate ideas for stories.
- Presentations to service organizations. Your community has many service organizations: Kiwanis, Rotary, Sertoma, and Lions among them. Many have weekly or monthly programs of topics of interest during which you can present information about the library/technology program in your school. The members are usually civic minded, supportive of education, and curious about anything

new happening in their communities. Plus they are often the opinion leaders in the community and can become great supporters of libraries if they aren't already.

- Open houses, events, and community meetings. Find reasons to bring the community into your library. Open houses and special events are one way. If you get new furniture for your library, hold an open house. If you have a guest author, see if he or she will give a program in the evening for adults. Encourage your parent–teacher organizations to meet in your library—and participate.
- If your district has public relations professionals, form an alliance. The public relations department is always looking for positive news to share and you need to get information out.

6. Make all communications efforts accessible

Keep all your communication efforts online with easy-to-find public links from your library website. Not everyone has time to read every e-mail or report when it arrives. You'll find yourself glad you can later retrieve much of this information yourself at a later date as well.

Speaking where people are listening

Oh, for the simple days of what seemed like a single means of communication—the printed newsletter that could be slipped onto a principal's desk, in a teacher's mailbox, or in a student backpack. (Alice Yucht created a "toilet paper" by taping the printed library newsletter to the back of bathroom stall doors.) Those of us who were "tech savvy" created our pre-Internet and e-mail newsletters in a word processor or desktop publishing program, adding headlines, columns, and clip art.

Most librarians quickly recognized that e-mail was an even more effective method of distributing newsletters and timely information. And that's what most of us have done. But we need to continually update our communication strategies—especially with our students, younger parents, and beginning teachers. We need to be speaking in places where the young are actually listening, viewing, and reading.

Here are some new avenues for information dissemination. Conveniently, once a message is created, it can be distributed through multiple channels.

- **Your library webpage** should be easy to find and include up-to-date, useful information including hours, services, links to resources, library goals and newsletters, and your contact information. Make it visually appealing and do not let it get dated.
- **A Facebook fan page** is easy to create if you have a personal Facebook account. The Facebook support center has good information on the topic. "Fans" don't have access to the rest of your personal Facebook account, so this is a safe and effective way to reach those who *only* seem to use social networking for communication. That includes a lot of students.
- **A blog with an RSS feed** is more effective than a static website. The interactivity of a blog will be appealing to those who like to respond to ideas. I've always thought Francey Harris's fantastic *Gargoyles Loose in the Library* blog is the model for this medium of communication.
- **Twitter** is popular among a growing segment of Internet users. The 140 characters are about enough to alert readers of an event or to provide a link to more substantial information posted somewhere else. "Tweets" can inform your staff and students about the latest books, effective resources, and reminders of continuing services available in your library. Build a "following."

- **Text-message, e-mail, voice message "blasts"** may be possible in your district. Our public relations department is the master of sending these alerts out. If you have some exciting news for parents, this may be the most effective means of information. Check with your PR department or student information system manager. There are free text-messaging services so you don't need to use your personal cell phone account quota.
- GoogleApps for Education has a wonderful tool called **GoogleGroups** that makes sending and archiving e-mails to larger groups really simple. Other e-mail systems also have this capacity. Check yours. It's e-mail, yes, but still an efficient way to get word out to your "mature" staff.
- While many of us are all about the written word, clever librarians are telling their stories in ways that **reach visual, auditory learners**. Look for year-end reports librarians have created using Animoto. Post library videos on YouTube or make podcasts. As long as people are walking around with things stuck in their ears with eyes glued to a tiny screen, they may as well be learning something cool about the library.

I am not convinced that e-mail is as dead as some might suggest. Nor am I convinced of the longevity of some of these other communication media. But I do know this: *Librarians must have regular and formal communication strategies for students, teachers, principals, and parents more now than ever.* People have to know what we do in order to advocate for us. Libraries in concept only or that are invisible are easy to cut.

Can a good library program be a marketing tool for your school?

You don't buy a quarter-inch drill bit because you want a drill bit.
You buy one because you want a quarter-inch hole.
—My dad

Mankato, Minnesota, is a small town of around 50,000 people. It's a nice place to live. We have short lines at the movie theaters, no rush hour traffic, a part-time accessible mayor, and neighborhoods where you actually talk to your neighbors. But Mankato has rapidly become a big city in one rather startling way: Parents here have a bigger choice of schools for their kids than they do of fast-food restaurants.

If as a parent I am not happy with the education my child is receiving at the school on a block in my neighborhood, I can:

- Send him to one of the other public schools in town
- Send him to our district's "magnet" school
- Send him to one of the charter schools in the region
- Send him to any of the neighboring districts' public schools through open enrollment
- Send him to any of the private and parochial schools in town
- Enroll him in a growing number of state-approved virtual high schools
- Homeschool him (Yeah, right.)

School officials here in Mankato and throughout the rest of the country are rapidly discovering that education has become a competitive commodity. And competition means marketing.

Librarians have a golden opportunity to increase their indispensability *if* they become a part of a district's marketing plan.

Imagine that you are a new resident of your community. How exactly would you as a consumer of educational services find information about schools for your children? How especially would you find information about the *quality* of instructional programs?

Our district, like most, produces a plethora of building and district newsletters, flyers, pamphlets, television public service announcements, and webpages. We try to have information about our excellent library/technology programs in every district communication.

If your district has a public relations director, buy him or her lunch a couple of times a year. These folks are always hungry for news, awards, and exciting programs to share with the public that makes the schools look good. They have a challenging job and welcome allies.

In your PR efforts, try to work in both concrete examples of the important things students are doing in the library program, as well as relevant studies about the overall effectiveness of library programs. Each kind of evidence will appeal to different types of parents, and the combined effect can be very powerful.

Quality school library programs help create quality schools, just like quarter-inch drill bits create quarter-inch holes. No doubt about it. And school leaders are beginning to realize that it's not enough just to have great schools and that test scores are not the only, or even most important determination of school quality, and that they have to let an increasingly education-savvy public know it. When parents can choose their schools as easily as they can choose their burger joints, let's make sure they order (and we can offer) a double child-centered, individualized experience with extra library and technology. And hold the pickles.

What are the basic rules of effective advocacy?

A number of years ago I was asked by a small school district's librarians to speak against library staffing cuts at one of their board meetings. They felt my "expert" opinion would help their cause. I gave a talk that I thought was most persuasive. But the board cut the library position anyway.

I left the meeting feeling rather sorry for the board for the hard choices they had to make. Along with the library position cut, a school bus route was eliminated; a two-hour-a-day mentally handicapped man who did lunchroom duties was let go; the head custodian's pay was reduced from twelve to ten dollars an hour; a vacant math position in the high school was not filled; and much-needed roof maintenance was again delayed. When one of the board members asked why there were no "administrative cuts," the principals reminded her that they had already absorbed the duties of the Title I coordinator, curriculum director, and standards coordinator without any additional compensation. Judging by the quality of his suit, the superintendent was not overpaid. None of the cuts were made without a good deal of thoughtful discussion, and few votes were unanimous.

But it was a question by one board member that really hit me hard. He asked, "Why, if this library cut is going to have such a serious impact on our students, have I not received a single phone call from a teacher, parent, or student objecting to it?" I thought it was an instructive question. Just a few teacher or parent voices (maybe only one) in support of the library position would have been far more persuasive than I could ever have hoped to be at that meeting.

On a regular basis, library organizations create sets of advocacy brochures for school librarians. Full of bright graphics and research summaries, the designers give librarians a good tool to use with administrators, parents, policy makers, and teachers. But I often worry such publications may do more harm than good. While I am pleased to see these materials made available, they, like any tool, aren't effective unless used correctly. Printing a copy of the brochure and stuffing it in your principal's mailbox will not save your bacon. Overreliance on such documents is dangerous indeed.

Here are some basic rules of advocacy.

First rule of advocacy: Never advocate for libraries or the librarian—advocate for library users. The biggest mistake we make is advocating "for libraries." When framing our comments from the standpoint of an impact on "the library," these statements sound self-serving: "The library needs a bigger budget" or "The library can't be used for study halls" or "The cut in the library paraprofessional's hours will hurt the library program." Look how a simple reframing changes these same ideas: "Without an adequate budget, students will not have access to the newest titles and reading interest will decline" or "If the clerical position is reduced, I will not have as much time to team-teach or do staff in-services" or "When the library is used for study halls, students who need to use the library resources and need a place to study find it more difficult to do so." I realize the reason we ask for anything is always because it has a direct or indirect benefit to our library users, but we have to make sure we connect the dots between what we want and why it's good for those we serve.

Second rule of advocacy: Use, but don't depend on, national studies, statistics, or publications. My cynical side says that if one looks hard enough, one can find a study to support almost any educational program, strategy, or theory, no matter how crackpot. And a lot of administrators share my cynicism. Your principal's goals might be different from the goals that advocacy materials say libraries help meet. And really, who trusts any study done in another state, let alone another country? Forget asking an administrator to read anything more than a page long. By all means use advocacy materials, especially as a discussion starter in face-to-face meetings. But don't depend on them alone to make your local case.

Third rule of advocacy: Build relationships so others will advocate for you. One parent telling a school board how important he thinks the library program is to his children is more powerful than a dozen studies. One teacher willing to tell the principal that library services have helped her class be more successful secures library funding better than any mandate. One community group that works with school libraries to build information literacy skills is more effective than any set of national standards. We need to make sure we build the kind of relationships with parents, teachers, and the community that are strong enough that members of these groups will speak on our behalf when needed. That takes a communication plan like the one described in this chapter. Make sure as many people as possible feel like they are responsible for the success of the program by doing collaborative library planning as described in chapter three. If the library is everyone's baby, no one will want to throw it out.

Fourth rule of advocacy: Don't depend on the library supervisor or an outside "expert" to make your case. A district-level library supervisor can be a wonderful voice for building librarians, especially when that person sits on administrative teams. But remember, no matter how forceful, how charming, or how much dirt he or she may have on other administrators, the library supervisor is always a single voice among many, each with its own set of priorities. We supervisors would love to be as powerful as you think we are, but we still pull on our superhero tights one leg at a time. There is certainly no guarantee that the advice of an "expert" on library efficacy will be effective, as my experience showed.

Fifth rule of advocacy: Advocacy must be ongoing. Advocacy is not an annual "project" or a one-time campaign. It's not something you can do once and move on to something else. Advocate before, not when your program may be in jeopardy. This is why our communication efforts must be planned, purposeful, and regular. Is advocacy a regular occurrence for you?

Use advocacy materials, but remember that they are a tool, not a magic wand.

As professionals, we believe in our efficacy and that our efforts benefit students and staff. We know how hard we work. We know that we cannot create resources to support good programs out of sweat alone. We see on a daily basis the excitement of children who have found books that speak to their hearts, computer programs that challenge their minds, or websites that answer questions they have about their world. We see children who are not served by textbooks learning because a teacher uses more than just the textbook. We know the more informed decision makers, critical thinkers, and lifelong learners we create, the better society will become. But for us alone to know this is not enough. We must share what we know and what we do in a systematic way. Then we can build a common cause in our schools and community through effective communications that help insure advocacy from others.

That's information power.

For reflection: What is transparency, and why is it critical to the librarian's success?

Don't take it personally, but teachers and administrators sometimes distrust their librarians. Why? Is it the shifty eyes? Their possibly subversive attitude toward school policies? The suspicion that after reading all the books in the library, the librarian really does know more than everyone else in the school?

No, it's not quite so dramatic. Unlike classroom teachers, librarians have both discretionary time and discretionary funds to spend. They may not have either in huge quantities, but most librarians do have these resources. Knowing about them engenders questions from other school staff members like "Just where does all the money in the library budget go?" and "What does the librarian do all day anyway?"

Educational change guru Michael Fullan makes transparency one of his six "secrets" of successful organizations (Fullan 2008). He contends that we have no choice but to be transparent in an environment of easy access to information and that the public demands accountability. He also argues that transparency is a good thing that is essential to success. Effective organizations develop a "culture" that realizes problems occur, are open about them, and solve them openly. In other words, you may as well let people know things they will find out anyway.

How can librarians develop a culture of transparency and build trust, helping insure the effectiveness and success of their programs? Let's open some windows.

Open budgets: Put your budget in an online spreadsheet that is available for anyone to read—teachers, administrators, parents, and the community. The format does not have to be complicated: list the vendor, the purchase order number, the amount of the order, and a short description of what was acquired. Invite everyone to the budget-making process.

Open calendars: Put every library calendar online and share it. This includes your own teacher calendar, your library calendar, your collaborative teaching calendar, and your computer lab calendars. The question might change from "What does she do with her time?" to "How does she manage to get everything done?"

Open goals: Your long-term goals and annual short-term objectives should be available online with a means for your stakeholders to comment and discuss them. Again, transparency means letting others have a role in creating your vision, plans, and goals as well.

Open statistics: Don't wait until the end of the year to file an "annual report." Keep a running list of total numbers of items circulated, students using the library, classes you've taught, and other things that "count." Make the numbers public—right on your library home page. If the statistics raise questions by other school staff, be open about finding the answers to them. "Our fiction circulation is down this year. What might be the reason?" Open up both the face-to-face and online conversations about such data. Set goals for statistics like numbers of items circulated—then celebrate publically when they are met.

Open doors: Take every opportunity to have parents, administrators, and teachers come into your library both during school hours and outside school hours. Let people watch you work, watch you teach, and watch you assist students and teachers. Think of making your library walls transparent.

Open opinions: People ought to know where you stand. If you think both kids and adults should have access to a divergent set of opinions about issues, say so. If you see that teachers and students are not taking advantage of fair use guidelines, say so. If you believe reading test scores will improve if students are given more opportunities to voluntarily read materials of their own choice, share the research. If you are concerned the principal has made a choice that will harm students, tell him or her (privately). Trust is built when a person acts in a consistent, open manner. Our stakeholders may agree or disagree with us, but they should certainly know our fundamental beliefs.

I've always thought that if somebody is not going to like me, I'd like it to be for something I've actually done, not just something I've been suspected of doing.

Make increased transparency a goal of your library program and practice.

Reference

Fullan, Michael. *The Six Secrets of Change: What the Best Leaders Do to Help Their Organizations Survive and Thrive*. San Francisco: Jossey-Bass, 2008.

Chapter Five

Managing Others and Collaboration

No library is an island.

Librarians cannot be successful alone, no matter how hard they work. Our program is directly dependent on how well we work with other people, like it or not.

In earlier chapters, we've discussed why it is important we seek input from stakeholders in our district about our assessment and planning efforts and why it's important to communicate effectively with them.

But we also work with others on a daily basis, not just on strategic, big-picture tasks. In this chapter, we'll look at three groups of people we rub shoulders with every day—the library support staff, the technology department staff, and our teaching staff—and examine some strategies for mutual success.

Working with the library support staff

It is not enough to be busy. So are the ants.
The question is: what are we busy about?
—Henry David Thoreau

Consider these two scenarios:

Each time Principal Jane walks by the library in her school, she sees a busy librarian. Jim is always fixing a printer with problems, checking books in or out, compiling overdue lists, or installing software in the lab. Jim often works late after school, takes home materials to read, and comes in during the summer to help install new computers, or process new books. Yet faculty and parents question Jane about the need for Jim's position being a professional one.

Each time Principal Bob walks by the library in his school, he sees a busy librarian. Laura is always teaching a class, tutoring a teacher, reviewing new materials, or supervising a volunteer. Laura also works late after school, takes materials home to read, and comes in during the summer to help write curricula or plan for staff development workshops. Faculty and parents never question Bob about whether Laura's position is professional. No one can envision how the school can run without her.

The question librarians need to ask themselves is not whether they are busy, but as Thoreau puts it, what they are busy about. In the examples above, the librarians are working, but they are busy doing two quite different kinds of tasks.

Jim is busy doing technical and clerical work. Fixing paper jams, installing software, reshelving books, and maintaining circulation and cataloging records are all tasks that do not call for professional library expertise. Laura's activities all revolve around teaching or selecting resources to meet school needs—professional tasks. It's easy to make the determination which type of activity has a more long-term impact on the educational program.

Shouldn't administrators figure out ways to straighten out the Jims of the library world? Perhaps.

But first we should be asking why a librarian might be doing clerical or technical work in the first place. To be sure, there are librarians who don't really like to teach and who given any opportunity to do other things will gladly do so. But a more common reason we have professionals performing nonprofessional tasks is that there is no one else to do them.

Clerical and technical tasks are usually imperative to the day-to-day operation of the library program. Computers have to run if students and teachers are to use them. Software must be installed. Books have to be reshelved. New materials need to be added to the catalog if they are to be found. Students in the library need to be supervised. When these things don't happen, important things can't happen either. It's sort of a Maslow's hierarchy of library needs—you can't teach a student how to use a resource or use a search engine unless the material can be found or the computer is running.

Library programs and librarians need good support personnel of two types: clerical and technical.

Libraries need paraprofessionals (aka secretaries or clerks) who handle things like circulating materials, processing new materials, checking in magazines, answering the telephone, and supervising students using the library independently. Again, if there is not a clerk to do these tasks they will still get done, but unfortunately by the librarian.

Libraries also need good technical support. Technicians install, troubleshoot, and maintain hardware and software. Schools too often have looked at technology upkeep as something that could be done as an extra assignment by a "techie" teacher. That may have worked when technology consisted of filmstrip projectors, an Apple II lab, and a single computer at the school secretary's desk. With the complexity of networks, the increased importance of school management systems, and the infusion of many kinds of technologies into classrooms and offices, the technology has become too mission-critical to the operations of the entire school for such minimal support. Buildings need access to a trained technician on a regular basis—preferably one housed in the school itself.

In some cases, schools are lucky enough to have volunteers who are reliable and long-term enough to do some of these tasks, but volunteers, especially parents, should be doing more important and interesting work like individual tutoring, creating special learning centers, or preparing exciting displays. Good programs cannot rely on folks whose presence on the job is discretionary performing nondiscretionary duties.

So how do we afford these support positions? It seems to me they should get funding priority. If we don't, we are paying professional salaries for nonprofessional work. If a building can't afford both library professional and support staff, it should consider sharing a professional among buildings who will be doing what teaching, planning, and supervising he or she can do at each building.

The better question is how can we *not* afford such positions when having them gives the professional librarian time to teach students and staff critical information literacy and technology skills? Without improved learning as the library's primary purpose, it really doesn't matter whether the books are shelved or the computers work or not.

Considering the important roles these support positions play, it's critical librarians know how to effectively supervise and work with them. Here are some ideas.

1. Honor their training needs. Paraprofessionals and technicians need and appreciate learning opportunities just as much as professionals. Learning about new trends in librarianship and technology, about new student educational resources, about new customer service skills, and about using new technologies are needed staff development opportunities for all support staff as well as professionals. More than most of us, technicians realize that additional training to develop new skills is a real investment—in oneself. In no field does one's skill set become more dated, more rapidly than in the computer science field. Generous training opportunities—school financed, of course—benefit both the technician and the institution. People feel better about themselves if they feel more competent about what they do. Library and educational technology conferences often have a strand for support staff. Watch for conferences especially created for paraprofessionals.

2. *Support their formal educational goals.* The path taken by some of our best professional librarians started with the person as a parent volunteer, then as a library paraprofessional, and finally as a professional librarian. If one of your support staff shows an interest in getting a library, teaching, or educational technology degree, encourage him or her to do so. Encourage your professionals to take on higher-level tasks and grow on the job. We need all the quality people in our field we can get.

3. *Value their contribution to the team and give them decision-making input.* Build on the understanding that you and your support staff's skills are complementary. While the librarian might have great planning, visioning, and teaching skills, the best paraprofessionals and technicians are well organized and detail-oriented. The simple acknowledgment that all skills used by the library's staff are important is essential. There is nothing more demoralizing to a technician than having a Dilbert-esque pointy-haired boss making ill-informed decisions that make the job more difficult than it has to be. There are days that I am sure my techs are convinced that I don't know my ASCII from a hole in the ground, but they also know that I seek, hear, and value their advice. Again, there are more ways of showing people that they have value than just money.

4. *Include them in planning and policy making.* One of my favorite stories tells of a janitor at NASA in the late 1960s. When asked what his job was, he replied, "To help put a man on the moon." Support staff members should know not just their jobs, but how those jobs are critical to the mission of the library program and school. One way to build this understanding is by making sure they have a voice in visioning, planning, budgeting, and policy making. That being said, it is also important that the role of the support staff is not to make policy themselves, but follow policies approved by the professional staff.

5. *Keep everyone in the loop.* If the techs are going to help give good advice, it means they need to be aware of the "big picture" as well as the details. When folks understand the educational goals behind the decisions made, it gives a higher purpose to one's job. For example, knowing that involved parents can significantly improve students' school performance, maintaining that website or e-mail server becomes important. I believe that education really is a calling, a vocation, and that paraprofessional and technician can truly be educators.

6. *Encourage their creativity.* If your paraprofessional wants to read the kindergarteners a story, what's the problem? If he has a dynamic idea for a display or reading promotion, why not encourage him? If a technician has found a new technology resource, why not try it? Maybe her idea about rearranging the computer lab for better supervision is worth exploring. Clerical and technical tasks can be stultifying. The chance for your paraprofessional or technician to do something creative, exciting, and different not only helps prevent job burnout but can be of genuine value to your program.

7. *Supply the tools and resources they need to do their jobs.* Technicians and paraprofessionals need to have their own workspaces, decent computers, and the proper tools for the job. Those tools include not just screwdrivers, chip pullers, line testers, book tape, spine labels, and book carts, but diagnostic software, program manuals, and telephone extensions or cell phones.

8. *Pay a competitive salary or be flexible.* Administrators don't always understand why a "technician" should be paid more than a beginning "professional" teacher. When skills, like materials, are in short supply, their value increases. And competent technicians are too often in short supply. All schools should know what

the competitive pay scales for these positions are in their area. Smart librarians can and do compensate folks in other ways as well. Being flexible with hours and days worked is a form of compensation. This gives us a larger pool of skilled workers from which to draw, including college students. Offering comp time works so long as it is documented. And just being "family friendly" by giving staff time to go see their daughter's music program or help a friend in need is not just humane, but wise.

9. *Run interference for them.* It's not the paraprofessional's job to take heat from disgruntled teachers or parents. The teacher's computer just crashed and he doesn't remember when he last backed up his files, and he blames the technician. An angry parent calls the library paraprofessional insisting her child returned a book. The librarian's job is to keep people communicating even when a technical fix doesn't work the first time or when a parent has an issue. Librarians must provide a buffer between a cranky user and support staff who are operating in good faith. Do it. It'll keep people loyal and effective.

10. *Keep in touch with reality.* It's not always easy to remember, but life continues even when not everything is working. A sense of perspective on everyone's part can lead to a happier work environment. Help your technicians and paraprofessionals to do their best, to strive to provide good service, to use good communication skills, to anticipate problems before they appear, and to meet their personal goals. The reality is that the satisfaction from doing a job well and from being perceived as important for many people is preferable to higher remuneration in a more stress-filled environment. Capitalize on it.

Working with the technology department

Is there any definitive answer to what should or should not be filtered to meet state and federal requirements? Our technology director has been checking more little boxes on our filter. Just yesterday he decided to block a site that students use to contact each other and experts for projects.

Our technology policies do not allow personal devices to access our network. Students and parents are asking why, if they have these tools, they can't use them in school, especially when it seems available computers in the library are always in short supply. Our new e-book collection won't be well used unless students can get access to it with their own readers.

The manager of our student information system just doesn't understand why it's important that the student data in our circulation system is updated on a daily basis. We're a school with a high student mobility rate, and monthly updates just aren't enough.

So why can't I have the management rights to the computers in the library's lab? Sometimes it's weeks before I get changes made that I need to teach my classes. And there are often small problems that I could quickly fix if I had the rights to do so.

Librarians and school staff members realize that technology is a double-edged sword. Almost any device can be used in ways that are disruptive, unsafe, unethical, and even destructive. Technology is neutral: The same hammer that builds the cathedral can be used to break its windows.

For some reason, many schools have not yet figured out how to create good policies and rules about technology use, and that results in complaints like the ones above. Under the worst circumstances poor or nonexistent policies have created what seems like a new range war between not cattle ranchers and sheepherders but between educators, often librarians, and the technologists. The technologists are winning by default since they have, as the librarian above puts it, the know-how to check "the little box." Knowledge of what is possible and not possible with technological devices combined with a carefully selected sharing of that knowledge gives technical staff power and credibility, and makes rules they set often difficult to dispute.

Table 5-1
It's not the technology that's good or bad. It's how it is used.

Technology	Appropriate use	Not-so appropriate use
The Internet	Source of great information for school projects	Source of pornography, ready-made term papers, and hate group propaganda
Cell phone	Means of communication in emergencies	Source of distraction for students
Personal computing devices	Devices used to access and read information, do schoolwork, keep schedules, and use specialize tools such as graphing calculators	Means of disrupting classes, cheating, and spreading viruses and malware
Social networking sites and e-mail	Ability to share ideas with experts, classmates, and teachers	Ability to harass others, waste time, and share ideas with dangerous strangers

Please don't think I am beating up on technology department personnel. (I am one in my district, after all.) They do indeed have knowledge that is critical to the vital operation of technology in schools. Plus they have the responsibility for data security, network bandwidth conservation, and the reliable operations of what are usually far too many machines for their staff to maintain. My sympathies are with them when they wish to make rules that will decrease the likelihood of more technical problems.

Yet these hardworking people often do not understand parent, teacher, librarian, or student goals and concerns. They may not understand why it so important that kids have access to as wide a range of information as possible. They may not understand that teachers need some flexibility to load software for preview on their computers. They may not understand why it is important that the library catalog and online reference sources are available from the homes of students and staff. They may not understand that the librarian needs the password to the desktop security program in the computer lab.

So who in a school *should* ultimately make the technology rules? These decisions need to be made by the district library/technology advisory committee, the same group that does technology planning as you read in chapter three. Remember that this committee is comprised primarily of educators—teachers, librarians, and administrators—but may also include parents, students, businesspersons, college faculty members, and public librarians. And of course the committee includes members of the technical staff for their important input on security, compatibility, and implementation issues. All members' views need to be considered and valued. Building technology committees should work in exactly the same way.

For example, on the difficult Internet filtering issue, one district's library/technology committee decided that as a result of federal regulations, the district was required to use a filter, but it would be set at its least restrictive settings, blocking only sites that were pornographic. Any teacher or librarian could have a blocked site unblocked by simply requesting it—no questions asked. Adults in the school are required to continue to monitor student access to the Internet as if no filter were present. The technology director now knows that it is the responsibility of the library and teaching staff to see that students do not access inappropriate materials, not that of the technology department alone. This is a good policy decision that could not have been reached without a variety of voices heard during its making.

An open dialog between professional educators and professional technology staff about concerns, responsibilities, and priorities related to technology is essential for its successful use in schools. Not everyone will agree with the decisions made, but at least everyone will have a better understanding of why they were made. Educational range wars aren't healthy for anyone—especially the little lambs we serve.

Librarians can actively promote such a dialog with their technology department by:

1. Serving on district and building technology committees. As indicated above, librarians taking an active and positive role in helping make good policy decisions is essential to positive relations with the technology department. While not all policies and priorities will be 100 percent acceptable to the librarians on the committee (or anyone else for that matter), they will know how and why the decisions were made.

2. Creating clear delineations of responsibility. Defining where technology duties begin and end helps everyone know what he or she must do. One simple guideline that works in schools is that the librarian has primary responsibility for teaching staff how to use technology and the technology staff has primary responsibility for doing the maintenance and support of technology. Exceptions must be made at times, but general guidelines for who-does-what are helpful in maintaining good relations.

3. Sharing ways other schools are using technology. Given the importance of administrative uses of technology in schools (we all like it when the payroll system is running well), educational technology use does not always get the priority it deserves. Librarians can share with the technology department leadership examples of how other schools are using technology effectively. This is especially helpful when encouraging the adoption of new resources (like social networking sites) or changes in policy (allowing students to access the wireless network with personal devices). Every technology director wants his or her school to be on the cutting edge of technology use. Librarians can help with that effort.

4. Asking for reasons and evidence for why policies are made. Unfortunately, too many technology departments are overly cautious and hyper-compliant when following good technology security practices and state and federal mandates. If such a reason is given for making what might be considered an overly restrictive policy, the librarian should diplomatically ask for evidence when given the reason for it. Documentation of such reasons is not an unreasonable request.

5. Framing requests in terms of student and teacher need. As we discussed when talking about library advocacy in chapter four, requests for services or materials for the library should always be framed by why the request is good for students and teachers. Rather than simply demanding the ability to access student usernames and passwords, explaining that the librarian can immediately help students who forget their passwords is more acceptable. Yes, technology departments do like security, but they also like students to be successful.

6. Accepting some limitations. Given the complexities and prevalence of computer and network security threats, librarians must accept that all systems cannot be as open and convenient to use as they would prefer. State and federal guidelines do limit what student and staff information can be accessed and by whom. And yes, a person who has not been trained in administering a complex technology system can really mess it up. A balance between security and access is necessary for the safety and reliability of all technologies.

7. Respecting each other's priorities. The "missions" of the library and the technology department may be the same: making sure all students receive a good education. But roles within that mission are different and can even be at odds. The technology department may place a priority on security, safety, reliability, and adequacy. The library program may emphasize availability, ease of use, and flexibility. The priorities of neither side are unimportant; they are only different. It is also apparent that neither side can function effectively without the other. A technology director understands that meaningful and effective use of technology is the key to his or her success. And librarians know that unless the technology is installed, operating, sufficiently powerful, and reliable, we may as well save our energies trying to get reluctant teachers to use it. Libraries and technology departments are "interdependent."

8. Combining the library and technology departments' physical spaces. People working in physical proximity have more opportunities for face-to-face communication. And such conversations lead to better understandings of each other. The library should house your building technology staff, and if there are district library and technology services, they should be located in the same offices. Not only is this better for internal communications, but it simplifies the lives of staff and students when trying to determine where to go for assistance.

  9. *Working under shared leadership.* While the building librarian may not have much choice in this matter, library and technology programs under a common district supervisor work better together. This person can schedule regular meetings between the technology department members and librarians to discuss day-to-day issues and often brainstorm future possibilities. When the librarians in the district meet, the supervisor can make sure technology support staff are available when needed. Ideally, the library/technology supervisor should:

- be an experienced, successful educator who recognizes that all technology efforts must be directed to meet educational goals. This is a person who has been a teacher, librarian, and possibly an administrator and can empathize with each role.
- be able to articulate a clear educational philosophy and the place of technology within it.
- be neither a technophobe nor technophile, having a balanced approach to educational technology, understanding its limitations.
- be both a model user and advocate for technology and libraries.
- have a broad understanding of the problems the district has and the goals it is trying to meet.
- be an efficient manager who can supervise others, create and administer budgets, and manage projects. This person may not need to know how to write computer code, extract data from the health services database, or replace the toner cartridge in a laser printer, but she or he knows the person in the district who can and sees that it gets done when needed.
- understand the ethical dimensions of technology use knowing technology has impacted the rules regarding copyright, materials selection, intellectual freedom, and privacy.
- be a leader—whatever that means. For me, it means creating and sharing a practical vision of a better system of schooling that serves more children in better ways. It means, as Tom Landry reminds us, of getting folks to do things they do not want to do in order to accomplish the things they want to accomplish. It means getting people to see and address their problems in constructive, effective ways, and helping them grow in the process. It means getting people to talk and work together, to be empathetic and patient. It means accepting risk, criticism, the need for continuous self-evaluation, and the acceptance that life will always be one long, steep, learning curve.

  No library/technology director may embody all these characteristics, but the best ones I have the privilege of knowing and working with come very close—and many of them have come from a library background.

Working with the teaching staff: The fundamentals of successful collaboration

  Effective collaboration with the classroom teacher is arguably the most challenging part of our jobs. There never seems to be enough time. Many teachers are very independent. Scheduling works against team efforts. Comfort, tradition, and school culture ("That's not the way we've always done it.") make changing teaching practices problematic. Librarians *know* the difficulties.

  Librarians can and should add genuine value to the educational process through collaborative planning and teaching. But this can only be done when the librarian is both proactive and reflective. While proactivity is widely touted by our professional organizations and many of us have become quite good at it, the art of being a reflective practitioner has not been as well explored.

A book worth reading is *Reflective Practice to Improve Schools* (York-Barr, Sommers, Ghere, and Montie, 2005). In it, the authors suggest that in order for us to truly improve our individual professional effectiveness, we should each deliberately and systematically analyze our experiences to determine why a practice worked or did not. Being a reflective practitioner means trying to look at something you've done as though you were an outside, impartial observer.

Below are a few suggestions drawn from professional literature, from watching really good library librarians at work, and from reflecting on my own successful and unsuccessful collaborative efforts.

As you read these suggestions, do this simple activity, alone or with a group:

1. Read each suggestion about initiating or improving collaborative experiences.
2. Think of an example of this suggestion from your personal experience.
3. Jot down notes about the factors that may have contributed to the success or failure of the experience.
4. Reread your notes to see if there are commonalities or trends within them.
5. Reflect.

1. Recognize what keeps teachers awake at night. The purpose of collaboration should be to help others meet their instructional goals—period. That cannot be done unless librarians know what they are.

- Use mastery of student learning objectives as the goal of the planning and activity.
- Know your school's curricula and how students will be assessed.
- Understand the expected mastery of skills on high-stakes tests in each content area.
- Know the research on effective practices in the content areas.
- Survey the teaching staff on their instructional needs.
- Be placed on grade-level and departmental communications e-mail mailing lists.
- Become a member and attend curriculum committees at both the building and district level.

2. Cultivate, use, and value your vital areas of expertise. All members of the collaborative effort should be bringing something unique to the table when working together and form a symbiotic relationship.

- Master and use teaching techniques, methods, and resources that the classroom teacher doesn't know.
- Clarify your role as librarian so as not to seem threatening to the classroom teacher.
- Continue learning new teaching techniques, methods, and resources as classroom teachers master the old ones and design practical applications that use them.
- Consider yourself a co-learner with your students and other faculty members.
- Teach skills, don't just provide resources. Librarian expertise should be the resource, not just the materials the library provides. Librarians can supply good information resources, but they also have the skills to help students and staff learn to produce their own information and data, synthesize it, and communicate it effectively.
- Keep track of past successful collaborative experiences and communicate those successes to others on the staff.
- Help create and participate in building-wide efforts such as writing across the curriculum or free-reading times.

- Respect yourself as a full-fledged teacher who may use different methods and resources than the classroom teacher, but who is just as important to the educational process.

3. Look for win/win situations. Good collaborations result in both the teacher and librarian meeting mutually agreed upon, but individual goals.

- Practice Stephen Covey's philosophy of "win/win or no deal" when collaborating (Covey 1989).
- Look for a shared passion or interest in a topic with other teachers.
- Coauthor and implement grants that support both the classroom and library program.
- Concentrate on helping teachers improve areas of their curriculum with which they are currently dissatisfied.
- Look for unusual areas of collaboration. Collaborate with the physical education teacher, principal, special education teacher, custodian, secretary, parent–teacher organization, and teachers of content areas that may not traditionally use the library and its resources, such as the math department.
- Recognize that there is no "one-size-fits-all" and that the teacher who is an early adopter of new teaching practices or technology and the teacher who is change resistant both need services.
- Don't let others take advantage of you by making sure the role you are asked to play in any collaborative effort requires professional skills and adds educational value. Don't relegate yourself to the role of teacher's aide.

4. Be likeable. The personality and interpersonal skills of the librarian are critical for successful collaboration. People don't work with people who are difficult or unpleasant.

- Seek guidance from research on improving interpersonal relationships. Respected authority on influence Robert Cialdini suggests these traits help make us likeable (Cialdini 2006):
  - Being physically attractive and well-groomed
  - Being similar to those with whom we work
  - Paying others compliments
  - Being familiar to others through contact and cooperation (and getting out of the library)
  - Being associated with positive happenings
- Brush up on your interpersonal skills. Seek out training and books on interpersonal skill building and effective communication techniques.
- Respond quickly to requests or at least acknowledge that the request has been heard and give a timeline for action on it.
- Build collaborative relationships by building personal trust and reliability.
- Send "thank-you" notes and create public statements of appreciation such as awards.
- Don't expect others to understand your problems—no whining.
- Understand "difficult people" and learn techniques to work with them such as working in teams instead of one-on-one.

5. Build slowly, but meaningfully. Most school cultures have been formed over years, if not decades. The expectation that the librarian will immediately become an accepted, valued collaborator on every classroom project or activity is unrealistic. But this does not mean this should not be the librarian's goal and that steps should not be taken toward achieving it.

- Don't try to work with everyone at once, but cumulatively do a few new or additional collaborative projects well each year.
- Start with personal friends on staff, but don't let it end with them. They can be a foundation on which to reach all teachers if they attest to your efficacy.
- Look for smaller, engaging activities for teachers who have "too much to teach" and are unwilling to work on major projects.
- Build administrative and curriculum department support of your program by focusing on creating library program goals that support building and curricular goals.
- Spend time working with others on critical problems, not just nice extras.
- Work with beginning teachers early and be a mentor to them.
- Never give up and never be satisfied. Remember that the library program will always be a "work in progress."

Too often we do not take the time to deliberately evaluate what we do and why it has been successful or unsuccessful. We need to purposely take time to evaluate and modify, and reflect.

And remember, napping, from a distance, looks a lot like reflection. Take advantage of it.

Some concerns

Collaborate:
1. To work jointly with others or together especially in an intellectual endeavor
2. To cooperate with or willingly assist an enemy of one's country and especially an occupying force

—Merriam-Webster Online

Collaboration is often viewed as the salvation of school librarianship. Those who do collaborate are sainted; those who don't are damned. Library professional literature is replete with books, articles, and training opportunities on collaboration, especially collaborative teaching.

But are we thinking critically enough about this rather vague word and its implications? Here are some reasons this professional obsession with collaboration makes me nervous.

1. Collaboration is too often viewed as a goal. What everyone seems to forget is that collaboration is just one means (and not always the best one) of achieving a goal, *not* the goal itself. Too many library studies say "such and such" led to greater collaboration. But the question such studies should answer is: "Did it lead to more measurable student learning?"

There are downsides to working with others. It takes more time to reach decisions and get work accomplished. It takes time to find the time to work together. Not everyone likes working with others. Defining specific responsibilities is difficult and too often neglected. Team players may get undeserved credit or blame for an outcome. Some people are just a real pain with whom to work. Genius and imagination may be dimmed through groupthink timidity.

If I am a principal or teacher who worries about literacy rates, I don't care if my teachers and librarian are being collaborative—I worry if my staff is doing what it needs to do to raise kids' reading ability and the test scores that supposedly demonstrate that ability. Collaboration may feel good, but it also has to get the job done.

2. Collaboration can encourage codependency rather than interdependency. I know a librarian who collaboratively taught a unit with a teacher for ten years. The classroom teacher had students write stories; the librarian taught students how to create webpages that display the stories. It was a wonderful activity by two talented professionals. The problem? Why, after ten years, was the classroom teacher not teaching her kids to do the webpages herself, and the librarian teaming with different teachers on different projects?

Too often our subconscious rationale for collaboration is not advancing common goals, but creating a codependence that might insure job security. (The teacher can't do this without me.) This doesn't work. People tend to dislike those on whom they feel codependent. We have more strength in the long run if we teach others how to do a thing than if we simply do it for them. Librarians should be people who empower others rather than being the wizards who keep dark skills to themselves. Librarians must develop inter-dependent relationships with others.

3. Collaboration doesn't make us indispensable. No matter how much the school budget shrinks, teachers still have to be hired—at least teachers who have a curriculum for which the public holds them responsible. Who is responsible for the teaching and assessment of information literacy and technology skills in the school? If it is the classroom teacher, and the librarian is "collaborating," the library position can be eliminated because these skills will still be taught. Not as well, certainly, but they will be taught. Power comes with responsibility for critical tasks, and if we alone are responsible for none of them, we have no power.

4. Collaboration is viewed as important at only the classroom level. As earlier parts of this book have stressed, librarians need to collaborate on planning, policy making, and assessment tasks, not just on class-room units. Librarians also need to collaborate by serving on leadership, curriculum, student assessment, and staff development committees, both at the building and district level. Which has greater, long-term impact—spending an hour co-teaching a social studies class or serving on the social studies curriculum committee? Think about it.

Collaboration is wonderful if we have a higher purpose for working together, if we have clearly defined roles in a project, and if it is the most effective means of achieving a worthwhile goal. But collaboration is not the Holy Grail of librarianship.

For reflection: What is the secret to successful supervision?

Johnson's First Law of Effective Supervision: Hire people who don't need to be supervised.

Really. That's the whole secret. While those who hear me say this think it is a sort of smart aleck re-mark, I sincerely mean it.

I've never taken a class in supervision, but over the last thirty years I have discovered that people who don't need to be supervised are developed as much as selected. Hiring self-starters is great, and do so when you can, but here are few ideas for creating staff members who don't really need much supervision:

- **Make sure everyone knows the big picture.** The "why" of a project, especially in education, is often overlooked. We in education have the greatest mission in the world: making kids successful. If that is at the root of all our efforts, we naturally do our best. But *everyone* has to see the link— although sometimes long and nearly invisible—to one's work and its impact on students.
- **Jointly set clear goals, establish timelines, and help prioritize work.** Then get and stay out of the way. Establish what needs to be done and the parameters under which it must be accomplished. Then let others figure out the best way to do it.
- **Provide resources for success.** The supervisor should be the go-to person if his or her staff needs training, equipment, or cooperation from other people.

- **Expect and analyze failures.** When one tries new and, hopefully, more efficient or effective ways of doing things, failures will occur. If you are not making mistakes you are probably not making anything, as the pundits tell us. Don't blame the person but figure out what went wrong and how to make a *different* mistake the next time.
- **Use employee evaluations to help build, not pull down.** My personal experience shows that formal evaluations of staff are worthless unless documenting for dismissal. Good people are self-aware of their strengths and weaknesses. Use evaluations to help people meet their personal challenges and goals.
- **Meet regularly.** Scheduled face-to-face meetings with a running agenda regarding tasks and projects keeps the lines of communication open and you informed without having to look over people's shoulders.
- **Accept and build areas of expertise.** You don't need to know the technical and other special skills of everyone in your department, thank goodness. But you need to know the reasons people do what they do and why those tasks are important in terms you can understand.
- **Be flexible with schedules.** It's reasonable to expect people to work beyond their normal paid hours when there are deadlines or emergencies. It's reasonable to expect that there will be times people come in late, leave early, or need a day off. Nine-to-five mind-sets are a thing of the past. Trust is implicit if you don't want to have to supervise people.

I have never liked to be micromanaged and fortunately I haven't been for many years. Isn't there this rule about treating others as you would like to be treated?

References

Cialdini, Robert B. *Influence: The Psychology of Persuasion*. New York: HarperBusiness, 2006.

Covey, Stephen. *The 7 Habits of Highly Effective People*. New York: Free Press, 1989.

York-Barr, Jennifer, William A. Sommers, Gail S. Ghere, and Joanne K. Montie. *Reflective Practice to Improve Schools: An Action Guide for Educators*. 2nd edition. Thousand Oaks, CA: Corwin Press, 2005.

Chapter Six

Managing Digital Resources

You know you are a 21st-century librarian when . . .

- You have to remind kindergarteners to turn off their smartphones before the story starts.
- You know what an IP number is but not an ISBN number.
- You have a student who does a better job troubleshooting the circulation system than the district technician.
- Your students think both *The Princess and the Frog* and *Meet the Robinsons* were written by Walt Disney.
- You know more librarians in Texas than you do in your home state because of your personal learning network.
- The best way to remind a student about an overdue book is through Facebook.
- You don't talk in the teachers' lounge about a project because it is not tied directly to a state test.
- When answering a reference question, *you* consult Wikipedia.
- You've started dressing like your avatar.
- Kids look at you funny when you call it the "the card catalog."
- You have more polo shirts with computer logos than you do book logos—and 25 percent of your wardrobe comes from vendor booths at conferences.
- Your students want to read the most popular YA lit on their phones.
- Your students show *you* how to get around the district Internet filter so you can teach a lesson.
- Your aid spends more time troubleshooting the network than reshelving books.
- You never see anyone copy out of the print encyclopedia anymore.
- Your index finger has a callous from tapping the interactive whiteboard.
- You didn't get your last grad class assignment turned in on time because the network was down.
- You've Googled the new teachers in your building—and all the kids have Googled you.
- You don't remember the last time you've had to alphabetize something.
- You have all your passwords and PIN numbers on your smartphone—and you can't remember the password for your smartphone.

One of our five district-wide library/technology goals reads:

Technology will be used to provide the most current, accurate and extensive information resources possible to all learners in the district and community in a cost effective and reliable manner at maximum convenience to the user.

As the opening section of this chapter suggests, libraries are in rapid transformation. And no part of what they offer is changing faster than "information resources" and how they are acquired, paid for, accessed, and delivered. Print reference collections are almost nonexistent. Videotapes and, increasingly, DVDs are disappearing. Few people even know what the *Readers' Guide to Periodical Literature* was, and library backrooms have few "back issues" of magazines. Students are demanding information that is digital, accessible from any location using their own devices, and don't necessarily want to come to a library to get it. What is the role, or is there a role, for libraries and librarians in such an information environment?

How has the library's role changed as information and books go digital?

Author Kevin Kelly calculates that everything humans have created and published, in formats from tablets to books, from webpages to videos, can be stored digitally on fifty petabyte hard drives. Using today's technology, a building the size of a small-town library could hold the entirety of human output.

But he goes on to predict that this same information will one day fit on a small portable device like an iPod, and that the "library of all libraries" may plug directly into one's brain with "thin white cords." And while adults might dread this change, our kids are asking, "What's taking so long?" (Kelly 2006).

Has Kelly's prediction already come true? When your smartphone accesses the Internet, isn't it already allowing access to "the library of all libraries"?

Chances are an increasing share of your library's materials budget is shifting to digital resources every year. Popular educational reference book publishers are publishing e-books and online databases. If you are adding a new encyclopedia next year, you are likely to consider an online version. Or you are asking yourself if Wikipedia has replaced the commercial encyclopedia, at least for students. Your teachers may well be using more instructional films from a streaming video source or YouTube than from your VHS/DVD collection. And we know our NetGen students prefer their information in bytes rather than pages.

Intelligently managing these intangible items is increasingly important, and it should be the librarian who has responsibility for doing so.

When we talk about the management of print and physical audiovisual resources, tasks and procedures can be organized into the following, semichronological, areas:

1. Needs assessment/collection development
2. Selection
3. Acquisition and access
4. Promotion and display
5. Cataloging, circulation, and control
6. Inventory
7. Evaluation

What we need to remember is that each of these resource management tasks is applicable to digital resources as well as to those in analog formats. But online resources have unique characteristics that make working with them quite different than the books, magazines, and AV materials we've managed in the past. And I'm sure you've already encountered some of those differences.

First, let's identify what digital resources need to be managed. Today's school libraries have most if not all these resources (I am listing only those items that have a purchase or subscription cost):

- Online databases such as full-text periodicals
- Online reference sources
- Streaming video collections
- Commercial search engines

- E-books
- Online tutorial or training services
- Productivity tools
- Curriculum programs

Do the management tasks above apply to these digital resources? Let's look at each task individually.

1. Needs assessment/collection development. Unless you have an unlimited budget, your digital resources must be selected to meet the needs of your school, its curricula, its students, and its teachers. Long gone are the days of the "balanced" school library collection where collection building meant having something available on *every* possible topic—just in case. While general reference sources are still needed, the "free" Internet, interlibrary loan, and local public and academic libraries give students access to a rounded set of materials.

Many states or regional consortiums also purchase general resources for all libraries, public, school, academic, and special, to use. A first question to ask in a needs assessment is "What do I need in addition to the resources provided by my state or region?" Some state collections of content databases and other resources are amazingly comprehensive. Familiarity with these resources is a must for every librarian for the collection development process.

The librarian should concentrate on building a collection based on specific needs down to course, unit, and even project level. Just as there is little sense in acquiring books on a topic that is not part of a curriculum, does not meet a reading program goal, or does not meet the needs of an identified group of students, there is no sense in selecting a subject-specific database for a subject not researched in your school. Traditional needs assessment methods can be used to determine areas of need in your collection (see chapter two).

Increasingly, the question about meeting those needs centers around whether digital or print resources are best suited to meeting them. How will your students and staff get the biggest "bang for the buck"? In making that choice, you need to ask a few questions:

- How timely does this resource need to be?
- How much access to computers or e-book readers do your users have in the library, in the rest of the school, in their homes, and in the community?
- What resources do your users seem to like using the most? Studies of NetGen students indicate they have a definite preference for digital information resources.
- How important is accessibility to this information from outside the school? For multiple users to have access at one time?
- Are there features some resources might have that would benefit special needs populations such English-language learners, special education students, or students with physical disabilities?

The "right" choice will depend on your own demographics and resources. While both you and your users may prefer a digital encyclopedia, if there are only a very few workstations in your library on which one might be accessed, the print version is still a better choice.

2. Selection. Just like choosing a print resource, good selection procedures need to be followed, including knowing the board selection policy and using unbiased review sources. Good reviews and comparisons are more difficult to find for electronic resources than for traditional ones. Given the changeable nature of online resources, reviews may no longer reflect the actual product (a full-text periodical database may have added or dropped titles or changed the number of years of back issues, for example).

One method of reviewing online resources, however, is available that is not traditionally used with print materials: the trial subscription. You and you patrons can use the product from fourteen to sixty days before deciding whether to subscribe or purchase it. One librarian tries to have at least one teacher use a database with students before he spends money on it. If there are glitches or the instructions are confusing, the problems will usually show up quickly. This method also helps determine if the reading and instructional levels of the information are suitable for the students who will be using the product.

Another important review challenge is that many digital resources tend to be collections of materials, not individual titles. It is one thing to purchase a single DVD title; quite another to select an entire collection of educational videos. This makes a review imperative since a hands-on, eyes-on examination of every title is certainly impractical if not impossible. It's also a good time to review a basic selection precept that we include materials based on their strengths rather than censor them based on a small percentage of material that *may* be objectionable. What happens when a health database is selected and made available online that contains material "objectionable" to a few parents? Is this any different from choosing any comprehensive reference source in print format? The potential for challenges here makes using an authoritative review source critical for information in any format—as well as having good reconsideration policies and procedures.

Additional considerations are operating system compatibility (less problematic with web-based materials, but not completely gone), network bandwidth needs, in-house maintenance support necessary, and on-site storage capacity required. Some companies will allow a school to house the product's digital content onsite so that only wide area network or in-building network capacity is a factor, not bandwidth to the Internet itself. When the medium being accessed is comprised of large files, like video programs, this is an important factor in selecting a resource. With the purchase of materials that are meant to be a permanent part of the collection, such as e-book titles, there is the question of how accessible such materials will be in future years as programs, operating systems, and storage media change. (Tried to read any files created on an Apple IIe lately?)

And finally, we also need to recognize that the resource interface, not just its contents, needs to be age appropriate. Happily, many companies recognize that younger users need less sophisticated search tools, larger icons, and brighter images.

3. Acquisition and access. Purchasing and accessing a digital resource may differ dramatically from buying a physical resource. Select a book, place a purchase order, catalog it, put it on the shelf, and you're done. But the same acquisition method may not apply to a database, online reference tool, or e-book.

Most online resources are not outright purchases, but subscriptions. In other words, the school is getting the right to use the resource for a set amount of time, not the resource itself. This has a couple of implications. Budgets will need to reflect the yearly cost of the item, and if the subscription is dropped, teachers and students will no longer have access to it. This may be problematic, as the discussion about evaluation below will suggest.

One management/budgeting tip is to make sure your subscriptions begin and end when your school fiscal year begins and ends. Most companies will work with you to bill your district for a partial year or, more likely, a year plus the months needed to end the subscription at the end of your school year.

Getting to a digital resource should be as easy as entering a URL—right? Not quite. Giving a school's users access means working with your technology department in most cases, and selection must be done in coordination with it. One decision to be made, when the option is available, is whether to give access to an online resource by password, IP address, or both.

If access is given by IP address, patrons at any computer within a range of IP numbers do not need a username or password to log on. The product recognizes the IP number as one in an organization that has purchased the product. This is convenient and reduces the amount of work needed to track usernames and passwords and is a fairly secure method of limiting access only to licensed users. However, access by username and password has advantages as well. Control of certain materials can be given to only select users;

users may have access to individual areas where they can store personal tags, results of searches, or favorites lists; users can get access to the resource from computers outside the school's IP range and on their personal devices without the school having to set up a proxy; and usage can be tracked more precisely. If access is given by individual rather than generic username and password, I would strongly suggest working with your technology department to set up a database, such as an LDAP (lightweight directory access protocol) directory, where usernames and passwords can be stored and used for authentication in multiple applications.

Home access is an important factor to consider when selecting a resource. The movement toward 24/7 learning increasingly requires learning resources to be available at all times. Online courses and hybrid classes will continue to demand access to good digital materials since a student may not be near the physical library for extended periods of time.

4. Promotion and display. How do you persuade kids (and teachers) to use authoritative online sources and not just "Google" the information they need? How do you teach your users to see the library as a portal to trusted sources? Online resources do not jump out at students and staff and scream "use me" any more than our library books jumped of the shelves. Digital resources also need to be promoted and displayed.

Library orientation programs must of course demonstrate online resources as well as the physical ones, but introductions to online resources are best done during research units themselves—when students actually need the information they contain. Any bibliography or webquest prepared for a unit should reference electronic tools as well as those in print. Teachers need to be informed about and trained in using these digital resources.

Library webpages should clearly mark links to their digital resources, either on the homepage or on a separate page that has a clear link from the home page. A note by the link that tells the user any special instructions for accessing the resource not only helps the user but also cuts down on questions. Oh, posting a generic username and password on a public website, no matter how convenient, is *not* appropriate.

Students and teachers can be subtly reminded of the schools' online resources if guides in the form of posters are visible near workstations. Again, these resources need to be actively promoted at teacher meetings and in teacher newsletters. The library's webpage with links to its digital resources should be the default page when any web browser is launched on every library computer.

Just because it doesn't fit in a display case, doesn't mean you can't make it visible.

5. Cataloging, circulation, and control. Should digital resources be cataloged? Well, of course. Many electronic resources come with catalog records. Online reference materials should be found when doing a catalog search just like their print cousins. When feasible, the ability to search digital resources using a federated search tool in your library catalog should be made available.

Few electronic resources circulate per se. Multiple users can access them all at one time—a major advantage of these tools.

E-books are the exception to this rule. Many e-book providers allow only single users to access titles with libraries determining "circulation" length as they would with any print resource. The specific rights for e-book use vary not only from supplier to supplier, but from publisher to publisher within suppliers' lists. This includes whether a title can be accessed by multiple users, if it can be downloaded and read by portable devices, on what devices it can be read, if selections from it can be copied and pasted into other programs, and if it can be printed. NetLibrary once suggested that most users treat their e-books as a reference source with an average use time of thirty-five minutes. Supplying digital materials like e-books or digital audiobooks may require the circulation of portable devices on which to read the materials such as e-book readers or digital audio players. When a single digital device may hold multiple items (one e-book reader with a dozen titles on it), counting circulation becomes very challenging. (See more on e-books later in this chapter.)

Regular checks to see if your users have access are important, as is checking the resources' links from the library's webpage to make sure they are working. Technology departments may change the district's external IP ranges without alerting the librarian and without realizing it has prevented users from being able to access those resources that are IP authenticated.

6. Inventory. Counting the number of resources to which the library subscribes is usual pretty simple since they aren't very numerous and impossible to steal, even by ingenious eighth graders.

Tracking licenses of software programs that are installed on computer workstations is more problematic. It's important to make sure that your school is not running more copies of an application than the number it holds a license for unless you want to run afoul of copyright. Every few years, our district, to help stay in compliance, runs a remote survey of all computers to get a list of licensed program files on each. These lists are then compared to licenses for which we hold records, and if any unlicensed software is found, our department takes action. Limiting the rights for installing software also helps keep licenses from being installed on more computers than allowed. Purchase site licenses for products when possible. It may be more economical, and help save the hassle of inventorying the product on individual computers. One major advantage to open source or free tools like GoogleApps for Education is that license accountability is unnecessary.

Do keep good records of your licenses and subscriptions. It may not be possible to be totally compliant, but your district needs to show it has made a good faith effort to do so.

7. Evaluation. Most vendors of digital information make it possible to track the usage of their products. It is, after all, in their own best interests to have librarians and their administrators know just how heavily a resource is being used. A typical report might look something like this (from TeachingBooks.net):

March usage statistics for Johnson Elementary School:
- 27,860 pages turned since the start of your license.
- 2,290 pages turned in the past month.
- 218 sessions in the main section of TeachingBooks in the past month.
- 58 sessions in the Educator Area of TeachingBooks in the past month.
- 276 total sessions in all of TeachingBooks in the past month.

Target usage figures can be established with resources meeting those targets retained, and those not getting the required use, dropped.

Usage analysis such as that listed above provides data on the volume of use but does nothing to show how useful your users found the resource. If you base your decision to subscribe purely on transaction logs, you are not getting the full picture. You need to combine log analysis with other forms of evaluation such as citation analysis and exit interviews done at the end of major products and student/staff surveys that ask about the importance of these resources.

The decision to keep or terminate a subscription to many of these products should not be done the first year. It often takes several years before teachers and students discover the usefulness of a resource. And a danger of switching content providers is that you might turn some teachers off if the links in their lesson plans to those resources need to be changed too often. Evaluate—cautiously.

The practice of effective analog resource management has developed over many years—even centuries. But the rapid pace of transition from print to digital resources does not allow today's librarian the luxury of a slow transition. We need to develop, test and share best practices with each other rapidly. After all, today's kids are asking, "What's taking so long?"

What is cloud computing, and how can librarians take advantage of it?

Ever heard these tales of woe from your students?

- I lost my flash drive with my homework on it.
- Our computer at home has a different software version than the computers at school so I can't open my file.
- I was at my grandma's house last night and my files weren't on her computer.
- I can't remember where I put my project.
- I ran out of storage space on the virtual drive.
- The computer's hard drive failed and I lost my files.

One area in which kids don't lack creativity is in excuse-making. As a student myself, I was pretty good at finding novel, yet believable reasons why my paper wasn't finished on time. And this was before there was technology to blame, just that poor old homework-eating dog.

Schools are rapidly moving to "cloud-based" networking environments. This is a radical shift on how schools provide access to resources, computer applications, and file storage to staff and students alike.

And librarians need to understand the implications and their roles in their implementation.

What is cloud computing and what are its advantages?

Anyone who has used a web-based e-mail program like Yahoo! Mail, stored a document using Dropbox, created a multimedia presentation using Animoto, or wrote a paper using GoogleDocs has experienced *cloud computing*.

Cloud computing relies on applications and file storage that reside on a network—usually the Internet itself—with minimal resources stored on local computers' hard drives. (A cloud graphic is often used to represent the Internet on network diagrams, hence the name.) As the examples above suggest, you may have already used cloud computing without even realizing it.

There are many genuine advantages to cloud computing. Since both applications and one's files reside on a network rather than on a specific computer, one can work on any project, anywhere regardless of the computer being used. Given a computer with Internet access—on one's desk at school, on one's lap at home, in any computer lab or coffee shop in the world, or at Grandma's house—one can work without worrying about transporting files on physical media like flash drives, keeping track of the latest version of a document, or having the right software to open a file. Students do not need to have access to specific workstations in a lab. Just as importantly, files are easily shared and collaboratively edited in a cloud-based application without having to resort to e-mail attachments and the confusion of multiple versions attachments can create.

Unlike much software that resides on computer hard drives, web-based applications that perform a wide array of productivity tasks are usually provided at no cost to the user. While not as comprehensive as commercial productivity titles like Microsoft Office, iMovie, Kid Pix, or Adobe Photoshop, these tools often have a surprisingly full set of features and are compatible with popular commercial programs. New features are added on a regular basis, and these programs often meet the needs of teachers and students.

Cloud computing requires less powerful computers such as netbooks, tablets, or even smartphones. Your library's technology costs can be lowered using these inexpensive computers, free file storage, and no-cost applications. Money that would have been spent on student workstations in labs, big file servers, support staff, and expensive software can now be used to pay for increased bandwidth, greater wireless coverage, or, maybe, just maybe, more library staffing.

One-to-one student to computer plans are more feasible using cloud computing. With a low-cost netbook or tablet and the cloud, student computers are virtually interchangeable, so if a device needs repair or is left at home, another machine can be easily substituted. Increasingly, K–12 schools will ask parents to provide basic computing devices for their children as a part of the school supply list. As a parent, I was asked to purchase a $130 graphing calculator for my son when he was in high school only a few years ago. How big a stretch is it to ask parents to provide a $250 netbook computer that includes a graphing calculator app that can be used in all classes for a wide variety of purposes today? These plans are referred to as BYOD (Bring Your Own Device) programs.

How can librarians take advantage of cloud-based computing today?

Before advocating for cloud computing for my staff and students, I decided to see if I could "live in the cloud" as a computer user—both personal and professional—myself. These are my top computer uses and how I moved my tasks to the cloud.

1. **Inexpensive hardware.** Rather than using a full-scale laptop computer, I used a netbook with a ten-inch screen that cost about a third of the cost of a regular laptop computer. The smaller keyboard and screen size took getting used to, but I found I could work on the computer for long periods of time. The speed was acceptable, the battery life was good, and the wireless connectivity was fast.
2. **E-mail.** Our district has successfully transitioned to Gmail accounts for all staff and students. I have long been a Gmail user for my personal e-mail.
3. **Web searching and bookmarking.** My delicious.com account has been a longtime cloud-based tool.
4. **Word processing, presentation creation, and spreadsheet use.** After years of using Microsoft Office, the move to GoogleDocs for my day-to-day productivity was surprisingly easy. In fact, getting away from Office's "feature creep" was refreshing. For 95 percent of my work and for storing my files, GoogleDocs works just fine, thank you. The work I create is compatible with Microsoft Office as well. Google adds features to its Docs suite on a regular basis. There are no skills in our information literacy/information technology curriculum that cannot be taught and practiced using GoogleApps for Education.
5. **Photo storage and editing.** I've been storing my best photographs on a commercial storage site for years and editing them with Photoshop Elements. But Flickr and Picasa are online applications that work just fine for this amateur's editing and storage needs. Picasa gives iPhoto a run for its money as a photo organizer. And Picnik allows me even more photo editing abilities.
6. **Webpage editing and webmastering.** My personal blog, wiki, and website are already hosted by application service providers who use online tools for management and editing. As does our school website. As do the professional association websites I've helped manage—my service club, our lakes association, and our state library/tech association.
7. **School-specific tasks.** All teacher gradebooks, reporting systems, and communications in our district are web-based, as are our accounting and other management systems. Period. Nearly every school document, form, and template I create and share is in GoogleDocs, not on my computer's hard drive.
8. **Library catalog and circulation system.** Both library staff and library users access our circulation/catalog system with a web browser. For a nominal fee, a regional telecommunications

agency hosts, maintains, and upgrades the system for us so there are no local storage or maintenance costs.

Cloud computing will impact our libraries. Now is the time to consider:

- If your school has a policy that allows, even encourages, student-owned devices that can be used to access the resources you provide in the cloud. (Parents will not allow a simple ban on them, any more than they allowed schools to ban cell phones.)
- If your school has the reliable, adequate, and secure wireless infrastructure to support dozens, if not hundreds, of student-owned computing devices designed to take advantage of cloud-based applications.
- If your district provides or is exploring cloud-based enterprise solutions like Google Apps Education Edition or Microsoft's Office 365.
- If your library is using cloud-based applications to lower its operating costs.
- If your library should repurpose its general use computer labs, providing instead a combination of wireless netbooks that can be used in and out of the library and fewer, but more powerful media production computers in the lab.
- The most important consideration for the librarian, however, is "If I am helping my teachers and students receive the training, resources, and strategies to use the cloud."

In rolling out a cloud-based resource like GoogleApps for Education librarians can play a critical role. Here are seven opportunities GoogleApps implementation presents to librarians.

1. This is the librarian's chance to be an information technology guru—again. Librarians are not just teaching face-to-face staff development classes, but are serving as role models by sharing documents, collaborating, and using these tools as teachers ourselves. One doesn't need to know much to be the "expert" in your school on GoogleApps—just be about five minutes ahead of everyone else. Such a reputation in a building is gold.
2. Librarians can be the daily "go-to" support for students and staff members for one-on-one help with the apps including using Docs for file storage/portfolios, sharing documents for viewing and editing, and solving log-on/access/password problems.
3. Librarians can teach students these tools as part of the information and technology curriculum, using GoogleDocs for activities they would have used desktop programs for in the past. Librarians must accept major responsibility for helping students use these new resources safely and responsibly.
4. Librarians can create templates and tools to help students during the research process. GoogleApps is less cumbersome than managing separate wikis, blogs, and other independent online tools for project-long documentation since everyone's work is in the same place and is easy to organize.
5. Librarians can use the tools for their own library information gathering efforts—conducting surveys, tracking classes via shared calendars, and organizing data. Do a search on "library" or "books" in the templates section of GoogleDocs and you will be amazed by what librarians have already shared—schedules, forms, surveys, worksheets, and dozens of other free and modifiable documents that can give a head start on any task.
6. Librarians can use e-mail, Groups, and chat for communication with their staff and students, making information available in real time—not relying just on monthly newsletters.

7. Librarians can use GoogleDocs for curriculum writing, lesson planning, and collaboration with teachers and with other members of the library department. Librarians can use and model self-made video tutorials shared via GoogleVideo.

Librarians as leaders can model the shift to a paperless, social, and ubiquitous learning environment where using technology productively takes precedence over just learning how to use it. If we don't, who will?

For some educators, especially technology specialists who have lovingly built in-house networks and fear the changes in their status and responsibilities, a move to the cloud will be a significant change in mind-set. They may see storm clouds—be warned. But remember—every cloud can have a silver lining, especially for our library users.

For reflection: E-books and libraries

I sense that the workshops I give on e-books don't deliver as many answers to librarians' questions about how to provide e-books to their patrons as they would like. As far as publishers and e-book vendors in attendance are concerned, I am sure I disappoint them by not recommending any particular product—or a full plunge into replacing print with electronic resources.

As I write this book, the e-book market is in full churn. Permitted uses, formats, degree of title availability, reading devices, and file formats change on a monthly basis. Publishers, seeing what has happened to the music industry as a result of unauthorized file sharing practices, are being very, very cautious. Some authors who count on royalties for their livelihoods may also be reluctant to step into this new form of publishing, while other authors are self-publishing with great success. Individuals, not libraries, are the target market for e-book sellers.

But there are a few things I can suggest that may be helpful to librarians and teachers.

The first is that we as digital resource professionals need to be more precise about how we use e-book terminology. Here is how I try to refer to materials when communicating about "e-books":

- **E-books** are downloadable files of individual book titles—those things you might acquire from Amazon, Barnes & Noble, or Project Gutenberg. Commercial titles usually contain some form of Digital Rights Management (DRM) code that controls the use of these titles.
- **E-book readers** are more-or-less single purpose devices on which e-books can be accessed, stored, and read. The Kindle, the Nook, the Kobo, and the Sony Reader are examples. I suspect this type of device will lose a lot of ground to multipurpose devices.
- **E-book reader applications (apps)** are small software programs that run on multipurpose computing devices such as the iPad, Android tablets, smartphones, and regular computers. Kindle and Nook apps as well as generic apps like GoodReader and Stanza are examples.
- **E-book apps** are self-contained programs that contain book content that are opened on tablets and other devices. They do not need a separate reader app to read them. Scholastic's I Spy Spooky Mansion, the Boynton picture books, and many other children's book titles are examples. Many of these titles have extensive interactive features. Broderbund's Just Grandma and Me computer program from the mid-1990s is their ancestor.
- **E-books in the cloud** are titles that are accessed and read with a web browser. The International Children's Digital Library and TumbleBooks—as well as reference books like WorldBook Online—are examples of these cloud-based books.

Some of our professional confusion about how to use digital materials might be lessened if we start using common terminology.

The second term we might want to think about more carefully is, perhaps surprisingly, "book" itself. The word "book" identifies a very broad range of content used in many different ways. From a dictionary, encyclopedia, or index that is used in a nonlinear way and only in small parts for short periods of time to longer works of fiction, biography, and narrative nonfiction that are read from front to back over a few days or weeks, the amount of access and portability needed for individual types of books varies greatly.

Providing access to a reference book on the library's computer workstations or on student devices through a browser makes perfect sense; providing the latest young adult novel in a computer lab makes no sense at all. And just where do picture books, textbooks, and anthologies fall along the "need for continuous access" continuum? Libraries will not be able to provide access to digital materials using any single method.

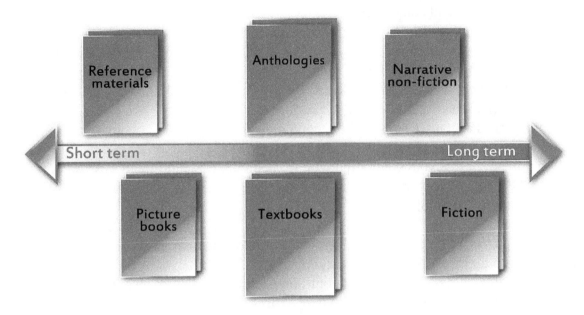

IMAGE 6-1   There are books and there are books

Finally, the third understanding that even in this time of uncertainly in e-publishing is that librarians still must be the digital content masters and that e-content carries with it all the collection development/management tasks of regular print as discussed earlier in this chapter.

As we transition from print to digital books librarians must constantly ask themselves and their vendors when considering digital materials:

- Is there a significant cost savings by providing my current resources in the new format?
- Will the new format improve learning opportunities for students and staff?
- Will all my students and staff be able to access these materials despite not having a computing device with Internet access at home.

And more specifically,

- What kind of device is required to read your e-books? What does it cost and how would you suggest I provide equitable, ready equipment access to all my students? Will your e-books work with many different devices or just one proprietary device? Can your e-books be read on a device that also allows productivity software to be used and that has a good web browser?

- Can my patrons put your e-books on their personally owned devices? Can more than one reader access an e-book at a time? Is there a time limit on how long a student can use one of your e-books? What is your electronic equivalent of the "first sale doctrine" that physical materials currently enjoy?

- Can text from your e-books be copy/pasted into student documents? Can students bookmark, highlight, and add notes to your e-text?

- How might your e-book collection be a better value than a print collection? Let's use these numbers as a starting point. Print collection of 10,000 volumes = $200,000 investment. Book life span = 20 years. Used by 500 students. Cost of print collection per year per student: $20 (at a 5 percent annual replacement rate) or $.002 per title. Remember to factor in the cost to purchase and maintain the equipment needed to read your e-books.

- Do your electronic texts offer any features that would help my learners, especially those who are beginning or struggling readers? Does your book convert text to speech, have a built-in dictionary, illuminate concepts with video or animation, or use artificial intelligence to offer help? Do your e-books actually help kids read or just keep nonreaders entertained? Are your e-books "social"—promoting group discussions, reviews, and commentary?

- If the collection is actually a subscription, not a purchase, how do I know that your company won't increase the price to a point we can't afford? Or change the collection so that teachers can't rely on having titles? Or that you won't align with some publishers and limit access to titles by other publishers? How do I know the titles you are offering are high quality, aligned to the curriculum, and developmentally appropriate?

Any e-book implementation plan must increase access to books to more students for more time, should increase learning opportunities, or save the library money.

It's urgent that all librarians start figuring out how to provide e-book resources in practical ways to their users. If we don't, the tech department will take on this task that they may not be trained or equipped to handle.

Reference

Kelly, Kevin. "Scan This Book." *New York Times*, May 14, 2006.

Chapter Seven

Curriculum

Putting technology skills in their place

The business community, higher education, and parents have made it clear that high school graduates need to be proficient technology users. Yet there seems to be only a vague notion on the part of the public and many educators of what "technology literacy" really means and how to make sure students have mastered it.

- Can a student who operates a computer well enough to play a game, chat, or maintain a Facebook page be considered technologically literate?
- Will a student who has used technology in school only for using reading and math programs have the skills necessary for survival in college or the workplace?
- What exactly are the "basic skills" of technology use all high school students should master before graduation, where in the school curriculum should those skills be taught, how should they be taught, and who should teach them?
- How can schools and families make sure children use technology, especially the Internet, in ways that are both safe and ethical?
- Are there dispositions and "soft skills" necessary for students to master before being truly adept with technology?
- What are the roles and responsibilities of the library program in assuring students are competent technology users?

Various organizations and institutions have attempted to identify what are popularly known as "21st-Century Skills." Recognizing that technology literacy is important but only a subset of skills needed to learn and work successfully in an information-based economy, a number of organizations have been writing or revising student standards intended to identify these skills. Three of the most popular are:

- ISTE's *NETS for Students*
- ALA/AASL's *Standards for the 21st-Century Learner*
- Partnership for 21st-Century Skills's *Framework for 21st-Century Learning*

While these sets of standards have different organizational structures and emphases, they all seem to agree that schools should be helping every student master:

1. Information literacy skills
2. Technology skills
3. Communication skills

4. Creativity and problem-solving skills
5. Digital citizenship (safe and ethical technology use)
6. Personal dispositions that enhance lifelong learning abilities like curiosity, tenacity, self-assessment, teamwork, and critical thinking

Many states have also written standards they expect students to master, but there seems to be no national or international consensus on what should be specifically taught and how it should be assessed.

One broadly held philosophy is that these skills need to be integrated into the content areas and not taught in isolation but applied in every class. Yet no effective, practical, and comprehensive K–12 set of technology skills and model for their integration exists. The broad standards above are good starting points for districts writing or modifying their own curricula but are not sufficiently specific. Too many classroom teachers still use computers only as electronic flash cards or worksheets, and neglect the productivity side of educational technology use. Tools, such as word processors, databases, spreadsheets, graphic tools, time-line makers, and video editing software, are still taught only in special classes like business or technology education—classes taken by a minority of students, despite the fact that most of these applications are of significant benefit to all students. And schools are skittish about using online tools like wikis, blogs, and social networking sites for educational purposes. Too many schools are banning, rather than embracing, the classroom use of student-owned technology devices such as smartphones.

Integrating technology skills into an information literacy curriculum

However, many schools have successfully integrated one set of skills into the curriculum—information literacy skills. The school library profession has long insisted that information skills not be taught in isolation, and the best library programs are designed around cooperative projects jointly taught by the classroom teacher and the librarian. The inclusion of a comprehensive, identified list of technology skills into an information literacy curriculum to create an information/technology literacy curriculum is a pragmatic model for teaching technology skills.

Information literacy curriculum models can be found in several places. The Big6™ information problem-solving model of Eisenberg and Berkowitz is a widely adopted example of such a curriculum. In this model, the curriculum is a process divided into several steps that can be taught to very young students and retaught at increasingly more sophisticated levels through high school and beyond.

One approach to integrating technology skills into the general curriculum is to revisit the steps of your school's current information processing model and add specific technology literacy skills. The technology skills become subsets of the broader information processing skills. They do not supplant, but supplement, the more general information skills listed (Eisenberg, Johnson, Berkowitz 2010). Using this approach assures that:

- Technology skills are not taught in isolation but integrated into the content area since information literacy skills are generally taught as a part of classroom projects.
- Technology skills are taught throughout the curriculum.
- Technology skills include the ability to produce and communicate information, not just access it.
- Technology skills are used to increase critical thinking, higher-order thinking, and problem solving.
- Technology skills are applied in meaningful ways with the instructional focus on solving a problem or answering a question rather than simply learning to use a specific digital device, program, or application.

Technology skills within an information-processing curriculum do need to be separately and clearly stated for a number of reasons:

- Many districts already have some form of technology skills curriculum, and those skills felt to be valid should remain clearly stated.
- It is not realistic to expect most teachers and many librarians to understand information literacy automatically assumes technology literacy.
- Clearly stated technology skills help determine the resources needed to effectively teach a skill. If it is the expectation that information be communicated through a computer-generated graph, then the need for a certain number of computers, types of software, and level of teacher proficiency is more easily established.
- The business world, academic community, and public are aware of the need for students to have technology skills, but the need for information skills is less recognized. The inclusion of readily understood technology skills may help raise the importance of and commitment to an information literacy curriculum.

The reality is that basic tasks in any information-processing model of accessing, selecting, evaluating, organizing, and communicating information realistically can no longer be done *without* the use of technology.

Here is one example of what the integration of technology skills into an information-literacy model looks like:

5. Synthesis

Students must organize and communicate the results of the information problem-solving effort. Students will be able to:

    A. *Classify and group information using a word processor, database or spreadsheet.*

    B. *Use word processing and desktop publishing software to create printed documents, and apply keyboard skills equivalent to at least twice the rate of handwriting speed.*

    C. *Create and use technology-generated graphics and art in various print and electronic presentations.*

    D. *Use electronic spreadsheet software to create original spreadsheets.*

    E. *Generate charts, tables and graphs using electronic spreadsheets and other graphing programs.*

    F. *Use database software to create original databases.*

    G. *Use presentation software to create slideshows and multimedia presentations. Use websites and online services to create and share multimedia products.*

    H. *Create media-rich presentations and use projection devices to show multimedia productions that include digital video, audio files and active links to HTML documents or other programs.*

    I. *Create Web pages and websites using hypertext markup language (HTML) in a text document or by using Web page creation tools; and know the procedure to upload these pages to a Web server.*

    J. *Use e-mail, ftp, shared documents, and other telecommunications capabilities to publish the results of the information problem-solving activity. Know specialized sites for sharing photographs, slide shows, and multimedia presentations.*

    K. *Use specialized technology applications as appropriate for specific tasks (e.g., music composition software, computer-assisted drawing and drafting programs, mathematics modeling software, scientific measurement instruments).*

L. Properly cite and credit electronic sources (e.g., text, graphics, sound and video) of information within the product as well as in footnotes, endnotes, and bibliographies (Eisenberg, Johnson, and Berkowitz 2010, 26–27).

Listing technology skills within a process framework is only a first step in assuring that all our students become proficient information and technology users. A teacher-supported scope and sequence of essential learner outcomes, well-designed projects, and effective assessments are also critical. Many librarians may need to hone their own technology skills in order to remain effective information skills teachers. But such a curriculum holds tremendous opportunities for librarians to become vital, indispensable staff members, and for all children to master the skills they will need to thrive in an information-rich future.

Building an information/technology literacy curriculum

It is easier to move a cemetery than to change a curriculum.
—Woodrow Wilson

Districts need to ask some questions about their "library" and technology curricula if they have not done so over the past few years. If these curricula were written before libraries were automated, before schools had connected to the Internet, and before most educators realized that skills are best taught as part of a process, rather than as discreet tasks, they are very dated, indeed. If the "computer" curriculum reflects the stand-alone, low-memory constraints of the computers in isolated labs, emphasizes drill-and-practice, focuses on keyboarding, and is taught in separate units or classes, it too is very dated, indeed. New state standards and graduation requirements that ask for student problem solving, decision making, and information literacy, all of which need to be authentically assessed, give a sense of urgency to creating an information/technology literacy curriculum.

At both local and national levels, critics are asking for evidence that the huge investment that education has made in technology is making a difference in how and what students are learning. When student attainment of technology skills is undocumented and taught inconsistently from teacher to teacher, grade to grade, and building to building, such critics will be difficult to answer.

So how, if "it is easier to move a cemetery," can librarians design and implement such a new information/technology literacy curriculum?

1. Create a district goal and shared vision. Significant curriculum revision needs district-level support. The district's library and technology advisory committee (see chapter three) can play an important role by making curriculum one of the library/technology department's primary goals:

All students will demonstrate the mastered use of technology to access, process, organize, communicate, and evaluate information in order to answer questions and solve problems and to practice digital citizenship.

This committee should make the request for support and cooperation from the administration along with curriculum and staff development departments.

There needs to be a common, shared vision of what an information/technology curriculum looks like. Meetings that have the primary purpose of creating such a vision are essential, both at the advisory level and among the library and technology staff. What are the elements of achieving the district goal mentioned above? Some may include:

- The curriculum will result in projects that create products using a variety of media and formats.
- The curriculum will teach meaningful technology skills using productivity software and online tools, including social networking sites.
- The curriculum will help students learn not just how to find information, but to evaluate the quality of information, and use information to make and communicate informed decisions.
- Student research will ask for original "higher-level" thinking, helping teachers and librarians combat both plagiarism and boredom.
- Information/technology projects will be integrated into the classroom's content areas and be team-taught between the librarian and the classroom teacher.
- These projects will be authentically assessed and the results of student skill attainment in these areas will be reported formally to parents, as is skill attainment in other areas such as reading, writing, and math.
- Projects will be meaningful, engaging, and therefore motivational.

Part of the vision should include a commitment to having all students complete the same curriculum so that a librarian's or teacher's personal enthusiasm (or lack thereof) does not determine whether a student learns and practices information/technology skills.

The work of the district-level group is to establish the vision for the information/technology and obtain district-level support. The library/technology department or a representative task force then needs to complete the following steps.

2. Identify a laundry list of current library and technology skills. The first task force work is to closely examine its district's current library and technology curricula and find exemplary models of curricula from other districts. In the attempt to improve how students are taught, care needs to be taken not to disregard important skills that are currently being addressed.

When this list of discrete skills is being made, a list of resources needed for each grade level that is available on a district-wide basis should also be compiled. In other words, as teachers and librarians plan specific units, they will know what tools are available to them. Consideration of cross-platform compatibility and affordability is imperative. The list may be relatively short:

- a productivity package that includes a word processor, spreadsheet, and presentation program
- a simple drawing program
- a graphing program for younger students
- e-mail
- a web browser and Internet access
- web-based access to the library catalog
- online full-text magazine databases that are age appropriate
- an online encyclopedia and other reference materials

Select "productivity" tools—programs that help students learn to manipulate and communicate information. While titles will change and more of these tools will become available online, there should be standardization throughout the district.

3. Select an information-processing model. The second step is to examine and choose an information-processing model to use district-wide. Use your state model if your state has one. If not, look at the national models or consider the Big6™ written by Mike Eisenberg and Bob Berkowitz. Most models contain many of the same elements and processes, only grouped and worded somewhat differently.

Make sure the model chosen is simple to understand but still comprehensive enough to be meaningful to all learners and that there are good support materials for it, including books, online user groups or mailing lists, and websites such as those available for the Big6™. Be sure the model is in the public domain, is under Creative Commons license, or that permission to use it is freely given by its authors.

4. Group skills within the process. The next step the task force needs to undertake is to group the laundry list of library and technology skills identified in step two within the information literacy model. This may be relatively easy. Most skills fall naturally into one or more of the steps in such a process, including technology skills. If a skill doesn't "fit," reconsider if it really is important.

My experience is that most librarians and teachers neglect skills related to formulating a good question, determining one's information needs, and evaluating the completion of a project. This is a good time to take a careful look at how to design research topics that ask students real questions of genuine interest that require critical, higher-order thinking skills.

5. Identify areas in the curriculum for integration. Major collaboration between the task force and classroom teachers is needed to complete these next steps. Since the vision requires a uniform curriculum and set of projects across the district, the participation of at least one teacher from each building from each elementary grade level or secondary content area should be sought at planning meetings. Meetings should be held for one grade level or one secondary content area at a time with all librarians initially.

These meetings should involve:

- **Familiarizing teachers with the district vision and directive of the project.** Making sure teachers know the "big picture" and obtaining buy-in are vital for the success of the work.
- **Familiarizing teachers with the concepts of information literacy.** This is best done by asking them to complete a series of simple, realistic information literacy activities including choosing a movie to see, planning a vacation, or helping a son or daughter choose a college. Each of these activities allows teachers to experience designing a good research question, identifying needed information, determining sources of that information, and evaluating the outcome.
- **Creating a simple curriculum map for each grade or content area.** A common complaint among teachers is that there is already too much curriculum to successfully teach. Identify units of study in which inquiry or technology use is already a requirement. On a practical note, select units that may be considered by the classroom teachers to be weak due to poor activities or little support materials currently available. Don't take the chance of possibly making successful units weaker—use the process only to make poorer units better. Information literacy projects need to be viewed as helpful to the classroom teacher, not just more work.
- **Brainstorm projects that have products other than the standard written report and that use mediums of communication other than print.** It doesn't take long to generate a list similar to this one: crossword puzzle, short story, game, video, model, drawing, audiotape, slide show, bulletin board, lesson, blog post, booklet, pamphlet, poem, newspaper, advertisement, multimedia show, puppet show, comic book, letter to the editor, photograph album, play, collage, mural, travel brochure, guide, manual, survey, chart or graph, animation, experiment, interview, map, book review, debate.

Examine how technology skills can be taught and practiced in creating these products. A skill, when applied, is better remembered.

6. Identify needed resources. Once there is an outline of what units and what projects will be undertaken, a closer look at the resources needed is imperative. It probably isn't realistic to ask all sixth grade students to do a multimedia project, for example, if there are only ten computers and no multimedia software available. But once the topics and project types are identified, the technology department and librarians can better focus technology resource purchases on these units. The availability of resources may also determine the phase-in period of the projects. The less resource-intensive the project, the earlier it can be implemented.

An important, but often overlooked "resource" is the skill level of the teaching staff. Look at the projects to see if there are definite areas where staff training is needed. While most teachers can help students with word processing, e-mail, and graphics use, fewer teachers may be comfortable enough with digital video editing, spreadsheets, Web 2.0 resources, or online productivity tools to use those applications as part of a project. This is where librarians can step in to offer their support by team-teaching newer, more complex technology skills. As librarians teach the student, teachers can learn as well (see chapter thirteen).

7. Develop assessment tools. Most of these projects cannot be evaluated effectively using a test. Moving beyond paper and pencil evaluations to asking students to demonstrate a working knowledge of the skills is one of the most important reasons for using an information literacy process. Such units demand authentic assessment tools like checklists, rubrics, and journals.

Working with teachers to describe in concrete, exact, observable language what students must be able to do is one of the most challenging parts of the curriculum redesign. But the work is helpful for both the teachers and the students. Even very young students can use checklists to self-evaluate their progress on projects and activities. Librarians can be genuine leaders in the district as they help others devise and use powerful assessment techniques.

8. Develop a record-keeping and reporting system. Part of the vision may be reporting the results of assessments of student skill attainment to parents. There must be a section on the elementary progress report for information/technology skills. Elementary librarians themselves should report whether students have achieved mastery of skills for each student in their school. Skills can be grouped into a few major areas for which grade-level benchmarks or essential learner outcomes have been written. The benchmarks and outcomes are important, especially for letting parents know what skills their children have or are expected to master. The benchmark skills reflect the information literacy curriculum and are tied to the project unit and their assessments. Secondary librarians should collaborate with the content area teachers to help make sure information/technology skill attainment is part of each course grade.

District-level librarians should aggregate and summarize the data on student attainment of these skills on both a building and district-wide basis for reporting to the school board and community.

9. Review and revise. Librarians and teachers need to review and improve information/technology literacy units nearly every year. Since the information literacy skills are taught within subject areas projects, the projects must change as other curricula change. Librarians who are members of the language arts, science, math, and social studies curriculum committees can keep the other librarians apprised of changes in those areas.

As technology resources change and grow, new projects become possible as well. The outcomes of the project may remain the same, but the tools may need to be updated frequently.

And as states' graduation standards change, district curricula must be adjusted to meet those requirements. (Minnesota changes state standards more often than some of its residents change their underwear, so this can be challenging as well.)

Practical advice:

- Focus on one or two projects per grade level or secondary course that are then shared among all librarians and teachers instead of developing individual projects at each school.
- Adopt common technology equipment and digital resources in order to more effectively develop good training activities and standardize student guides and activities. As more schools encourage the use of personally owned computing devices, the selection of resources that can be used on as wide a range of platforms as possible is another consideration.

- Don't try to "teacher-proof" the curriculum. Individual approaches to completing the projects are expected. But every child should be taught the same skills to the same level of proficiency of use.
- The impetus for the curricular change must come from a group representing a wide segment of both the school and the community and have administrative support. Don't even begin until administration is on board.
- Approach this curriculum not as an add-on to the current content areas, but a different and more effective method of teaching content objectives as well as information/technology skills.
- Skills taught in the library must be reinforced in the classroom, and vice-versa.
- Help teachers understand that students are more motivated when skills are applied in meaningful ways and to topics of personal interest. This is especially true with technology. The "why" of learning, not just the "how," is keeping our schools and classrooms relevant in children's lives.

Elements of projects that motivate

Ms. Lu's seventh grade health class must meet a state standard dealing with "avoidable diseases." Traditionally, she had asked her students to read a chapter in their textbook, held classroom discussions, and required the students to write a short paper on a disease she assigned to each individual. There was a multiple-choice test at the end of the unit. Ms. Lu always felt the students didn't pay much attention to this important topic and quickly forgot anything they'd learned in the unit.

This year, at the urging of Mr. Ojampa, the librarian, Ms. Lu decided to try a different strategy. Students:

- *Surveyed their families to determine if there are any hereditary illnesses in their family and listed them.*
- *In small groups identified by common family illness, the students worked with both Ms. Lu and Mr. Ojampa to answer this question: "What are the best ways of reducing my chances of developing this disease—or minimizing its impact on my life?" Students had to use at least one print resource, one website, and one interview with a local health professional as part of their research. Mr. Ojampa introduced students to the new health subscription database and showed students how to access it from home using a link from the library website.*
- *Using checklists they and the librarian created as a guide, the students developed an oral presentation supported with a slide show that helped communicate the supported answer to their question. The use of multimedia in the slide show was worth extra credit.*
- *Students gave the presentation to the class and posted their slide show on a website that could be accessed and commented on publically.*
- *Teams did an assessment of the other teams' presentations and did a self-assessment of their own slide show using the checklists.*
    At the end of the unit, Ms. Lu and Mr. Ojampa reviewed each project and their own efforts. They agreed that students were concerned about both the quality of the information they used and the quality of their slide show. Ms. Lu felt she needed to improve the presentation rubric and figure out how to share the projects online in a less time-consuming way. Mr. Ojampa's short survey of students after the conclusion of the project told him that the students found the new database useful in completing the assignment and they were likely to use it again.

While the curriculum described in the last section is essential, its success will depend on the quality of the individual projects that support it. Good projects don't just happen. They have some common elements that tend to group themselves into three categories: Assignments, Activities, and Assessments.

Assignments that matter to the student

1. **Motivational research projects have clarity of purpose and expectations.** By working on a project about a disease to which their family is prone, students recognize they are learning ways to avoid or mitigate its effect on their own lives. Ms. Lu made sure the students knew that the purpose of the unit was not just learning about diseases, but also knowing how to evaluate information sources—a skill that will be useful to them for the rest of their lives. The checklists of expected quality criteria were given at the beginning of the assignments along with a timeline for completion. Students knew exactly what Ms. Lu and Mr. Ojampa expected them to do.

2. **Motivational research projects give students choices.** If the purpose of the assignment is to teach a basic understanding (that certain diseases can be avoided) or a set of skills (how to communicate effectively using a slide show), it doesn't make any difference what the specific disease might be. Dig down and look at the core concepts that research assignments are trying to teach, and let the students pick a specific subject that interests them.

3. **Motivational research projects are relevant to the student's life.** For our students, osteoporosis or diabetes or heart disease are conditions only suffered by people who may be impossibly old (over thirty). But by asking her students to interview their families, the teacher added real faces and lives to these diseases. The stories resonate with those doing the interviewing. So many times we ask our students to research important topics—environmental, historical, or social issues—but fail to help them make the vital connection of why the findings are important to the people in the town in which they live. Strive for projects that are relevant because they are timely, local, or personal.

4. **Motivational research projects stress higher-level thinking skills and creativity.** Think how different the results of a project that asks for a creative solution to a problem are from a paper that simply asks an "about" question. (List ten facts "about" strokes.) Find ways to move up Bloom's taxonomy from the recall level to analysis, evaluation, and creativity. (What are the three most important things a person can do to prevent having a stroke? Justify your rankings.)

5. **Motivational research projects answer genuine questions.** At the beginning of the project, most students didn't know their family's medical history. They didn't know how some illnesses can be prevented. Ms. Lu and Mr. Ojampa probably didn't know these things either. Genuine questions are ones to which the teacher or library does not have a preconceived answer. Unfortunately, adults rarely ask questions to which they do not believe they already know the answer. Good projects try to answer only genuine questions.

Activities that involve the researcher

6. **Motivational research projects involve a variety of information finding activities.** As librarians we are comfortable with the familiar primary sources of reference books, periodicals, and trade books. Yet the answers to many personal, local, and timely questions cannot be found in them. They can provide excellent background information, but often we need to talk to experts, conduct surveys, design experiments, or look at other kinds of primary sources to get precise information. The learners in this example spent time with secondary sources, but the generation of new knowledge by talking to their families and to a local health care provider was involved.

7. **Motivational learning tends to be hands-on.** Students in the example above conducted interviews, did online database searches, created a digital slide show, and gave an oral

presentation. Many of them used cameras to take photographs and videos to be used within the slide shows. They learned how to upload and share digital files. Students were learning by doing, not just listening. Notice, too, how many corollary skills are practiced in this "research" project: writing skills, interviewing skills, photography skills, layout and design skills, and speaking skills.

8. **The use of technology can be exciting for many students.** Whether for planning, for research, or for communication, many students find the use of technology motivating. Ms. Lu's students used computer programs that were *not* purposely designed to be "motivational." It is the challenge of designing containers for a message that give good productivity tools like graphic programs, slide show creators, and webpage construction kits—the virtual equivalent of a set of LEGOs—their motivating qualities.

9. **Good projects use formats that take advantage of multiple senses.** Ms. Lu's students were asked to communicate their finds not only with words, but sound and sight as well. Our ability to digitize and present information is no longer restricted to the written word but now can include drawings, photos, sounds, music, animations, and movies. All are formats that carry important and often unique information.

10. **Interesting projects are often complex, but are broken into manageable steps.** One of the first things Mr. Ojampa helped students in Ms. Lu's class do was outline the tasks to be done and establish a timeline for their completion. Checking off completed tasks is satisfying, and students learned some corollary planning and time management skills in the process. Large projects can be overwhelming even for adults, but planning smaller steps, building timelines, creating frequent deadlines, and scheduling multiple conferences turn complexity into manageability. It's also clear that some tasks in effective projects often require sustained periods of time to complete, so the regular 50-minute block of "library time" doesn't always work very well, making flexibly scheduled library time important.

11. **Collaborative learning is often stimulating and results in better products than individual work.** Ms. Lu asked her students to work in teams. Joint problem solving, assigning and accepting responsibility, and discovering and honoring individual talents helped create a synergy that resulted in better, more satisfying presentations than students working alone would have produced. Not every project needs to be a joint effort, but real-world work environments increasingly stress teamwork. Teamwork in school is not only more enjoyable, but leads to the application of practical interpersonal skills as well.

Assessments that help the learner

12. **Motivational research projects have results that are shared with people who care and respond.** Ms. Lu's kids got the same credit as those who may have simply taken a multiple choice test or written a short paper on "preventable diseases." So why would kids go to all the extra work a project like the one described entails? Kids get hooked because adults take the time to really look at the work they have done and comment on it. The community, both physically and virtually, visited the students' shared slide show presentations and left comments—both compliments and criticisms. Assessments and reviews by peers, experts, and neighbors (any audience beyond the teacher) are common in scouting, athletics, dramatics, 4-H, and music groups. Students who know they have a public audience tend to have a higher degree of concern about the quality of their work.

13. **Learning that is assessed by an authentic tool is more meaningful than a paper and pencil test.** Students had the checklists at the beginning of the project and used them several times to

determine their progress during the project. It was easy to recognize both what was completed as well as what needed improvement. When students are given quality indicators like rubrics and checklists with the assignment, they can use them to guide their learning and keep guesswork to a minimum. As students become more sophisticated in the assessment process, they should be expected to choose or design their own "quality indicators"—one of the attributes of a genuinely intrinsically motivated person.

14. **Examples give the learner a clear idea of what quality work looks like.** Ms. Lu's class next year can use some of the diseases slide shows as exemplars. Topics may need to change enough from year to year so that copying is not possible.

15. **Well-designed projects allow the learner to reflect, revisit, revise, and improve their final projects.** While Ms. Lu's class had a completion date, students continued to edit and revise their work as they received feedback from website visitors and their peers. There is satisfaction to be gained from observed growth. Good projects, like gardens, musical repertoires, and relationships, are probably always works in progress.

Why don't all teachers design projects with some or all of these elements? Well, a fourth "A" sneaks in.

(Teacher and librarian) Attitude is everything

16. **Teachers and librarians who enjoy authentic, project-based learning are comfortable with a loss of control over time, the final product, and "correct" answers.** If some parts of the curriculum don't get "covered," if conflicting evidence causes confusion, or a controversial solution to a problem is suggested, these educators roll with the punches. They have the intellectual confidence to handle ambiguity.

17. **These teachers and librarians enjoy active students rather than passive students.** They have developed new rules of behavior that stress student responsibility, and have trained their principals to differentiate between active learning and students out of control.

18. **The professional's belief that given enough time, resources, and motivation, all students are capable of high performance is critical.** It's not just the talented and gifted student who can make choices, solve problems creatively, and complete complex tasks. These teachers and librarians know that all students rise to the level of performance expected of them, and that great ideas can come from anyone in the class.

19. **Librarians and teachers who do exciting projects recognize that their expertise is in the learning and research process rather than in any particular subject area.** No longer is the primary role of the educator that of information dispenser, but of guide for information users and creators. The happiest teachers and librarians are co-learners in the classroom, especially when learning new technology tools. And students get the satisfaction that comes from teaching as well.

20. **Teacher and librarian enthusiasm becomes more important than ever.** Teachers who are enthusiastic about what they are doing and how they are doing it design the best projects. The downside to this is that it is very difficult to create recipes for specific projects that can be easily adopted by other teachers. We can all use principles and guidelines like the ones in this chapter, but to say a project, no matter how well designed, is going to work for every teacher, every librarian, or every group of students is impossible.

21. **Teachers and librarians who work on these kinds of project know that they don't always work the first time.** But they keep trying.

Research must matter. The research needs to be important to the researcher. If it isn't, students will go through the motions. And Johnson's First Law of Schoolwork will kick in: *A job not worth doing is not worth doing well.* One of the best things librarians can do is work very hard to make sure research projects are well designed and intrinsically motivating. Use the rubric below to evaluate the quality of your project. Every project should be at Level Three. Fortunate students will get to do a few Level Four tasks during their school years.

A Research Question Rubric

Level One: My research is about a broad topic. I can complete the assignment by using a general reference source such as an encyclopedia. I have no personal questions about the topic.
  Primary example: My research is about an animal.
  Secondary example: My research is about the economy of Minnesota.

Level Two: My research answers a question that helps me narrow the focus of my search. This question may mean that I need to go to various sources to gather enough information to get a reliable answer. The conclusion of the research will ask me to give a supported answer to the question.
  Primary example: What methods has my animal developed to help it survive?
  Secondary example: What role has manufacturing played in Minnesota's economic development?

Level Three: My research answers a question of personal relevance. To answer this question I may need to consult not just secondary sources such as magazines, newspapers, books, or the Internet, but use primary sources of information such as original surveys, interviews, or source documents.
  Primary example: What animal would be best for my family to adopt as a pet?
  Secondary example: How can one best prepare for a career in manufacturing in the Duluth area?

Level Four: My research answers a personal question about the topic, and contains information that may be of use to decision makers as they make policy or distribute funds. The result of my research is a well-supported conclusion that contains a call for action on the part of an organization or government body. There will be a plan to distribute this information.
  Primary example: How can our school help stop the growth in unwanted and abandoned animals in our community?
  Secondary example: How might high schools change their curricula to meet the needs of students wanting a career in manufacturing in Minnesota?

Enjoyable learning experiences that are both motivating and meaningful don't just happen. They require thoughtful preparation and the conscious use of lessons learned from previous successful projects. All of us who work with students on projects need to keep asking ourselves questions like:

1. What are the barriers to better information and technology literacy projects?
2. How do we create meaningful assessment tools that can help us become more comfortable with ambiguity?
3. How do I make sure all students are intrinsically motivated to keep learning throughout their lives by finding, evaluating, and using information?

Lifelong learning is a reality for all of us, student and librarian alike.

What new skills are needed to survive the information jungle?

Research for most of us who finished our formal education before 1995 was conducted in an Information Desert. Those five or ten sources required for a "term paper" were darned tough to find in our schools and even in our public libraries. Librarians performed much the same role as that of any desert guide: helping the students and teachers locate scarce resources. Remember how happy you were to find that last, perhaps only partially relevant, magazine article that met the minimum number of sources required?

And we librarians were pretty good as desert guides. We taught kids to use the card catalog, the *Readers' Guide to Periodical Literature*, the vertical file, reference sources, and indices. We knew where to look for that hidden waterhole, patch of shade, or edible lizard. We could because we were taught these exact skills ourselves as students. Libraries changed little in the first nine decades of the 20th century.

Today's student who has access to online sources of information has been thrust into the Information Jungle. A quick search using just a single search engine can yield thousands of potential sources of information. And the "free" Internet access by common search engines is just one trail in this great tangle. Wandering slightly off the well-trod path, the searcher discovers subscription databases, blogs, massive online union catalogs from which print materials can be interlibrary loaned, newsgroups, digital multimedia collections, chat rooms, wikis, personal websites, and e-mail contact with individuals. Now all educators have the challenge of acting as jungle guides—helping learners to find, evaluate, and select resources of genuine value. With resources being overwhelming rather than scarce, avoiding snakes, telling the good berries from the poisonous ones, keeping away from the quicksand, and finding a way out of the undergrowth are the "skills" we as librarians need to help our students rapidly acquire.

Let's look at some of these survival skills more closely

Information jungle survival skill one: Know where you are going and make sure the trip's worthwhile. How do your research questions stack up? (See a "Research Question Rubric" above.) Helping students prepare good questions to answer or problems to solve using information is more important than ever for a number of reasons:

- The vast amount of information available makes research that tries to be exhaustive impossible for nearly every topic. Even in the Information Desert era, students would too often choose a subject like World War II as their research topic. I would then show them the volumes already written on the subject and ask if they really wanted to rewrite all of that information. A clever way of helping students narrow the focus of their research is by helping them find a question, preferably of personal interest, about the broader topic. For the student who wants World War II as a topic, the librarian might ask, "What other interests do you have?" A student who expresses an interest in horses might then try to answer the question. "Did horses play a part in the battles of World War II?"
- Plagiarism can only be avoided by having the learner ask genuine questions that require original higher-level thinking. Plagiarism has come of age on the Internet. Now when Mr. Fogy assigns a paper on the Olympics of Ancient Greece, the savvy student heads for an online term paper mill where a variety of papers are available for downloading on that topic. The copy, paste, find, and replace commands make quick work of a topic that does not ask for any original thought on the part of the writer. However, change Mr. Fogy's assignment to read, "How might your favorite athlete of today have done in the Olympics of Ancient Greece?" The student now not only needs factual information but also must apply the higher-level thinking skills of analysis, synthesis, and evaluation—and those cannot be downloaded.
- In order for all students to master information literacy skills, the problem or question must be of interest to the individual. Librarians and teachers who can identify the core knowledge to be

gained through a problem-solving process understand that students can have a variety of topic choices. If the purpose of an activity is to help students understand how the geography of a state affects its economy, it shouldn't make much difference to the teacher if the student looks at Florida, Nebraska, or Oregon. But it may make a big difference to the student who has a favorite state. Personal choice leads to intrinsic motivation.

Information jungle survival skill two: Learn to stay on the main trail to avoid the quicksand of irrelevant information. Searching for information on the Internet is a pretty simple affair. Find a search engine like Google or Ask.com or Yahoo!, type a term in the search box, and find hundreds, if not thousands, of possible sources. Students need three basic skills to help them improve the results of such searches:

- Start with the best search engine: Google sorts results by interpreting the number of links to a page as an indicator of that page's value. It seems to work. Ask.com allows users to ask natural language questions. KidsClick! searches only preselected websites. Students and adults should get to know one or two search engines well.
- Use advanced search operators in constructing a search. The more descriptive the term searched, the better the results. A search on "twins" will provide links to both siblings and the baseball team. Using the Boolean operator NOT (twins not baseball) will cut down on the number of hits returned.
- Discriminate relevant hits from irrelevant. A child using a search engine to find information about "cougars" is as likely to find pages on sports teams and automobiles as big cats. Most search engines return some descriptors that indicate the general topic of the page. Students need to read these and determine those relevant to their needs. This is especially true when students search on topics that might have sexual connotations.

Information jungle survival skill three: Learn to tell the good berries from the bad berries. Even very young students can and should be learning to tell the bad information berries from the good ones. Since junior high students make websites that often look better than those of college professors, we teach students to look:

- For the same information from multiple sources.
- At the age of the page.
- At the credentials of the author.
- For unstated bias by the page author or sponsor.

As students use research to solve problems about controversial social and ethical issues, the ability to evaluate and defend one's choice of information source becomes very important. Here's a scenario:

Your students have been researching current diseases and they find information from these sources. Could you help them determine which are the most reliable? Might you as a librarian have a different opinion than some parents about the validity of information from some sources?

- *Centers for Disease Control*
- *A weekly news magazine*
- *A nonfiction bestseller*

- *An insurance company or HMO website*
- *A personal webpage or blog*
- *A phone call to a local clinic*
- *A radio talk show*

Information jungle survival skill four: Don't just gather sticks. Make something with them. Traditional research assignments asked students to gather factual information and present it in an organized fashion. But if problem-solving activities are to help students master critical thinking skills, they must also require that learners:

- Organize information to help determine importance and spot trends.
- Determine the importance of discrete pieces of data.
- Anticipate critics of the findings or solutions and be able to defend one's choices.
- Offer conclusions and solutions that show insight and creativity.
- Advocate an action or actions that can be taken by the audience of the research findings.

This is how information problem skills will be used throughout students' lives. Whether using information to select a community in which to live, political candidate for whom to vote, or camera to purchase, we gather sticks of information for the purpose of determining a course of action.

Information jungle survival skill five: Learn to play the jungle drums to communicate purposefully. One of technology's very best attributes is how much it can help us improve the communication process. Most technology curricula include how to use a word processor, spreadsheets, presentation programs, webpages, blogs, podcasts, videos, and dozens of specialized digital storytelling tools. Learning such technologies simply for the sake of learning them leads to what pundits call "powerpointlessness": glitzy webpages, noisy slide shows, or colorful animations that are devoid of meaningful content.

Using technology to communicate the findings of a problem-based activity keeps this from happening. The emphasis is not on the use of the technology, but the effectiveness of the information problem-solving process that includes communicating one's findings.

Information jungle survival skill six: Prepare for the next journey by learning from the last. Information problem-solving skills are sufficiently complex that complete mastery of them is probably not possible. Assessment tools that help students continue to improve their information searching, evaluating, and communicating skills are necessary, rather than simple evaluative tools. Checklists and rubrics that describe specific criteria for both content and technology mastery give students direction for continued improvement.

Librarians who help students formulate and answer meaningful questions and solve real problems take chances. Critical thinking often leads to messy solutions; information literacy activities are tough to schedule; and higher-level thinking by students can lead to genuine intellectual challenges for educators. To be successful, librarians need to collaborate with technologists, classroom teachers, and assessment experts in order to design effective projects. And the results of such projects can be both spectacularly good and spectacularly bad.

But librarians who do help others learn to survive in the information jungle have the satisfaction of knowing that their students are using information and technology as a real-world application; that whole-life skills are being reinforced through application; and that they are providing meaningful, motivational experiences for their students. Getting students excited about learning powerful skills is the best reason of all for trekking in the Information Jungle.

How can librarians support the development of "right brain" skills?

The popular book *A Whole New Mind: Moving from the Information Age to the Conceptual Age* (Pink 2005) stresses the need for "right brain" skills in tomorrow's workforce.

Labor outsourcing to developing nations, technology use, and rising worldwide affluence are shifting our economies from the Information Age to the Conceptual Age—and successful players in this new economy will increasing be required to develop and use the right-brain abilities of high concept (seeing the larger picture, synthesizing information) and high touch (being empathetic, creating meaning).

Because of this shift, Pink suggests we work toward developing in ourselves and by implication, in our students, six right-brain "senses," to complement our left-brain, analytic skills:

DESIGN. Library programs can:
- Introduce and read picture books. Study illustrators and their work, not just authors.
- Buy and promote graphic novels.
- Assess not just content, but appearance of student work.
- Teach visual literacy.
- Teach design principles as part of desktop publishing, multimedia presentations, and webpage development.

STORY. Library programs can:
- Ask for student writing using the narrative voice.
- Teach speaking skills.
- Use storytelling as a part of teaching.
- Give students opportunities to both hear and tell stories.
- Promote the reading of narratives—fiction, biography, and narrative nonfiction.

SYMPHONY. Library programs can:
- Help design classroom projects that cross disciplines.
- Ask for the application of skills and concepts to genuine problems.
- Ask for multiple sources of information when doing a research or information literacy activity.

EMPATHY. Library programs can:
- Emphasize reading literature about people from other cultures and socioeconomic groups.
- Give students service learning and volunteer opportunities—including as library volunteers.
- Dramatize stories and give students the opportunity to take part as an actor in theater productions and puppet shows.
- Design group projects.

PLAY. Library programs can:
- Teach with games. Provide access to both physical and online games.
- Use storytelling techniques that require action and music.
- Teach through riddles and jokes, and encourage students to create and tell them.

MEANING. Library programs can:
- Share stories from comparative religion, myths, and legends.
- Teach ethical behaviors as a part of every project.
- Ask for writings to include statements of personal values.
- Teach the skills and sensibilities of digital citizenship.

I will also be bold enough to add a seventh "sense" of my own to Pink's list:

LEARNING. Unless a person develops both the ability and the desire to continue to learn new skills, to be open to new ideas, and to be ready to change practices in the face of new technologies, economic forces, and societal demands, he or she will not be able to successfully compete in a global economy. Library programs can:

- Teach processes, not facts.
- Encourage students to research areas of personal interest (and tolerate a diversity of interests).
- Give students the ability to learn in nontraditional ways (online, early enrollment in college, apprenticeships), and support students in such learning environments.
- Provide access to a wide range of information sources.

Our society and educational system sadly sees many of these opportunities that develop conceptual age skills as extras—frills that are often the first to be cut in times of tight budgets. It's tragically ironic that we are doing a disservice to our students as future workers and citizens by doing so. In the age of educational accountability, too many classrooms seem to be gearing all their instructional efforts to helping students master left-brain skills, since that is what standardized tests measure, of course.

Library programs should be developing design sense, storytelling abilities, synthesis, empathy, humor, and the ability to detect the importance of the information—right-brain skills needed by all students in an economy that is changing dramatically.

For reflection: What does a library for a postliterate society look like?

> . . . the fact is that people don't read anymore.
> —Steve Jobs

Next time you wander an airplane's aisle, do a quick scan over the shoulders of your fellow passengers. What are they doing?

If your observations are similar to mine, well over 50 percent of air travelers are listening to portable music devices, playing games on handhelds, working on laptop computers, or watching video on diminutive players. Paper book and magazine readers are in the minority.

Reading is declining—primarily the reading of novels and longer works of nonfiction. Attention spans are shrinking. As Jobs' quote above suggests, we are becoming a postliterate society.

YouTube is replacing Google as the primary search engine for young people. Why? They want their information in video, not text.

Wikipedia describes a "postliterate society" as one "wherein multimedia technology has advanced to the point where literacy, the ability to read written words, is no longer necessary." I would modify that definition and define the "postliterate" as those who *can* read, but *choose* to meet their primary information and recreational needs through audio, video, graphics, and gaming. Print for the postliterate is relegated to brief personal messages, short informational needs, and other functional, highly pragmatic uses such as instructions, signage, and time-management device entries—each often supplemented by graphics. The postliterate's need for extended works or larger amounts of information is met through visual and/or auditory formats. (Postliteracy differs from aliteracy in that the demand for information and new learning is present, only met in other means than print. Aliteracy simply means choosing not to read.)

The term "postliterate library" may at first glance appear an oxymoron. But it is not. Our best libraries are already postliterate, increasingly meeting the needs of users who communicate, play, and learn using media other than print. And the attitudes librarians adopt toward the postliterate may well determine whether libraries continue to exist.

Education and librarianship have a current bias toward print. This communication/information format has served civilization well for a couple of millennia. The majority of today's professionals demonstrate high levels of proficiency in print literacy skills and they can be expected to defend the necessity of such skills vociferously. They are competent readers, writers, and print analysts but neophyte video, audio, and graphic producers, consumers, and critics. And it is human nature to be dismissive of those competencies that we personally lack.

But I would argue that postliteracy is a return to more natural forms of multisensory communication—speaking, storytelling, dialogue, debate, and dramatization. It is just now that these modes can be captured and stored digitally as easily as writing. Information, emotion, and persuasion may be even *more* powerfully conveyed in multimedia formats.

Libraries, especially those that serve children and young adults, need to acknowledge that society is becoming postliterate. These are some critical attributes of a library that serves a postliterate (PL) clientele:

1. PL libraries budget, select, acquire, catalog, and circulate as many or more materials in nonprint formats as they do traditional print materials. The circulation policy for all materials, print and nonprint, is similar.
2. PL libraries stock without prejudice age-appropriate graphic and audiobook novels and nonfiction titles for both informational and recreational use.
3. PL libraries support gaming for both instruction and recreation.
4. PL libraries purchase high-value online information resources.
5. PL libraries provide resources for patrons to create visual and auditory materials; promote the demonstration of learning and research through original video, audio, and graphics production; and provide physical spaces for the presentation of these creations.
6. PL libraries allow the use of personal communication devices (MP3 players, handhelds, laptops, etc.) and provide wireless network access for these devices.
7. PL library programs teach the critical evaluation of nonprint information.
8. PL library programs teach the skills necessary to produce effective communication in all formats.
9. PL library programs accept and promote the use of nonprint resources as sources for research and problem-based assignments.
10. PL librarians recognize the legitimacy of nonprint resources, and promote their use without bias.

While I recognize this may look frightening, even culturally destructive, to many of us "print-bound" professionals, we cannot ignore the society of which we are a part and are charged with supporting. Culture determines library programs; libraries transmit culture.

School libraries are often the bellwether programs in their schools. If we as librarians support and use learning resources that are meaningful, useful, and appealing to our students, so might the classroom teacher.

In *Phaedrus*, Plato decries an "alternate" communication technology:

The fact is that this invention will produce forgetfulness in the souls of those who have learned it. They will not need to exercise their memories, being able to rely on what is written, calling things to mind no longer from within themselves by their own unaided powers, but under the stimulus of external marks that are alien to themselves.

The Greek philosopher was, of course, lamenting the new "technology" of his day: writing. Plato might well approve of our return to an oral tradition—in its digital forms. But his quote also demonstrates that sometimes our greatest fears become our greatest blessings.

References

Eisenberg, Michael, Doug Johnson, and Bob Berkowitz. "Information, Communications, and Technology (ICT) Skills Curriculum Based on the Big6 Skills Approach to Information Problem-Solving." *Library Media Connection*, May/June, 2010.

Pink, Daniel. *A Whole New Mind: Moving from the Information Age to the Conceptual Age.* Riverhead, 2005.

Chapter Eight

Budget

Educational funding is a "zero-sum game." School districts have a finite amount of money in their budgets to spend on programs and have reached a level of funding that the public seems reluctant to substantially increase. Regardless of how much your principal or school board may support your library, they simply may not have extra money to allocate toward it. Does this mean no additional funds for your program?

Not at all. When working in a zero-sum situation, you can ask that money be taken away from other programs and given to yours. This, however, puts many of us outside our comfort zone. Aren't we librarians really "givers" of resources, skills, information, time, and effort? Fighting for funding, especially if it means butting heads with department chairs, band directors, coaches, custodians, or union reps, certainly feels like being a "taker" instead. And threatening the funding of a program that is near and dear to another person is not the best way to make friends.

Budgeting as a library ethic

Librarians, however, have an ethical obligation to work for fiscally well-supported programs. If we believe deep in our hearts that what we are doing is in the very best interest of our students and community, that spending what is necessary for an effective library program is better than buying new textbooks for science or replacing the saxophones in the band, or that smaller class size has less impact than a well-funded library, we have no choice but to enter the budget battle.

You need two psychological weapons when fighting to make your program a budget priority: a thick skin and a deeply felt mission. Without them, you'll get eaten alive; with them, you can accomplish anything.

Strong feelings and fearlessness must be supported by a strong rationale for your budget. Every school budget committee, not just the library's, needs to be asking serious questions like:

- What programs teach the skills that will be vital to tomorrow's citizens?
- What programs, skills, and attributes does your community believe are essential?
- How many teachers and students will benefit from or be harmed by a particular spending decision?
- Are there other sources of funds for activities that could be considered "nonessential"?
- How might a budget decision affect the school's climate?
- Is there research to support the effectiveness of a program or specific spending decision?
- How much budgeting is being done simply for sentimental reasons, out of tradition, or for convenience?

As librarians, we need to do our homework. Our budgets must be goal driven, specific, and assessable. They must be accurate and easy to understand. They need to be supported by research and sound reasoning. They need to be developed and owned by not just the library staff, but by all library stakeholders.

No matter how poor a district may be, odds are that it has at least one exemplary, well-funded program. Maybe it's the science department, maybe it's the debate team, or maybe it's the girls' tennis program. Why should it not be the library/technology program? Others in your organization should not spend funds that could be better spent by you. Librarians must learn to be effective "takers" if we are to have the resources to be good "givers."

Ten strategies of effective library budgeters

Good budgeting is not magic. Librarians with good budgets aren't just "lucky" or work in districts with lots of money. Librarians who practice skillful budgeting techniques get bigger budgets.

Library budgeting must be considered a process, as are program evaluation, planning, and communications. Budgeting is interrelated to each of these other important tasks. Here is a simple flowchart that can be applied to the budgeting process:

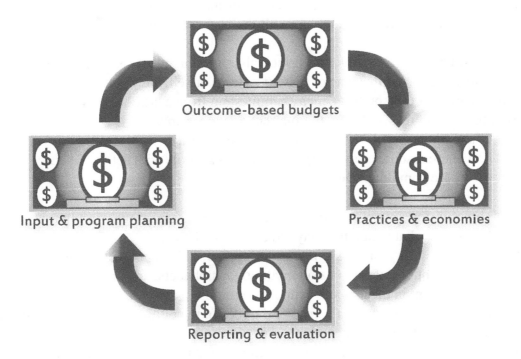

IMAGE 8-1　Budget process

Effective library budget makers:

1. Submit budget proposals even when they have not been requested or when the chance of the budget being fully funded is slim. Too often librarians confuse having a budget with having a fully funded budget. Every librarian needs to submit every year a *written* budget proposal. If students are to have access to an effective program, librarians must accurately inform decision makers of the cost of the resources needed. The outlays necessary for digital resources and the technology needed to access them make this more critical than ever.

Good budgeting is the responsibility of the building librarian, even when there is district-level library budgeting as well. Building librarians play a large role in determining the funding for their programs, especially when their districts are decentralized. When funds are allocated by building, site teams determine staffing and resources. District library supervisors, superintendents, and even principals will have less ability to support or protect programs when buildings are site-managed.

A good budget can increase the effectiveness of your program even if the effort does not result in increased funds. More money is only a part, and perhaps not always the most important part, of developing better services to staff and students. When a good budget is based on planning, prioritizing, and accountability, better programming is the result—even without an increase in funds.

2. Actively counter the argument that the free Internet will replace libraries, books, and purchased online information sources. There is a bumper sticker that reads, "Libraries are for people who can't afford the Internet." An extreme sentiment to be sure, but one that echoes these more common statements that librarians sometimes overhear.

- "Now that we have the online encyclopedia, we don't need to buy the print version."
- "Buying books is investing in an outdated technology. All the information anyone needs is available on the Internet—for free."
- "These online fees will have to be taken out of your magazine budget."
- "Our new school won't need a library since all the classrooms will be networked."

What motivates otherwise knowledgeable principals, superintendents, school board members, and legislators to advance such ideas? While some of these questions arise from wishful thinking about ways to reduce expenditures in times of tight budgets, many simply stem from a lack of knowledge about how teachers and learners use library resources and what the Internet actually contains.

Good teachers and librarians understand how different resources in school libraries are used for different purposes and how these resources are complementary. In schools with active, resource-based programs, the following scenarios are commonplace:

- A student comes in for a novel, and in passing an empty terminal, runs an Internet search on the book's author to see what the author may have published recently.
- A student using the library catalog to research Egypt now finds not just the books in the geography and history section, but locates books on mythology, alphabets, and costumes—since a keyword search turned up Egypt in those books' annotation fields.
- A teacher finds a brief reference to a historical figure in the online encyclopedia and then checks out a full biography on his e-book reader.
- A student doing research on an explorer in a print source requests a digitized map that can be modified with a graphics program and imported into a slide show.
- A teacher, having stirred the curiosity of his class with a video on plate tectonics, now wants a pathfinder of both print and online resources on geology.
- A class doing research on diseases scatters throughout the library with some students heading to the print reference sources and some to the Internet terminals since no single source can accommodate all the learners in the class and each resource contains unique information.

Adding technology to a library is like a strip mall adding a new store—all the stores get more traffic. Experienced teachers and librarians know that it takes newer technologies and print together to create meaningful learning experiences. This will be the case for some time. Humans are not given to simply replacing old technologies with new ones. Television did not replace either radio or motion pictures. Video photography has not replaced still photography. E-books will not replace all print books.

Decision makers need to be reminded that when using books, magazines, and subscription reference sources, student researchers are getting edited and verified information. Unlike the Internet where anyone can present credible-*looking* material, publishing houses go to great lengths to protect their reputations by ensuring their writers are expert and authoritative. The cost of print includes not just the paper, ink, and cover, but careful editing, including fact checking.

Purchased materials are still needed to provide students with information of both currency and depth. Often costly equipment and networks are needed to access "free" online materials. Keep in mind that a true library program is not simply a collection of "things"—print or electronic. It is a vital combination of resources, curriculum, activities, and professional expertise that help students acquire not just information, but the skills and judgment to make good use of that information.

3. Construct outcome-driven budgets that are specific in supporting curricular and school improvement goals. Budgets can basically be divided into two groups—those that are arbitrarily created and those that are outcome-driven. Some librarians are allocated a set sum of money and then told to make the most of it, while other librarians submit budgets targeted to meet specific needs, goals, and outcomes. All library budgets should be outcome-driven.

Budgeting needs to be considered integral to the long and short-term planning described in chapter three. Good outcome-driven budgets have three major components:

- Goals and objectives—This is how this budget ties in to the long-term goals and annual objectives of the collaboratively written planning document.
- Specificity—This is how much money the library needs, and this is exactly how it will be spent.
- Assessment—This is how stakeholders will know if the money in the budget helped the library meet its goals.

Too often budgets have relied on state or national standards as a rationale for funds for resources and collection building. While such standards can be useful as a discussion starter or a means of doing a program assessment (see chapter two), a budget based on the specific needs of your individual curricula, students, and teachers is more likely to be funded. The fact that Mrs. Green's science students need more current and varied resources for their solar system unit will carry more weight that a state rule or national standard.

Just as your library's goals and objects draw from library assessments, your district's and building's goals plans, and curricular objectives, so should your library's budget be designed to support these specific needs.

You will need to be able to clearly show decision makers how much money your program requires if it is to meet the goals and objectives of the library program and to help meet building goals. No one can or will give the library program what it needs if the librarian can't determine it or communicate it.

The librarian must develop stakeholder ownership of the library budget in the same way ownership of the library's goals and objectives are developed. Library budgets that come as a recommendation of a library/technology advisory committee and with an endorsement from the principal (as described in chapter three) carry more weight than those developed by the individual librarian. Administrators are reluctant to deny the request of a group, especially if that group includes parents, students, and teachers.

4. Describe the "consequences" of an underfunded budget in concrete terms. Letting stakeholders understand what *won't* happen if library funding is inadequate may be as important as letting them know what *will* happen. We need to make the case that inadequate or reduced library funding will have an impact on not only the library, but on other school programs, the classroom curriculum, and student achievement.

This is easier to do if your budget proposals are specific and goal driven. In visiting with the person or team that makes budget decisions, you can say:

- "I won't be able to purchase the 25 books that support the revised ninth grade history class that the teachers requested."
- "Teachers will only get to print 200 copies in the lab instead of 500 copies as in past years."
- "Only four students will be able to use the research terminals in the library at a time."
- "With the reduced clerical staffing, I won't be able to update the school webpage as often as in the past."
- "Students will not be able to participate in the state children's book award program if the books can't be acquired."

You will need to use your very best interpersonal skills to make sure these predicted outcomes don't simply sound like threats or whining. Give decision makers the entire budget and be open to their ideas about how to economize.

5. *Recognize the sources for budget dollars and who controls those dollars.* Educational institutions get funding from a variety of sources. The percentage that any one of these sources contributes to a budget can widely vary from state to state, and even from district to district, from type of school to type of school. But nearly all public schools in the United States get some funds from:

- A state aid formula. This is usually a baseline amount paid to all districts on a per pupil basis. It comes directly from the state budget.
- Local revenue. Often from property taxes, these dollars are often a large percentage of many states' school budgets. It is this source of revenue that sometimes creates large funding disparities among districts.
- Special local levies. These are passed to fund new buildings or facility upgrades, large investments in technology, or to supplement the operating budget. These usually require a public referendum.
- Federal funds in the form of grants. These monies are a small percentage of most school budgets, but are critical to specific programs like Title I.
- Private dollars from educational foundations, parent organizations, or endowments. These funds are becoming increasingly important to districts with lots of community involvement and some wealth.
- Private and government agency grants. These are a source of revenue for individual projects that address specific needs. Competition for large grants is fierce, and good grant writing takes time, experience, and talent. Rather than writing library-specific grants, you may be better off collaborating with other grant writers who may need library and technology resources.
- Fundraisers. Book fairs, candy sales, and car washes can make small amounts of money for those who wish to hold them. Such activities are best sponsored by a "Friends of the Library" than directly by school personnel. Online donation programs and some businesses provide funds to libraries.

Librarians need to exercise caution if they rely too heavily on funding sources from outside the school's regular operating budget. If library and technology programs are to be viewed as core to the educational process, then funding for them should be from the core budget, not fundraisers.

Private schools rely on tuition and endowments for primary funding rather than state or local public funds. Librarians in these institutions should still be knowledgeable about the source of school revenue.

Savvy librarians know how much money their schools operate on each year. They know where the money comes from and how it is spent. Your school's business manager can help you determine these budgets. In public schools finances are, by law, public information. Visit with your school board representative and get his or her perspective on finance and the budget. Serve on your teacher salary negotiations committee for a crash course in school finance. Learn the difference between capital funds and general funds. Know what tax abatements are. Take a school finance class at the local university. You will be able to amaze your friends, baffle your enemies, and never have to worry about running out of stimulating conversation.

Like other librarians, I have taken my budget requests to my principal and been told there is no money in the budget. My follow-up questions then were, "Is there money in the budget for textbooks, for science supplies, for the office copier, and for summer school?" If the answer to any of those questions was yes, then both the principal and I knew that the question was no longer one of "Is there money in the budget," but "How do we choose to spend the money in the budget?" An important difference that opens the door to budgeting for reasons rather than tradition.

The librarian of course needs to know who controls the overall budget in a building. Does the superintendent, the principal, or a site team determine how budget dollars are allocated? Does your district have a hands-on kind of school board? Knowing to whom to submit a budget proposal is critical.

You also need to know and follow district budgeting schedules. If your capital outlay requests are due February 15, then have them in on the 14th.

Here's a little trick many librarians have learned: A good time to ask for money for a special project or piece of equipment is a month or so before the end of the school's fiscal year. Principals and others may be looking for ways to spend the small balances of their accounts (budget dust). Have a list of items your library needs that can be quickly acquired and paid for.

6. List the areas for which one needs to budget. One way to ensure specificity in your budget is simply to create a spreadsheet of each item your library program needs to purchase in the coming year. Here is generic example:

Table 8-1
A library budget worksheet

Item	Relevant data	Rationale/goals to be met/ department requesting	Amount requested
Print and e-book collection maintenance	Collection size X replacement rate X average cost per title	Maintenance of core materials collection *(see "Create maintenance and growth budgets" in this chapter)*	
Print and e-book collection maintenance growth	User requests/ program goals	This may include new units, building goals, or long-range plan related to collection size	
Periodicals	Number of titles	Person or department requesting each title and circulation data	
Online subscriptions and fees (periodical databases, online encyclopedias, online tutorials, e-book collections, etc.)	Specific titles and cost per title	Amount of previous year's use and assessment data collected from users	
Multimedia materials such as videos, kits, audiobooks, and royalty-free audio and visual materials	Collection size Replacement % Average cost per title	Include new units and requests	

(continued)

Table 8-1 (*continued*)

Item	Relevant data	Rationale/goals to be met/ department requesting	Amount requested
Software and apps	Number of computers	Include new units, teacher requests, and curriculum requirements	
Licenses and support costs (for library systems, servers, etc.)	Specific programs requiring support licenses		
Library, computer, and lab supplies	Amount used previous year and statement of adequacy	Be as specific as possible. Show allocation per teacher if the library is responsible for providing	
Library equipment—maintenance	Current amount Replacement % Average cost per replacement	Maintenance of current inventory (*see "Create maintenance and growth budgets" in this chapter*)	
Library equipment—growth	User requests and program goals	This may include new units, building goals, curricular needs, and long-range plan related to student access	
Other items specific to my program or school		Special projects that require one-time expenditures (furniture replacement, for example)	
Professional expenses	Anticipated costs of professional training, supplies, association memberships, and travel	Specific professional development events and resources, specific learner outcomes as a result of participation, and explanations of benefit to school program, staff, and students	

What you need to include in your budget will vary by district and by level of responsibility. If you have district-wide or building-wide budgeting responsibilities, you may need to calculate library personnel salaries and benefits, networking costs, administrative system expenses, classroom technology costs, staff development needs, and equipment maintenance and repair costs.

Use the multiple "worksheet" feature of spreadsheet programs. The first worksheet is a broad overview of all areas in the budget, then separate worksheets can be created for detailed accounting purposes. Balances can be linked between worksheets. Remember that public copies of this spreadsheet should be shared if you are working toward transparent budgeting as suggested in chapter four.

7. Create maintenance and growth budgets. Administrators understand maintenance. They regularly budget for replacing roofs, tuck-pointing brickwork, and resurfacing parking lots. They understand why windows, furnaces, and pencil sharpeners all need to be replaced now and again.

What administrators don't always understand is that library collections and instructional technologies need to be maintained as well. But once it's pointed out to them, they "get it" and budgets become more realistic.

Use the following formula with your print and e-book collection and your library equipment, share the results with your administrator, and see if it makes a difference.

Doug's Magic Formula for a Maintenance Budget

Here's one way to calculate what funds you should be spending to keep your resources up-to-date:

Maintenance budget = replacement rate X total number of items X average cost
(Replacement rate = 100%/number of years in the life span of material)

Here are examples:

If a library has an agreed upon supported collection of 12,000 books with an average cost of $18 per volume with an estimated life of a book at 20 years, then the maintenance budget should be 5% X 12,000 X $18 or $10,800 (remember the replacement rate is 100%/life span or 1.00/20 or 5%).

If a school has 20 DVD players which cost $100 each and have a life span of 10 years, then the maintenance budget for players should be 10% X 20 X $100 or $200.

Here's one for you to try:

A school has 40 computers with a life span of 5 years. The average replacement cost of a computer is $1000. How much should be spent each year to maintain the computers?

Replacement rate = 1.00/ _____ years

Maintenance = _____ X _____ X _____
                       Replacement rate   Total number of items   Average cost of an item

or

$_____ Maintenance budget

How do you determine a "supported collection size"? There is no one right way, but it does need to be mutually agreed upon by the librarian, the administration, and the library/technology advisory committee. Here are some things to look at when determining this number:

- Current collection size and how well it serves the curriculum
- Any standards regarding recommended collection size
- Size of school population, number of grades served, and special needs of student groups
- Other digital resources available to students

Current, well-maintained materials, even if in smaller quantities, better serve staff and students than larger amounts of dated and unreliable materials. If maintenance budgets are inadequate, your materials will get older, fewer in number, less reliable, and have less relevance to the user and program. Those who allocate budget dollars need to know this. A maintenance formula will make sense to them. Remember that this is an annual expense, not a onetime outlay.

If your collection is not at "supported collection size," you will also need to create a growth budget. A growth budget formula looks like this:

Supported collection size – current collection size / years to achieve target size X the average cost of a book.

So if you now have 6,000 volumes in your collection, you have a supported collection size of 8,000 volumes, you want to achieve your supported collection size in 5 years and the average cost of a book is $20, then you will need a growth budget of (8,000 volumes – 6,000 volumes = 2,000 additional volumes) / 5 years = 400 volumes X $20 per volume = $8,000. Remember that this should be in addition to your maintenance budget.

8. Report to budget decision makers how past budget dollars have been spent. One powerful way to convince others you should be given adequate funding is to inform them of how successful you have been with your past budgets. Remind them about how many people your program serves and how much of the curriculum depends on it.

Don't just deal in numbers. Let decision makers know how individuals, both teacher and student, have been helped by your program. The one common denominator that all effective salespeople have is the ability to tell a good story—to personalize the facts. And who can tell stories better than librarians? "You should have seen the kids lined up before school opened to get into the library to use the new computers. You all know how Johnny Smith never gets excited about anything in school. If you'd have seen him find the NASA website, you wouldn't have recognized him."

The formal communications efforts that were discussed in chapter four need to include budget reports. Link what has been spent by the library program to how students and staff have benefitted regularly to targeted audiences.

9. Know the importance of serving in school, professional, and political organization leadership roles. Woody Allen once quipped that 80 percent of success is showing up. Your ability to get support for your budget will increase if you "show up" on school governing committees. It's surprising how few individuals in an organization actually want to be decision makers. Serving on these bodies always takes extra time, but one learns to love those 7:00 AM meetings.

Make a list of groups who make decisions in your school. Schools may use:

- A site council or a committee that writes building goals and improvement plans
- Curriculum and textbook selection committees
- Staff development committees
- A parent–teacher organization
- Committees that interview and select new staff members
- Accreditation teams

If you have a chance to take a decision-making role and do not, you've lost all whining rights about the choices that are made for you.

There are other groups in schools that have educational goals and political agendas, some of which may be closely aligned with those of the library program. Some districts have legislative committees that create a platform of issues important to the district, and find ways to let their local legislators understand those issues.

Nearly all state and national educational associations have legislative platforms—the school board association, administrators associations, parent–teacher organizations, and state and national teacher organizations. These groups often hold forums for local politicians. Attend, get informed, and get active. State library organizations may sponsor a yearly library legislative day that gives librarians a chance to visit with their legislators.

If one of your faculty, a neighbor, or community member is in the legislature, visit with them, write letters, and send them e-mail. Local political party meetings and fund-raisers often give you a chance to visit with a variety of local politicos. It's effective to be able to start a conversation with your senator by saying, "As we were discussing at the fall fundraiser . . ."

Help pass bond referendums and elect school board members. Members of the community who have children in school and therefore a vested interest in schools are becoming a smaller and smaller percentage of the total population. It's therefore increasingly taking more work to get referendums passed and progressive board candidates voted in.

Offer to give short talks at service groups like Kiwanis, Sertoma, Rotary, and Lions. Inform the community about your program, and fill the talk with specific times your program helped individual students.

Of course one can always make the ultimate sacrifice: run for office. We all wanted to know about the skeletons in your closet anyway.

10. Use technology to improve their budgeting and communication skills. These tools are ones that every budget maker needs to master.

Spreadsheets come with a variety of names, features, and price, but all basically do two main tasks for budget makers—to easily add and subtract numbers and display those numbers in readable columns and rows or as charts and graphs.

Budget makers can create easily "what-if" scenarios using a spreadsheet: If books' average price changes to $18.50 from $21.00, what is the impact on the total budget? What if we order fifty computers with extra RAM at a cost of $50 more per machine?

Spreadsheets are an efficient means for keeping track of the money you have allocated. A simple bookkeeping system that records the date, purchase order number, vendor, item, and amount can do wonders in solving any discrepancies between your records and your business office's accounts. Remember to make this spreadsheet available online for both viewing and comments if striving for transparency (see chapter four).

A word processor and layout skills can help sell your message. One of the most popular questions from children in writing classes has always been, "Does neatness count?" It did, and it still does.

A clear and readable narrative of your budget helps others understand it. Good organization, correct grammar and spelling, and a clean layout are all more easily accomplished using a word processor. A sophisticated user can create effective layouts for eye appeal and ease of reading, select appealing fonts for impact, and add graphics for illustration and interest. The purchase of a primer on design is a great investment.

Good integrated software makes it easy to add spreadsheets and charts to the budget narrative. Cloud-based word processors like those in GoogleDocs, Zoho, or Microsoft Office 365 make access and collaboration simple.

A slide show presentation program can help your audience literally "see" the points you are making when pitching your budget to a decision-making group. Full-colored slides containing text, illustrations, graphics, charts, animation, and sound created on a computer and then displayed on a projection screen using an LCD projector help clarify your message as the presentation is given. Find and follow good visual communication advice regarding the number of words on a slide, font size requirements, and the effective use of graphics. A bad slide show is worse than none at all.

Good purchasing strategies

Congratulations. You've submitted your budget and it's been approved. Now make the most of the money coming to your program.

Some simple strategies can get you the most "bang for your buck," especially when it comes to technology purchases. You can stretch your budget by:

- **Limiting the life of your equipment.** Set a supported lifespan of equipment and then don't repair anything that is past that age. Don't throw a piece of equipment away just because it's over its lifespan, but do put it in a non-mission critical place, so if it breaks down it won't need immediate replacement.
- **Getting price quotes on EVERYTHING.** Watch the legal requirements for getting bids. Over a certain amount, state law may require getting formal bids. Get at least two or three quotes on

everything, even if it is on a state contract. This takes only a little time and can save a lot of money. Even with tried and true vendors, get quotes now and then just so they keep their pencils sharp.

- **Taking advantage of group purchases.** Check costs in your state equipment and services contracts and statewide purchasing plans. Take advantage of regional purchases when possible. You may also be able to take advantage of regional support/training.
- **Purchasing warranted reconditioned computers and other equipment.** There are pros and cons to this. If a computer is in a lab setting and does not need a lot of power, reconditioned computers can provide a low-cost alternative. Make sure they come with at least a three-year warranty and are from a reputable company. (If a lab needs 30 computers, buy 32 or 33 when buying reconditioned.)
- **Using free and open source software and moving to the cloud.** In many cases, products like OpenOffice, TuxPaint and GoogleDocs have all the features needed by students and even staff members. Cloud-based services may reduce local costs significantly (see chapter six).
- **Standardizing.** It's easier to stock parts, maintain, cannibalize, and train when you have a single model of about anything to support. This is not always possible, but strive for it.
- **Making sure all equipment purchases go through a single department.** Individual teachers should go through the library or technology department to acquire any materials. This assures that the new equipment will work with current systems in place, can be supported, and is of good quality.
- **Not supporting obsolete technologies.** While these devices may need to be ripped from some teachers' hands, they are no longer viable classroom technologies:
  - 16mm film projectors
  - filmstrips
  - cassette tape players
  - opaque projectors
  - Microsoft Works and Appleworks software

  I would add that we should be phasing these obsolescent technologies out
  - overhead projectors
  - CRT television sets
  - VHS tapes and players
  - desktop, rather than web-based, software

  Budgets need to be focused on technologies that still have a long lifespan, not propping up those that are dying.
- **Budgeting for training.** How can you make the most powerful and expensive technology worth absolutely nothing? Drop it? Spill coffee on it? Let an eighth grader hack into it? While those things do often work, a far more common and effective way to stress your educational budget and get nothing in return is to buy a new system, hardware, or software and not provide sufficient training in its use.
- **Buying early in the school year.** While this may not save money, it does stretch your materials budget. Why not get nine months' use out of a new book by purchasing it in August instead of just two or three months if you wait until March? Keep a little money back for those "must-have" new titles, but spend the bulk of your materials budget early and then keep a file of new titles to order early the next school year.

For reflection: Weed

Remember Bertha from chapter three and how during her thirty-five-year tenure, she never threw anything away? Most of the books in the collection I took over from her were well over twenty years old.

Many titles could and should have retired. One book had not been checked out since two weeks prior to Pearl Harbor.

The reason I can state with confidence she threw nothing out is because the bottom left drawer of her desk contained nearly a dozen years of the *Sports Illustrated* magazine swimsuit editions in pristine condition. I could just envision Bertha's dilemma. "I can't put this out where children might see it, but I can't throw it away. I can't put this out but I can't throw it away. I can't put this out but I can't throw it away." It must have cost her sleepless nights.

Dated collections are not the sign of poor budgets but of poor librarianship. Only two things can happen if library material replacement budgets are inadequate. The collection ages or gets smaller depending on whether the librarian actively discards outdated materials. Weeding must be ongoing despite the adequacy of the materials budget. Small, but high-quality collections are far better than large collections of mostly worthless stuff. Continuous, thoughtful weeding rids your collections of sexist, racist, and just plain inaccurate materials and makes the good materials easier to find. But it also is important to obtaining better budgets.

A well-weeded, and thus smaller, collection sends the message that the library may not be adequately funded. If you went into your neighbor's pantry and saw the shelves filled with boxes of breakfast cereal, you'd conclude your neighbor had plenty to eat. But what if those boxes were empty? Shelves filled with books of no value are the equivalent of pantries full of empty cereal boxes. Visitors don't look very hard at book collections. They only see whether shelves are empty or full. Your budget is unlikely to increase if the perception is that you have a library full of materials already.

When accreditation standards call for minimum collection sizes, what needs to be understood is that these are minimum size collections of useful, usable materials—not just objects.

Many individuals regard books as sacred objects and have difficulty throwing them away. A teacher from Bertha's school glares at me to this day, claiming he hurt his back climbing out of the dumpster into which I had thrown away some "perfectly good" books. What he did not understand and what we need to remember is that it is not books that are sacred, but the thoughts, inspiration, and accurate information they contain.

Chapter Nine

Facilities

It's painful to admit, but I don't go to libraries as much as I once did. Whether I am at my desk at work or in my favorite chair at home, the information, guidance, and social experiences for which I once went to my public or university library now are delivered to me electronically.

For nearly 100 years, elementary and secondary schools have been building or remodeling their libraries, creating spacious rooms that contain thousands of physical materials to support reading programs, aid research projects, and expand the content area curricula. Studies indicate that schools with good library programs are more successful than those without, validating the wisdom of the leaders in those schools (Scholastic 2008).

Today's reality is that all readers and information seekers, including those in schools, are having increasingly less need to visit a physical library to meet their basic information needs. Digital information sources, readily accessed from classroom, home, or mobile computing devices are the choice of many students and teachers. The NetGen student increasingly prefers the visual and the virtual rather than the printed text. Why, many school leaders ask, does a school need a physical library when seemingly all resources can be obtained using an inexpensive netbook and a wireless network connection? Might these large physical spaces in our schools be repurposed for greater educational impact?

I would argue that the best school libraries are not just surviving, but thriving, in this new digital information environment—but not without seriously repurposing their physical spaces. This chapter looks at three ways today's school library can and should adapt to the digital age, new learning environments, and 21st-century skill expectations of today's students and then goes on to examine if some traditional library design rules are still relevant when building or remodeling a school library today.

Why should I go to the library when the library will come to me?

The purpose of our library's physical space needs to encompass more activities than simply retrieving materials in physical formats—books, magazines, and audiovisual resources. To stay relevant in an increasingly digital world, today's school libraries must provide:

1. Social learning spaces. Students still want to meet and learn in physical environments—check any shopping mall, coffee shop, or teen center. Online bookstores did not kill the physical bookstore. But like bookstores, libraries are becoming "high-touch" environments in a high-tech world.

Comfort and aesthetics are increasingly important in today's school library. High school libraries are following the example of bookstores and public and college libraries by adding coffee shops. Upholstered seating, flexible furniture arrangements, and attention to aesthetics in lighting and colors help make libraries places where students and staff *want* to be. Many small, intimate spaces are being carved out of one grand space.

There is an increasing body of evidence that supports the value of student collaboration. Studies demonstrate that the ability to form "learning groups" in which participants collaboratively construct personal meaning for content studied is *the* most important factor in college students being successful (Brown and Adler 2008). As collaboration and social learning grows in importance, libraries are becoming places for teams to work together, both formally and informally.

For many students, school libraries fit the description of a "third place"—an area for informal social gathering outside of home (the first place) and work (the second place). Oldenberg suggests such environments are necessary for a healthy society and healthy individuals. He writes that the third place is "marked by a playful mood" and is "remarkably similar to a good home in the psychological comfort and support that it extends" (Oldenberg 1989).

Like the student commons or playground, the library can provide spaces for recreation and play, especially before and after school. Allowing gaming, research on topics of personal interest, and a more liberal definition of what constitutes "constructive activities," the library space may be the only place that provides some students "psychological comfort." A third place library might contain:

- Social interaction spaces where small groups can work and play
- Gaming both physical and virtual
- Collections of popular books, manga/graphic novels, music, and high-interest magazines
- Access to workstations for social networking sites
- Displays of information on high-interest materials (teen drinking, job opportunities, eating disorders, popular culture, etc.)
- Computer workstations for the creation of personal communications and art
- Comfortable chairs and tables
- A coffee shop

The term "learning commons" is growing in popularity among educational institutions. Popularized by David Loertscher, the school library as "learning commons" can be defined as "where exemplary teaching and learning are showcased; where all professional development, teaching and learning experimentation and action research happens; and where various specialists of the school have offices" (Loertscher, Koechlin, and Zwaan 2008).

The use of the library as a "learning commons" will mean different things to different organizations, but flexibility, a wider scope of use by more school personnel, and a less narrow definition of "library" will be the hallmarks of the library/learning commons. A space that has tutoring, vocational education, gifted and talented services, and a raft of educational support services including library services provides synergistic service to students.

2. Multimedia production and presentation spaces. School librarian and writer Joyce Valenza reminds today's educators that we need to stop thinking of the library as a grocery store—a place to "get stuff"— and start thinking of it as a kitchen—a place to "make stuff" (Valenza and Johnson 2009). The kitchen metaphor is a good one when looking at how technology should be a part of the physical library.

Student access to technology has evolved over the past twenty years. Providing access to information and digital productivity tools is requiring less and less school real estate as schools move from computers in labs housed in separate classrooms, to labs in or adjoining the library, to classroom mini-labs, to carts of laptops, and increasingly to 1:1 device projects. Students are increasingly using personal mobile devices such as tablets, netbooks, and smartphones that decrease the need for school-supplied computers even more.

As digital access moves from workstation to mobile devices, the physical library needs to provide a robust wireless network infrastructure. Electrical outlets throughout the library to power and recharge mobile devices are necessary. Indirect lighting that reduces screen glare is important throughout the area, not just in labs. Workspaces on which laptops can be placed at a good ergonomic height are needed.

Signs of a welcoming library

As students enter the Left Overshoe School Library, they always pass this sign posted boldly by the entrance:

Welcome to the Left Overshoe School Library

- No cell phones/no texting
- No personal computers or other equipment
- Computers for school use only

- No talking
- No eating or drinking
- No book checkout without ID
- Library is for schoolwork only

As students enter the Right Overshoe School Library, they always pass this sign, posted boldly by the entrance:

Welcome to the Right Overshoe School Library

- Please use your phone quietly
- If you need help connecting to the school network, let us know
- Hard time finding something online?—We can help you search
- We have social learning areas

- Please consume carefully—Have you tried our coffee shop?
- Can we help you find a book or magazine to read?
- The library is for learning—What interests you?

Gamers meet from 3–4 Monday–Thursday. Join us!

Increasingly information, entertainment, and assistance comes to the end-user digitally instead of the end user having to go to the information, entertainment, and assistance traditionally found in libraries in analog formats.

Why would anyone go to your library at all if it's not a genuinely welcoming place?

Some library terminals need to remain available for quick access to the library catalog and reference queries. Workstations with good processing speed, adequate memory, and software for video and still photo editing, music production, voice recordings, computer programming, and multimedia construction are still important. While portable devices are growing more powerful, desktop computing is still needed for some applications, and by placing these machines in the library, everyone throughout the school has access to them.

Libraries have traditionally contained presentation areas for librarians to read stories, do storytelling, create puppet shows, and produce skits. These spaces are still useful but need to be expanded for student and staff use as electronic presentation areas. Student demonstrations and presentations that take advantage of multimedia enhancements such as video, computerized slide shows, and sound need good audio amplification, video projection systems, interactive whiteboards, and student response systems. Every class in a school can use such presentation areas when they are universally accessible in the library.

While not a glamorous role, the library is often the best choice to serve as the technology hub of the school. Often located in a central location, the library's controlled backroom spaces are well suited to be wiring closets containing servers, routers, patch panels, and other networking equipment. Building technology integration specialists and technicians' offices and workspace should be a part of the library where students and staff have ready access to their expertise and where collaboration between technology and library staff is more convenient and likely.

3. Teaching spaces. The library's tools (print to electronic information sources) have certainly changed, but not its mission: teaching people to effectively find and use information to meet their needs. Skill emphasis has shifted from finding and organizing information to evaluating and using information. The teaching role as opposed to the "providing" role of librarians has grown. But students and teachers need guidance and instruction more than ever. Teaching spaces remain vital.

Large group instruction is still a useful means of imparting information, giving instructions, and holding discussions. This requires having a classroom-sized seating area or areas (depending on school size), in or attached to the library. A room attached to the main area in the library provides noise containment going in both directions, but tables in a corner of the main library works as well. In either case, a whiteboard or interactive whiteboard, projector, a means to show video, sound amplification, and other large group teaching tools are needed. The "library" classroom should serve as the "model" classroom in a school—the place where new teaching technologies can be piloted and taught before installation in regular classrooms.

Seminar and small group spaces are popular in all libraries. Spaces serving four to twelve learners can be created by sectioning-off part of the main room with furniture or dividers. Many groups throughout the school appreciate separate conference rooms (with windows for visual control) for meetings.

And the librarian's desk needs to be on the floor of the library, not in an office, for ready one-on-one assistance.

What about books? Will all books be replaced by digital resources? Should we start ripping out bookcases now? Much of this may well depend not on technology, but on how publishers rise to the challenge of digital publishing, balancing control with convenience, profitability, and willingness to allow libraries to loan digital resources.

If U.S. intellectual property laws don't change and ownership of the 70 percent of books that are not in print but not in the public domain remains in question, a lot of information will remain accessible only in print form. Libraries will definitely become digital information centers, but not as quickly as one might think since conversion speed is not a technical issue, but a legal, moral, economic, and social one. Books will be available in multiple formats for a very long time. Print, audio, and digital will continue to coexist quite nicely much as radio, television, and the Internet do now.

Design for the technologies that are available *now*, not those just over the horizon. The horizon might be further away than you anticipate. And make flexibility one of your key goals as you reimagine the library space.

Look at places where kids DO want to be and see what might be learned from those spaces. The coffee shop should guide us, telling us kids want a social learning space. Online preferences suggest we need to give kids a lot of access to digital resources. Gyms and theaters indicate that libraries should be performance spaces where kids can share information, not just absorb it. And finally, the popularity of social networking sites and media sharing sites like YouTube demands that we make libraries knowledge production areas.

Be broad-minded about the functions of the school's library and get planners thinking less about designing an effective library, but an effective school with a library program that supports the school's goals.

A good library is a physical indicator that a school embraces certain values regarding education—that multiple points of view have value; that teaching kids how to think, not just memorize, is critical; and that self-exploration should be encouraged. The school library must be a space dedicated to honoring those who use its resources to meet whatever informational, educational, socialization, and personal needs they might have.

The fundamentals of good school library design and why they are still important

After having helped plan multiple new and remodeled school libraries, I have developed a short list of questions that a planning team needs to answer, and another list which needs to be asked of the architect or project leader. As schools change their instructional program and as technology evolves, a simple list of "do's" and "don'ts" for building or remodeling may be outdated nearly as soon as it is written. These questions need to be answered as close to the time of building as possible.

General rules for planning

1. Use a steering committee with a range of stakeholders to help answer these questions. Visit other new school libraries and ask "what's right" and "what's wrong" with their design. Look for recent best practices on facility design of libraries of all types in the literature.
2. Work with the architect as early as possible. A good one will be involving you in the planning anyway. Rather than supplying him or her with a layout or floor plan, be able to describe the activities that will take place in the library, the kinds and quantities of resources you have or will have, and how many people you serve. Share your library's philosophy, mission, and goals statements.
3. Look ahead, but don't design for technology that does not yet exist. Despite the rise of wireless networking and projects that give every student a computing device, wired networks and computer labs have a purpose into the foreseeable future.
4. Remember that older technologies are rarely replaced by new technologies. As previously mentioned, the book, the radio, the motion picture, the television, and the Internet all currently provide people with information, and all will probably continue to do so for a very long time.
5. Learn to read the architectural plans and double- and triple-check the location of data, electricity, phone lines, and light switches. Walk through a typical day using the floor plan or model. Are you having to wheel equipment carts through the reading area? Are there unsupervisable blind spots when standing at the circulation desk or from your own desk? Will you have to walk a long distance to complete common tasks?

Planning committee's questions

1. How will the new library facility be used and by whom? How many students and classes should be able to work in the library at one time? Will future classrooms make more or less demand on library resources? (Remember that libraries with too much seating may become study halls, test centers, or dumping grounds.)
2. What kinds of things will students be doing in the library? What major projects or activities will require library resources?
3. What areas of the school should the library be near, and what areas should it be distant from? Libraries, gyms, and music rooms don't always make good neighbors unless serious noise abatement is planned.
4. How will the library be staffed? How will the area be supervised? Will there be times only one person needs to be able to see what is happening throughout the space?
5. Will the resources (books, computers, magazines, etc.) be made available to the public beyond regular school hours? Will the rest of the building be accessible as well, or does the library need

to "stand alone" in regard to bathrooms, drinking fountains, and climate control? Does there need to be an outside entrance with parking nearby?

6. Can other departments, programs, or public agencies share the new area? Think of the Learning Commons concept and be open to the gifted and talented program, a study center, career guidance, special education services, and other student services as part of the library space. What will be most convenient for students and staff? Remember, the more adults in a space, the less need there is for student supervision.

7. Should the library have a computer lab or labs in or adjacent to it? Should the computers all face in one direction or be placed in a more lab-type design with perimeter placement?

8. Decide what things are vital in your requests, and which things would just be nice to have. Pick your battles.

The architect's questions

1. Does the library allow for different kinds of student use—individual, small group, and large group? Are there areas that can be used for both social learning and quiet study in the library? Are all forms of information access and communication provided for, both physical and digital?

2. Does the design eliminate any areas that cannot be seen from a single location? Is the library on a single floor for effective supervision and accessibility? Is shelving not over 30" high, accessible to children and those with disabilities?

3. Do the traffic patterns make sense? Are the circulation areas and the computer labs(s) near the entrance? Is equipment storage near a hallway?

4. Are new technologies being accommodated? Is there a controlled space for the network wiring closet, work area for technology maintenance, and office space for technicians and technology integration specialists? Does the library space serve as the building's "head end" for video, telephone, and computer networks?

5. Have acoustical considerations been made? Do the ceiling tiles and flooring have sound-damping properties? Does the design allow for windows to the computer labs, conference rooms, and multimedia production areas for visual control, but sound containment?

6. Is the lighting adequate and nonglare? Are the light diffusers adequate? Is there a natural light source that will not fade the carpet and materials or wash out computer screens? Are there zones that can be darkened, especially where projectors are being used? Are the light switches in a single bank in a controlled area?

7. Has consideration been give to the aesthetic qualities of the area? Are colors coordinated, is there visual interest, a variety of textures, and warmth? Are there display areas for student work and new materials near the high-traffic areas? Does the library look "interesting" while still being very functional?

8. Have security issues been discussed? Can some parts of the library be restricted from student and/or public use? Can computer labs be locked? Are student entrance points easily monitored? Could a security system be installed if needed?

9. In addition to large labs, are there areas for individuals and smaller groups of students to use computers and do research or complete multimedia projects? Are there places for these technologies made available to students and teachers?
    *   scanners
    *   video and still digital cameras

- computers for video and audio editing
- microphones
- graphics pads or tablets

10. Are there conditioned electrical outlets and data drops throughout the area? Can a 10' × 10' electrical and data floor grid be installed for maximum room use flexibility? Are there places where library users can plug in their computers and other devices? Do all walls have data drops? Where monitors are ceiling mounted, are video and electrical outlets near the ceiling? Is there robust wireless connection throughout the library space?

11. Is there a "wall to the future" for expansion if additional space is one day needed?

12. Are all areas and resources accessible by the physically challenged? Have all Americans with Disabilities Act (ADA) requirements been met, including space between shelving and shelving unit height?

13. Does the library have a work area for teachers?

14. Is there sufficient space to house an adequate print collection? Does the shelving have backs, is it height appropriate for the age of the student user, and can it hold materials of a variety of sizes? Is there a periodicals area for both display of new titles and a place to sit and read them?

15. Is the furniture of high quality? Does it have a matte finish to reduce glare and eyestrain? Does it resist scratching and marring? Are upholstered chairs provided for reading and studying, as well as tables for planning and writing?

16. Does the furniture invite collaboration? Can chairs and tables be easily moved close together for informal learning and farther apart for individual reading and studying as needs arise?

17. What atmosphere are you trying to create? How do you want the user of the library to feel when entering?

18. Is there a presentation space for both students and adults to use? Does the elementary library have a story area?

19. Does the library have:
- a work area for the library staff
- a book drop accessible when the library is closed
- a coat closet for employees
- a sink

20. Is the library designed for maximum flexibility? Can furniture, shelving, and even walls, be moved and reconfigured as needs and services change?

Ten common design pitfalls and how to avoid them

I once caught a glimpse of what purgatory must be like for school librarians. While student teaching in the mid-1970s in a small Iowa town, I watched the most hapless librarian I have ever met trying to do her job—which at that time was mostly keeping study hall students quiet and busy.

Her library was simply two classrooms pushed together with bookshelves around the walls and a high circulation desk at the front of this long room near the door. The floor held just two tables near the circulation desk. The main seating was provided in rows of tall-sided study carrels running in long aisles down the length of the room.

The librarian spent most of the time I observed her running up and down those aisles of carrels trying to detect which students were making the little bird noises they knew drove her crazy. I believe this happened every hour of every school day. At least it was going on each time I visited the library. (That school building

bird noise

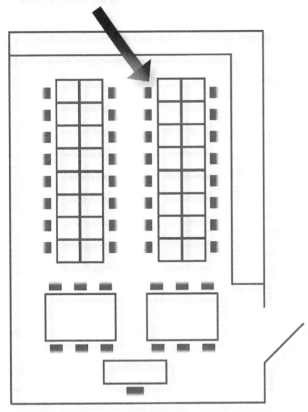

IMAGE 9-1 Study carrels and bird noises

has since burned down. I like to think it was the act of a merciful god.)

A few years later when I was a school librarian myself, I overheard my principal say that he thought tall-sided carrels would be just the ticket for helping students work quietly in the new school's library being planned. My ears pricked up quicker than a dog's. I decided it might not be a bad idea to be a bit more involved in the library design process.

I avoided getting study carrels in that new library I actively helped design. Since then, I've managed to find and avoid a number of other pitfalls when helping plan about a dozen more new and remodeled libraries. Below are ten of the deepest pitfalls of library design. Seek to avoid them.

1. Not planning for a physical library at all. Messages like these from practicing librarians are too common:

> *Help! My boss is seeking information about what size a school library should be. It seems that the old argument of "Why do we need physical libraries when we have the Internet?" has reared its ugly head again. As you can imagine, this is giving me a knot in my stomach.*

For some reason, remodeling tends to bring out the "visionary" in school planners and architects—especially when that vision holds within it a means of cutting construction costs by shrinking or eliminating the library from the building project. What these folks forget is that while some information resources might become digital, the folks who use them will remain "analog" for a very long time. And these analog people will continue to need a physical facility in which to place their physical bodies and gather to meet very human needs.

Even if all books suddenly disappeared tomorrow, we will still need bricks and mortar libraries. We forget sometimes that society has given our K–12 schools three major charges:

1. Teach young people academic and technical skills.
2. Help socialize its future citizens.
3. Contain and protect its children while Mom and Pop are busy (and to keep children out of shops and off the streets).

Each of these societal charges is getting stronger, not lessening. Hence all-day kindergarten, longer school days and school years, and after-school programs.

The physical space of the library helps a school meet each of these charges. In most schools, there is project-based, collaborative work done by students at all grade levels, often required by state standards. There are increasing needs for students to have access to digital technologies that help them access and communicate information. Flexible learning opportunities like online coursework, interdisciplinary units, extended school days, service learning, and secondary/postsecondary class schedules create needs for school spaces that are not the traditional classroom.

We are social creatures and social learners. Although we have the Internet, we still gather at shopping malls and libraries. We may have e-mail, but we still phone and visit. We can watch movies streamed to our televisions, computers, or cell phones, but we still go to motion picture theaters in record numbers. Our analog selves like physical places to gather to work and learn.

2. Not having a planning team. A steering committee with a range of stakeholders can help design a library space that does not just fit an existing program, but allows an envisioned program to happen (see chapter three). Your committee should visit other new exemplary school libraries and programs and question the people actually working in those libraries. ("Having the windows shine directly on the bank of computer catalog computers was not a good idea.")

Involve the architect as early as possible. A good one will be asking you questions.

Rather than supplying him/her with a layout or floor plan, you and the planning team should be able to describe the activities that will take place in the library, the kinds and quantities of resources you have or will have, and how many people you serve. Share your library program's philosophy, mission, and goals statements. Be open to innovation, but make sure that "form" follows "function."

Progressive planners will invite other departments, programs, or public agencies to share their new area. Think about spaces for the gifted and talented program, a study center, or community access in your library. Lots of adults working in the library tend to help make a more productive center all around. Does your library have a work area for teachers, complete with laminator, telephone, sink, comfy chairs, and coffeepot?

3. Planning for only one kind of learning. The amount of physical floor space necessary can only be answered by determining how the new facility will be used and by whom. How many students and classes should be able to work in the library at one time? Will future classrooms make a greater or smaller demand on library resources and space? The number of students and classes working productively at one time will be dependent on the level of staffing in your library. One professional will have a difficult time helping more than two classes do research at one time.

A rule of thumb is that an essential library has workspaces and tools for three classes to work researching and producing projects. Assume that one of these classes will probably be working in the library's computer lab or multimedia production area.

The library needs to allow for different kinds of student use—individual, small group, and large group. This means conference rooms or zones for collaborative work, enough tables in an area to seat a class, and upholstered chairs in which individuals can read and study.

Storage and access to all formats of information and communication need to be provided for—including print. Plan sufficient space to house an adequate print collection. Purchase shelving for your current, well-weeded print collection and buy all the shelving at the time of construction. It won't match if you buy some of it now and some of it later.

At least one of the building's general-use computer labs should be a part of the library area, preferably separated by well-windowed walls for visual supervision and for sound containment. While the current and correct push is to place as many computers in individual classrooms or in individual students' hands as possible, most teachers still like to use a lab occasionally for whole class instruction. Every building should have at least one, and the library is a practical place for it since it is accessible to all teachers.

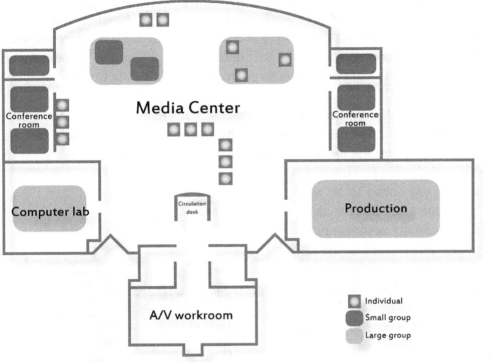

Media Center

Conference room

Conference room

Computer lab

Circulation desk

Production

A/V workroom

□ Individual
■ Small group
▢ Large group

IMAGE 9-2   Multiple uses

In addition to a large lab, the library needs to provide a generous number of research and productivity terminals for individual users. There should also be an area for individuals and smaller groups of students to use technology to complete multimedia projects.

Remember too that all areas and resources need to be accessible by the physically challenged. Your architect should be able to help you meet all ADA requirements. Look carefully at things like shelving height, aisle widths, and floors on multiple levels that need ramps. These things all require a surprising amount of floor space.

Design a "wall to the future" in your plans. If your library one day needs to grow, is there a logical wall that can be removed to accommodate that growth?

4. Designing the library for school use only. It's good to determine the areas of the school the entire library should be near and the areas from which it should be distant. Classes that use the library and its technology labs the most need to be located near it. Noises from the band room, technology education shops, gymnasiums, cafeterias, or air-handling units create unnecessary distractions.

There is another "location" factor that is becoming increasingly important. In many communities less than 25 percent of the households have children in any school system. If schools want to pass bond or operating referendums, they need to market schools as resources that can and will be used in the evenings, on weekends, and throughout the summer by the community as a whole. It's becoming common practice to have resources, especially the technological ones, available to the public after school hours through adult education classes or other open lab opportunities.

This really means you need to ask if you want the whole school building accessible, or if the library should be a "stand-alone" facility for after-hours use with its own bathrooms, drinking fountains, and climate control. Does the library need an outside entrance with nearby parking?

5. Designing for technologies that do not yet exist. Look ahead, but don't design for technologies that do not yet exist, let alone for ones that haven't yet been proven to work in a school setting. Even as inexpensive, wireless, handheld, battery-operated devices come on the market, we will be living with legacy equipment that is not wireless or battery-operated for many years. You'll still need lots of power and wired network drops. It is far better to hide the unused outlet or data plate than to go back and ask for the funds to drill new holes soon after construction.

Avoid visible goofs like placing the electrical plates and video jacks near the floor beneath the ceiling mounted television monitors. Those wires and extension cords running down the wall look tacky. If your data projectors are ceiling mounted, make sure the electrical and data outlets that supply them are on the ceiling near them. (Seems obvious, but I've seen extension cords run across ceilings.)

Whole building network technologies need to be accommodated. The library is a practical place for the network wiring closet, work area for technology maintenance, and the network head ends. In a controlled space in the library this equipment can be easily monitored and accessed by the librarian and the technician who works for her or him. Schools that locate the technology department in one wing and the library in another simply make getting help less convenient and more confusing.

Learn to read the architectural plans. Get permission and a hard hat to do onsite construction visits on a weekly basis as the facility is being built. While you're at it, make sure the doors and windows are in the right places, too.

Here are a few lessons from Johnson's Technology Implementation School of Hard Knocks. With any technology implementation:

IMAGE 9-3   Unsightly wiring

a) Know the educational benefits of any new technology.
b) Always go with the industry standard.
c) See it in action in a school and talk to users before you buy it.
d) Check consultants' references. Hire the person, not the firm.
e) Allow at least a year for networks or systems to "settle in." Don't evaluate them until that year is up.
f) Double the amount of time you estimate for staff development for learning new systems. Then double it again.
g) Hire or train on-site tech support.
h) Specify capacities and purposes, not specific technologies.
i) Get documentation—as-builts, drawings, and test results.
j) Don't pay the whole bill until everything is working to your satisfaction. Have a checklist that can be completed before the final bill is paid.
k) Expect to be working with crabby people during the process, but don't turn into one yourself.

6. Creating libraries that are difficult to supervise. If I were going to be working in a new library for 20 years or so, I would determinedly insist on a number of things that will help in student supervision including:

- Areas of the library that can be restricted from student and/or public use.
- The ability to lock conference rooms, computer labs, and production areas.
- Large and multiple windows into conference rooms, computer labs, and production areas.
- Easily monitored student entrances.
- A security system, if needed. Do you need a security system? Estimate the value of missing items in one year. Subtract those taken by staff. Multiply by five. Only if the amount is greater than the total cost of a security system, buy one. Most kids I know see such systems as only an easily beaten challenge.

Seek to eliminate:

- Any areas that cannot be seen from a single location such as the circulation desk.
- Any freestanding floor shelving over 30" high.
- The placement of any computers where the screens cannot be easily seen.
- Any plans for a two-story library.
- And especially, no high-walled study carrels.

The library must be on a single floor. While most of us could use the aerobic exercise associated with climbing a couple of sets of stairs a few hundred times a day, two-story libraries are impractical for reasons of supervision, security, and accessibility. You really need an upstairs/downstairs librarian arrangement in such facilities. I have also had the heart-stopping experience of watching one young daredevil work his way around the perimeter of my library's balcony on the outside of the railing. Liability suits are such unpleasant things.

Use the floor plan to look for unsupervisable blind spots.

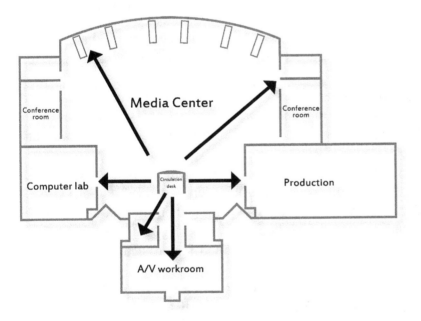

IMAGE 9-4   Visual control

7. Designing libraries that have poor traffic patterns. Lay out any proposed floor plan on a table. Get your favorite Monopoly piece. Walk through a typical day using the plan. Get a piece of equipment. Answer the phone. Answer a reference question. Plan with a teacher. Help with an Internet question.

Now do the same as a library user. Get a book or read a magazine. Come in as part of a class to use the computer lab. Return a book. Use the library catalog. You get the idea.

Library traffic patterns that make sense place the circulation areas, reference collection, displays, and labs near the entrance. Equipment storage should be near a hallway. The reading/study area should be away from high-traffic areas where users may be repeatedly distracted. Increasingly the goal is to create separate "zones" for social learning and group work and for quiet, independent reading and study.

Ask your architect about placing tile or replaceable carpet squares in the high-traffic areas and laying carpet in the rest of the library for more uniform wear throughout the room.

Is the library easily accessible from the rest of the building, but cannot be used as a convenient passage between areas of the building?

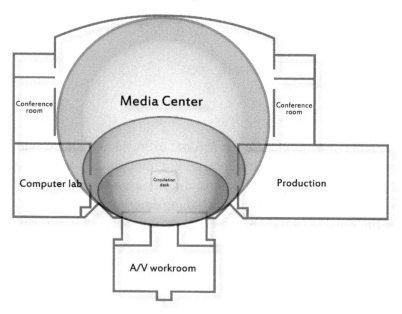

IMAGE 9-5   Traffic patterns and zones

8. Forgetting the importance of good lighting and sound dampening. As anyone who has used a computer for extended lengths of time can tell you, the importance of good lighting is more important to our physical comfort in the digital age than ever before.

Lighting needs to be adequate, adjustable, and nonglare. Architects have the lumen numbers and nifty gadgets to determine the amount of light in areas like book stacks and reference areas. Make sure light levels are checked in the final walk-through. Light diffusers need to be in place to reduce reflection and glare, especially on computer monitors.

Natural light sources are desirable, but they should be designed so that they will not fade the carpet, destroy materials, or create glare. Point of interest: "Under full spectrum light students attended school 3.2 to 3.8 days more per year, had nine times less tooth decay, grew an average of 3/4 inches taller, and had more positive moods and better academic performance than students attending schools with other lighting" (Rouk 1997).

Your library should have a specific area that can be separately darkened for projected presentations, and light switches in a single bank in a controlled area.

Make sure the furniture you choose has a matte finish to reduce glare and eye strain. Light-colored woods are easiest on the eyes since they provide the least contrast with the generally lighter-colored materials placed on them.

Good carpeting and ceiling tiles can help mute the necessary noises associated with learning. The days of the deathly quiet library are past, but it's still hard for both students and the librarian to work in an echo chamber of din.

9. *Ignoring aesthetics.* The first rule of decorating is to never let someone who is not a professional select the color of anything. Even if someone on your committee thinks he or she has taste, double-check with a real interior designer. It is money well spent.

Consideration needs to be given to the aesthetic qualities of the area. Colors should be coordinated, not just throughout the library, but throughout the building. Find ways to create visual interest in the architectural design while still having usefulness as the primary goal. Add warmth through fabrics and woods in your seating and shelving. Display areas for student work and new materials near the entrance help personalize a library. Consider what atmosphere you are trying to create, how you want the user of the library to feel when entering. When designing secondary libraries, I strive for the look of an office where I think I would be happy working—pleasant, comfortable, businesslike, and efficient.

Taking the time and making the effort to make your library not just functional, but attractive as well sends a very clear message to your patrons—I respect and care about you.

10. *Forgetting about all those things that will drive you nuts day in and day out.* Here's my short checklist:

- No nightlight by the door. You have to stumble though the dark barking your shins to get to the bank of light switches.
- No backs on shelving. Books slip back . . . and down.
- Too tall, nonadjustable shelving.
- No area for the display and reading of current magazines and newspapers.
- No dedicated story area in an elementary library.
- Low-quality furniture that doesn't resist scratching and marring. Get good laminate and strong legs.
- No upholstered chairs for comfortable reading and studying.
- No work area for the librarian.
- No after-hours book drop.
- No coat closet for the library staff or place to store dripping umbrellas.
- No sink.
- No water fountain.

I like visionaries. Without them I would never have gotten to dream about beeburgers, personal helicopters, self-cleaning houses, or all digital libraries. When it comes to facility design however, I think I'll let practicality take the front seat. Bricks and mortar last a very long time. And remember, even if the future is digital, it's where you'll be spending the rest of your analog life.

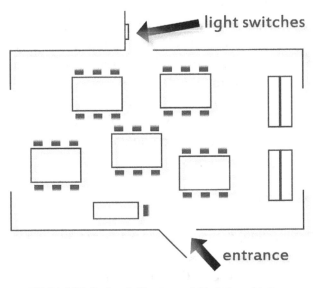

IMAGE 9-6   Misplaced light switches

For reflection: Are there schools that don't need a library?

Building a library would be a waste of money if you find your school's administrators and teachers:

- Are content to have their instruction be textbook and test-driven. Given the number of standards in the state-mandated curriculum and the state's test-based accountability requirements, your staff does not see the need for in-depth study of topics, problem-based teaching, or authentic assessment. Textbooks are meeting the needs of your teaching staff.

- Are unconcerned about providing quality information sources to staff and students. If your staff does not feel that edited sources of information—books, commercial databases, or reference materials—are necessary when "everything is free on the Internet." Questions of information reliability and authority are deemed irrelevant.
- Believe students and staff can locate information without assistance. Citing the ability of students to do a search in Google and find pages of information on which the search terms appear, your staff dismisses the notion that more sophisticated strategies and search tools are needed. "Kids can always change their topic if they don't find what they need with Google," a teacher would conclude.
- Feel that the ability to process and communicate information in formats other than print is unnecessary. Students in your schools use standard written term papers as the sole means of communicating the results of research. That they are word-processed is cited as proof of "technology integration." When asked about having students communicate using audio, video, photographic, or visual productions, teachers dismiss these formats as irrelevant to preparing students for college.
- Use computers only for testing and as online worksheets. Online testing and computer-assisted instruction now uses approximately 75 percent of your schools' computer labs' schedule, leaving little opportunity for students to use the technology for creative work.
- View independent voluntary reading as a waste of time. Strict adherence to the basal readers and reading "skill building" software has resulted in students scoring acceptably on standardized tests. Both administration and teachers are reluctant to "mess with success." Developing a desire to read is not part of the district's strategic plan.
- Believe differentiated instruction is just babying the slackers. Providing materials at a variety of levels, in multiple formats meeting the needs of learners with divergent abilities, interests, and learning styles is given a low priority by teachers in your schools.
- Small classroom book collections that support the reading series and a word-processing lab with access to Google are all that your school currently requires. Since the skills of librarians and technology specialists are viewed as unimportant, the library can be staffed by clerks and by technicians who can keep the student information system running from a hidden location until it is outsourced—and you don't need much of a space for that.

References

Brown, John S., and Richard Adler. "Minds on Fire: Open Education, the Long Tail and Learning 2.0." *Educause Review*, Jan./Feb. 2008.

Loertscher, David V., Carol Koechlin, and Sandi Zwaan. *The New Learning Commons Where Learners Win: Reinventing School Libraries and Computer Labs*. Salt Lake City, Utah: Hi Willow, 2008.

Oldenburg, Ray. *The Great Good Place*. New York: Paragon Books, 1989.

Rouk, U. "School Sense." *PROBE*, Spring 1997.

School Libraries Work! 3rd ed. Scholastic, 2008.

Valenza, Joyce Kasman, and Doug Johnson. "Things That Keep Us Up at Night." *School Library Journal*, October 2009.

Chapter Ten

Digital Intellectual Freedom

It really isn't fair. Nutcase book burners get all the attention. In 2009, a float in a small-town Wisconsin Fourth of July parade presented a washing machine with a sign that read "keep our library clean." This was in response to a controversy over some books about homosexuality in the public library. And of course, there was the traditional call for book burning. The brouhaha got a lot of press (Hanna 2009).

What I would like to ask is where are the headlines proclaiming the far less egregious but more widespread and harmful censorship that is an ongoing occurrence in many, if not all, public schools today?

As professional librarians, our role in helping others understand the principles and importance of intellectual freedom is among the most important duties we have. The profession has risen to this challenge as it has related to print and multimedia resources. But as information, opinion, recreation, and communication shift to digital platforms, our efforts in maintaining access to the widest possible spectrum of resources must shift as well. And that's what this chapter is about.

Freedom to learn

The professional who prepares my income taxes says that good citizens pay every penny they owe in taxes—but not one cent more. That pretty well summarizes a sensible view of compliance with any law. Follow it, but don't go overboard.

A driver is not more law-abiding when going ten miles per hour *under* the speed limit.

Unfortunately, too many school technology decision makers "hyper-comply" with the Children's Internet Protection Act (CIPA). Tumblr, Wikipedia, YouTube, and even the Google search engine have all been singled out as violating CIPA by schools around the country. Some school districts have just flat out blocked any sites that encrypt data because Orwellian administrators can't see what their network users are reading and writing when sending or receiving data from these sites. Since GoogleApps in Education uses encryption, schools have been blocking that very useful tool as well.

Just as a reminder, CIPA reads: "The protection measures must block or filter Internet access to pictures that are: (a) obscene, (b) child pornography, or (c) harmful to minors." The law does *not* read, "sites that are uncomfortable for adults."

Smart schools practice due diligence in preventing access to things that are "harmful to minors." This means filtering at a reasonable level. It means adult monitoring of student computer use. It means having, teaching, and enforcing an understandable Acceptable (or Responsible) Use Policy (AUP).

Due diligence can have different meanings to reasonable people, but it does not mean using scare tactics to block access to useful information, tools, and experiences. It does not mean relying solely on over-blocking by web filters. It does not mean knee-jerk blocking decisions made by single individuals in an organization.

The Federal Department of Education's director of education technology, Karen Cator, states "sites . . . deemed appropriate . . . can be unblocked. So having the process in place for unblocking sites is definitely important" and reminds educators that unblocking sites deemed appropriate will not put E-rate funding at risk (Barseghian 2011).

The librarian's real concern with filters themselves should not be over-blocking or under-blocking. The primary concern of anyone who believes intellectual freedom is important is who decides what is blocked and how the decisions are made. Do I seriously think my students' education is jeopardized because they can't get to a music streaming service from the computers in our district? Not really. What I do worry about is when decisions about what is blocked are unilaterally made—whether by an administrator, a technology director, a technician, or a noisy parent. Today it may be Pandora that's blocked. Tomorrow it may be the websites of Planned Parenthood or Rush Limbaugh. The day after that, any website or web tool that a left- or right-wing nut community member may object to. Where does it end?

Librarians need to take a leadership role in addressing school district policy making—working with our advisory committees, our administrative groups, our school boards and our professional associations to teach, maintain, and extend the principles of intellectual freedom to the online world. Decisions about allowing access or limiting access should be done following a procedure and with input from a group representing a wide range of stakeholders. Much like what librarians have been advocating (and largely succeeding in getting) in response to book challenges.

When your school blocks a website, is there a "reconsideration" process in place? Does the one wishing to take or keep the resource away from learners need to file a formal challenge? Does an established committee meet to examine the site, discuss its appropriateness, look at reviews, and examine if and how it has been used in other districts? Does the recommendation eventually go to the school board for a final decision about keeping or removing access? If not, why not?

Banned Books Week has been a successful effort by the American Library Association for raising public consciousness about the dangers of print censorship. It's helped keep Harry Potter, Anne Frank, Lucky, Holden Caulfield, and Huck Finn a part of students' cultural experiences. Banned Book Week is a good, good thing.

But if we are truly committed to "Freedom to Read," what we *really* need in today's world is also a Blocked Bytes Week that addresses the egregious blocking done not to just information online, but productivity tools and social networking sites as well.

Perhaps we could create a new manifesto: "Freedom to Learn."

Maintaining intellectual freedom in a filtered world

> We trust Americans to recognize propaganda and misinformation, and to make their own decisions about what they read and believe. We do not believe they need the help of censors to assist them in this task.
> —American Library Association's "Library Bill of Rights"

> Young people have First Amendment rights.
> —American Library Association

The concepts of intellectual freedom as expressed in the statements above are as relevant to information in electronic formats as they are in print.

As a proponent of intellectual freedom, I advocated and received administrative support for unfiltered Internet access in my district from 1994 through 2001. But because of the Childhood Internet

Protection Act (CIPA), our district installed an Internet filter in order to remain eligible for some federal funds. I was expecting a raft of problems.

I was concerned that students would rise in revolt after having Internet sites unreasonably blocked as they searched for information. I was worried that by installing a filter, teachers would abandon their roles as guides and supervisors when students were on online. I feared the light of education would glow less brightly as a result of the filter's installation with diminished staff and student access to a variety of information sources and opinions. I was certain I was violating my long-held personal beliefs that every individual, regardless of age, has the right to access and read a multiplicity of ideas and viewpoints, free of censorship in any form.

My pragmatic side had its doubts about the wisdom of our district's *not* having a filtering device installed as well. Technology had indeed opened floodgates of information into our schools by way of the Internet, and those rising waters included flotsam and sewage. Materials and ideas that had been in the past physically inaccessible to students now could be viewed, both purposely and accidentally, right in our libraries and classrooms.

The potential of student access to unsavory and possibly unsafe materials on the Internet has made support of intellectual freedom extremely challenging. It is difficult to justify a resource that allows the accidental viewing of graphic sexual acts by second graders searching for innocuous information, communication by anorexic teens with supportive fellow anorexics, or access by seventh graders to "Build Your Own Computer Virus" websites. Well-meaning teachers and administrators today express concerns over the dangers of Facebook and the distractions of YouTube.

Defending unfiltered Internet access is quite different from defending *The Catcher in the Rye*.

But the sky has not fallen in the years since we installed our filter. The complaints about over-blocking and under-blocking from teachers and students have been few and far between. I was surprised in light of what I had been hearing from librarians in other school districts who complained about the filters and filtering policies in their districts.

How does a librarian help maintain some semblance of intellectual freedom in a filtered information environment?

Are Internet filters mandatory?

Must public schools install Internet filters? If they wish to remain eligible for federal funds, including E-rate, the answer is clearly yes. The Childhood Internet Protection Act reads:

> To be eligible to receive universal service assistance under subsection (h)(1)(B), an elementary or secondary school (or the school board or other authority with responsibility for administration of that school) shall certify to the Commission that it has—
> (A) selected a technology for computers with Internet access to filter or block material deemed to be harmful to minors;
> (B) and installed, or will install, and uses or will use, as soon as it obtains computers with Internet access, a technology to filter or block such material.

CIPA defines "technology protection measures" as a specific technology that blocks or filters Internet access to visual images that are "obscene, child pornography, or harmful to minors." Internet filtering software clearly meets both the letter and the spirit of the law.

Yet, filtering is not a perfect solution. Using and relying solely on these products to limit students' access to "sites deemed harmful" may:

1. Under-block, leaving inappropriate sites accessible.
2. Over-block, preventing access to appropriate sites.
3. Block sites deemed not politically acceptable (including anti-filter sites) to the filtering authors.
4. Leave access to inappropriate peer-to-peer networks, chat rooms, or images that cannot be blocked.
5. Be easily disabled or worked around by our clever and ambitious students.
6. Give teachers, librarians, administrators, parents, and legislators a false sense of security.
7. Permit student access to inappropriate materials when they use personal Internet access on their own computers and phones.

Studies, like those of the Electronic Freedom Foundation (Electronic Freedom Foundation 2003) that examined nearly a million web pages, should raise concerns. The researchers found:

- For every web page blocked as advertised, blocking software blocks one or more web pages inappropriately. Ninety-seven to ninety-nine percent of the web pages blocked were done so using non-standard, discretionary, and potentially illegal criteria beyond what is required by CIPA.
- Internet blocking software was not able to detect and protect students from access to many of the apparently pornographic sites that appeared in search results related to state-mandated curriculums.

And, as anyone who has worked with children knows, a certain percentage of young people will see any "block" as simply a challenge to find a way around. Students can circumvent filters by:

- Disabling stand-alone software through simple keyboard combinations.
- Using specialized software such as that available from Peacefire's website.
- Changing a browser's proxy to an unfiltered site.
- Logging into the filtering server using a default administrator's password if not disabled.
- Simply using their own smartphones with personal Internet access.

As clever as we adults might think we are, we are usually at least two steps behind many of the students in our schools.

Maintaining intellectual freedom and a safe Internet environment when filters don't necessarily work very well

There are a number of proactive measures schools should take to make sure students and staff can operate in the least restrictive Internet environment possible, keep students safe, and yet meet the requirements of CIPA.

1. *Base the choice of filters not on cost or convenience, but on features and customizability, and chose the least restrictive settings of the installed filter.* Internet filters have a wide range of restrictiveness. Depending on the product, the product's settings, and the ability to override the filter to permit access to individual sites, filters can either block a high percentage of the Internet resources (specific websites, e-mail, chat rooms, etc.) or a relatively small number of sites. The Electronic Freedom Foundation study revealed some other interesting numbers:

- Schools that implement Internet blocking software with the least restrictive settings will block between .5 percent and 5 percent of search results based on state-mandated curriculum topics.
- Schools that implement Internet blocking software with the most restrictive settings will block up to 70 percent of search results based on state-mandated curriculum topics.

Another study conducted by the Department of Family Medicine at the University of Michigan Medical School (*JAMA* 2002) examined how well seven Internet filters blocked health information for teens at settings from least restrictive to very restrictive. They found that at the least restrictive setting only 1.4 percent of the health information sites were blocked and 87 percent of the pornography sites were blocked. At the most restrictive setting, 24 percent of the health information sites were blocked with still only 91 percent of the pornography sites blocked.

2. *Generously use the override lists in the Internet filter and make sure librarians can override the filter or have access to a machine that is completely unblocked in each library so that questionably blocked sites can be reviewed and immediately accessed by staff and students if found to be useful.* Any teacher or librarian should be able to have a site unblocked by simply requesting it—no questions asked. The technology department need not have the responsibility, beyond correctly installing and configuring the filter, for students accessing possibly inappropriate materials, and all school staff members must be required to continue to monitor students while on the Internet as if no filter were present. The technicians should know that it is the responsibility of the teaching staff to see that students do not access inappropriate materials, not theirs, and there is less tendency to "block everything—just in case."

3. *Treat requests for the blocking of specific websites like any other material challenge.* When any staff member, parent, or community member requests that a specific Internet site be blocked, that request must be treated like any other material challenge in the district. Most districts have a "reconsideration" policy outlining procedures to follow when someone requests that any material be removed from our schools, whether it is a book from a library or classroom, a textbook chapter from the curriculum, or a video from the collection. A good policy calls for the person making the request to complete a form specifying what is objectionable about the material. Once completed, a special committee is formed that carefully reviews the material and then makes a recommendation to the school board about the material—whether to retain it or remove it. The school board then decides the issue, based on the recommendations of the committee. Online resources are given the same rigorous review process before being blocked.

4. *Take a proactive approach to ensuring good Internet use by students.* Librarians and classroom teachers should:

- Articulate their personal values when using technology, talking to students about ethical online conduct, and setting clear limits about what is allowed and what is not allowed. All staff members need to be knowledgeable about the school's AUP and work to help students understand it.
- Build student trust. If an inappropriate site is accidentally accessed, adults should be encouraged to use the incident to teach some strategies about finding and interpreting clues in search result findings to discriminate between relevant and nonrelevant sites.
- Allow students personal use of the Internet. If the Internet computers are not being used for curricular purposes, students can research topics of personal interest (that are not dangerous or pornographic). The best reason for allowing this is that students are far less likely to risk loss of Internet privileges if that means losing access to things that they enjoy.

- Reinforce ethical behaviors and react to the misuse of technology. Technology use behaviors are treated no differently than other behaviors—good or bad—and the consequences of such behaviors are equal. We try not to overreact to incidents of technological misuse. If a student were caught reading *Playboy* in paper form, it's doubtful a school would suspend all his or her reading privileges.
- Model ethical behaviors. All of us learn more from what others do than what they say. Verbalization of how an adult personally makes decisions is a very powerful teaching tool, but it's useless to lecture about safe and appropriate use when that adult may not follow his or her own rules.
- Create environments that help students avoid temptations. Computer screens that are easily monitored, passwords kept secure, and required logging into and out of network systems help remove the opportunities for technology misuse. An adult presence is a far more effective means of assuring good behavior than filtering software.
- Teach and assess children's understanding of ethical concepts. Do not give technology use privileges until a student has been taught and can demonstrate that he or she knows and can apply school policies. Test appropriate use prior to students gaining online access. (After over fifteen years of Internet access in schools, the latest E-rate requirements finally require that teaching safe Internet use be a part of a school's AUP.)
- Educate staff and parents about ethical technology use. Through school newsletters, talks at parent organization meetings, and through school orientation programs, librarians can inform and enlist the aid of teachers and parents in teaching and enforcing good technology practices.

Maintaining both the concept of intellectual freedom and providing a healthy and educational online environment may seem to be a difficult balancing act. But so far, many districts have been able to both meet the requirements of CIPA and give staff and students access to the greatest possible range of online resources.

But as an intellectual freedom advocate, you should be monitoring the situation very closely.

Best practices for meeting CIPA requirements

I was visiting a school district not long ago and had a chance to visit with its curriculum director. In passing, she referred to their technology director as the "Tech Nazi"—a title she admitted was borrowed from *Seinfeld*'s character the Soup Nazi. He had been taking on the job of unilaterally blocking websites.

This is not the first time I've heard folks holding the position of technology director in other districts described in less than endearing terms. One librarian refers to her tech director as "Bob God." I heard a teacher refer to her district's technology department as the "Education Prevention Department." And of course there are those other names that shouldn't appear in a professional publication.

Tech directors have two strikes against them coming out of the box. First, educators have not always embraced technology (not to state the obvious). Its complex and often unreliable nature often makes it a source of irritation rather than delight. Second, technicians have an appreciation of the vulnerability of the equipment they are charged with maintaining that normal people simply don't. They see those viruses, hackers, software conflicts, power surges, and foolish acts by the laity that are always surrounding the fort, waiting for the smallest breach, and then sneaking in and wreaking havoc.

By their very nature, policy and rule making are influenced by human values. Nowhere in schools is this more evident than when it comes to the selection of teaching resources.

Controversies have swirled around textbook content (intelligent design in science texts), book censorship (Harry Potter's place in our libraries), and video content (a film's R-rating automatically earning it exclusion from the curriculum). Public schools' parents and community members can be at both ends of the political and religious spectrum. As Larry Cuban suggests, such values conflicts present not solvable problems, but an ongoing dilemma that needs ongoing management (Cuban 2001).

Access to the vast resources of the Internet has added a twist to the selection of ideas and images readily available to students while in school. Without using a filter, the Internet is an either/or proposition—either students have ready access to all of its content or none of it. Given that valuable, arguably essential, resources are available only online, not giving students Internet access is educationally unsound. Given that inappropriate, and arguably dangerous, materials are also available through this medium, giving students complete Internet access is educationally irresponsible.

There is little disagreement that websites that are prurient in nature should be blocked. Most educators would agree websites designed especially for students should be available. The problem is that the great bulk of sites fall somewhere on a continuum between these two extremes. When the Internet is filtered at a district or even regional level, both high school seniors and preschoolers have the same degree of access.

Maintaining both the concept of intellectual freedom and providing a healthy and educational online environment may seem to be a difficult balancing act. But some districts have been able to both meet the requirements of CIPA and give staff and students access to the greatest possible range of online resources by providing a mechanism for all stakeholders to have a voice in policy-making decisions.

Values issues often play out in very tangible ways. A high school social studies teacher may want students to analyze a hate group site and compare it to the Nazi movement, while a parent group wants such sites blocked. A librarian, tired of keeping students from accessing games, may want all game sites blocked, while an elementary teacher uses game sites that reinforce math skills. A language arts teacher might encourage students to use e-mail to contact experts on term paper topics, but the district has "banned" student e-mail. And students themselves see Facebook as a vital means of communication and collaboration while many educators see it only as a frivolous time-waster.

Below are some best practices in insuring that good decisions about Internet filtering are made in a district.

Policies, rules, and guidelines related to filtering need to be created through a formal, collaborative process undertaken by a group consisting of educators, students, technicians, and community members (see chapter three). Such a group, whether a policy committee, technology advisory group, or building site team, needs to address the following issues and make recommendations to the school board and administration.

1. Whether a filter should be used, which filter should be used, and how the filter should be initially configured.
2. How requests for sites to be either unblocked or blocked are handled.
3. By whom, how, and under what circumstances filters can be overridden.
4. How the effectiveness of the district's filtering practices and policies are evaluated.
5. How other practices that help ensure appropriate student access are developed and used.

Librarians should facilitate informed decision making. Like all policy decisions, those helping construct them should have good information about the national and state laws and local school board policies regarding student Internet access; what types of filters are available and the strategies they use to identify sites to be blocked; research (and opinion) on the efficacy of filtering software; and local network and hardware configurations.

Policy-making groups need to understand the requirements of CIPA and the financial consequences should a district choose not to meet its requirements.

Studies that demonstrate that even the best filters both over-block and under-block and offer only a partial solution to controlling access to Internet resources should also be made available and discussed. Overreliance (or worse, sole reliance) on filtering programs can lead to a lack of monitoring student use by adults and few efforts to teach good evaluation and selection skills.

And finally, good decisions should be based on the principles and guidelines of other professional organizations such as the American Library Association's web resources on CIPA.

Access to these documents allows committee members to base arguments on more than "gut reactions."

Districts must develop clearly articulated filtering guidelines. Any guidelines, policies, or procedures need to be documented, distributed, and discussed among all stakeholders. Should questions arise, should school administration, technology administration, or school boards change, there will be no change in practice without a formal reevaluation. Too often we confuse practice with policy—at our peril.

Effective school leaders have long harnessed the power of building policy ownership through collaborative decision making. New technologies, tech-savvy students, and vocal publics make good policy creation more important and more challenging than ever. But it can be done.

Seven myths about Internet filters

There are some common myths created both through ignorance and intent about Internet filters. These mistaken beliefs often result in poor decisions about the use of this software, leading to censorship of online resources. You and your school will be more successful in developing good policies about filtering if you have good information. And it will be up to you, the librarian, to bring intellectual freedom into the conversation.

1. *The Childhood Protection Act (CIPA) is specific and broad in what must be filtered in schools.* CIPA reads: "The protection measures must block or filter Internet access to pictures that are: (a) obscene, (b) child pornography, or (c) harmful to minors." That's it. Karen Cator, the Department of Education's director of Education Technology, reassures teachers that schools will not risk losing E-rate funding for unblocking YouTube or giving teachers broad access to the Internet. And no, Facebook does not have to be blocked, as a clarification in the FCC Order 11-125 of August 2011 states implicitly (Barseghian 2011).

2. *It's the filtering company that determines what is blocked.* Most filters have a great deal of customizability when it comes to what is filtered. Broad categories of blocked sites can be enabled or disabled. Schools can override filters by adding specific sites to "white lists" of allowed sites or to "black lists" of blocked sites. Filtering can (legally) be turned off in schools on specific computers by user category, by specific IP address of a computer, or by using a filter bypass login.

3. *Some sites must be blocked due to bandwidth limitations.* A common reason for blocking sites like YouTube or Pandora is that they use too much bandwidth. While it is true that most districts have a limited amount of Internet connectivity, devices called packetshapers can be used to prioritize traffic on a network, eliminating the need for bandwidth intensive sites to be blocked completely.

4. *The processes for reconsideration of print materials don't apply to online resources.* Digital resources are as legitimate as print resources and the same criteria for removing online resources apply to them as apply to library books, textbooks, magazines, and videos. Once a district has

decided that the Internet is an educational resource, any removal of a specific resource on the Internet must follow board-adopted policies and procedures on the reconsideration of educational resources.

5. *The technology department must determine what is blocked.* The major intellectual freedom issue related to filters is not whether a particular resource is blocked or not blocked, but who makes the blocking decision and how it is made. Determinations about the availability of Internet resources should be made by a formal group of educators, technicians, and community members at two levels. The first level is the broad filter level—selection of the filtering product itself and the categories settings of that filter. The second level is the individual Internet site level (Planned Parenthood, SarahPAC, YouTube, Facebook, etc.) Single individuals should not make blocking decisions.

6. *Internet filters are so good that supervision of students while online and instruction in online safety and appropriate use are not necessary.* One of the biggest dangers of Internet filters is overreliance on them. No filter catches 100 percent of all pornographic sites. Users can use proxies and other work-arounds to bypass the school's Internet filter. And increasingly, students are using personal devices such as cell phones and tablets that use cell phone carrier data plans for Internet connectivity that are completely unaffected by school filters.

7. *Internet filters and intellectual freedom are mutually exclusive.* When chosen, configured, and monitored carefully a filter can become a selection tool. A limited filtering system that keeps the little ones from accidentally accessing inappropriate or even dangerous websites is ethically responsible. It's not the technology but its application that can lead to censorship.

For reflection: Getting websites unblocked

There are few situations more frustrating for a librarian than learning of an Internet resource or tool that would be of value to students but finding it blocked by the district. Here are some strategies for dealing with this problem:

1. Know and be able to articulate the educational value of the blocked site. Cite the specific standards the resource helps meet. Make sure the curriculum director gets this information.
2. Be able to share examples of how librarians and teachers in other districts are using the resource.
3. Ask to have the resource provided on a limited basis—for a certain period of time or on specific computers. Report at the end of the test period if any problems were encountered and what uses students made of the resource.
4. Speak as a member of a group of teachers that wants the resource unblocked.

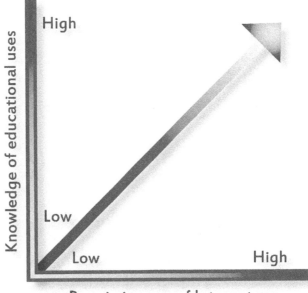

IMAGE 9-6 How filtering policies are made

5. Know exactly who makes the filtering decisions in your district and if there is a formal process for getting a site unblocked.
6. Know local, state, and federal laws pertaining to filtering and student Internet access to avoid "hyper-compliance" by your district.
7. Communicate in writing your requests and responses when seeking to get a site unblocked. Always copy the supervisor of the decision maker, the curriculum director, and your building principal on all communications.
8. Seek to establish a formal review process for unblocking Internet resources or seek to have the reconsider policy in your district revised to cover online resources.
9. File a challenge on the resource to start the due-diligence process on school materials. (Yes, you can do this as a staff member.)
10. Don't give up after the first denied request. Come back with other uses, examples, and partners. Sometime the squeaky wheel gets some grease.

References

American Library Association. The Children's Internet Protection Act. American Library Association website, nd. http://www.ala.org/advocacy/sites/ala.org.advocacy/files/content/advleg/federallegislation/cipa/cipatext.pdf (accessed Jan. 21, 2013).

Barseghian, Tina. "Straight from the DOE: Dispelling Myths about Blocked Sites." *Mindshift* blog, April 26, 2011.

Cuban, Larry. *How Can I Fix It?: Finding Solutions and Managing Dilemmas*. New York: Teachers College Press, 2001.

"Does Pornography-Blocking Software Block Access to Health Information on the Internet." *JAMA*, Dec. 11, 2002.

Electronic Frontier Foundation. "Internet Blocking in Schools." 2003. https://www.eff.org/node/67552 (accessed Jan. 21, 2013).

Chapter Eleven

Ethics and Technology

At a workshop on technology ethics for students, I was (to put it mildly) surprised when one of the thoughtful, lively school librarians attending revealed that she did not realize that one should not publicly post to the school website lists that linked student names and titles of overdue materials. It seemed to me to be an issue that was, as our students put it, a "no-brainer"—librarians have an ethical duty to protect the privacy of their patrons. But apparently it is not.

The sweeping impact that information technologies have had on school library programs suggests that we continually revisit the American Library Association's "Code of Ethics" as technologies change. We have accepted as part of our mission and charge the ethical education of our students and, to some degree, our fellow educators and parents. But in order for us to do this with understanding and without hypocrisy, we need to look at the ethics of our own professional practice as it relates to use of information technologies.

While it is impossible to visit every ethical issue that technology touches, this chapter deals with those that are the most significant or most confusing. We need a continuing dialog in our profession about our own ethical practices. A reexamination of the ALA's "Code of Ethics" is a beginning.

How has technology impacted the ethical practice of librarians?

One of the things that makes a profession a profession is that it has a written code of ethical practice. ALA's Code of Ethics for librarians has been around since 1930 and is revised on a regular basis. As of this writing, it was last changed in 2008.

While the Code doesn't get down to specific cases, it does provide a broad framework for guiding the day-to-day, often confusing and controversial decisions all professional librarians must make. It takes a brave, values-driven practitioner to follow this Code. But it is what makes librarians unique and invaluable as professionals. These values, if lost, would truly diminish educational opportunities for all children.

Let's look at each of the eight statements in light of how technology decisions need to be made.

ALA Library Code of Ethics Statement I: We provide the highest level of service to all library users through appropriate and usefully organized resources; equitable service policies; equitable access; and accurate, unbiased, and courteous responses to all requests.

Information technologies—the automated catalog, online databases, and access to the Internet—have allowed even the most humble school library to offer services and a range of resources of which even research libraries could only dream just a couple of decades ago. But, our jobs have become increasingly complex as a result.

Resources

School budgeting is a "zero-sum" game: there is a finite, and usually inadequate, number of dollars that can be spent by a school district in any one year on the total educational program including class size, basketballs, toilet paper, staff development, and superintendent's transportation allowance (see chapter eight). What this means is that every dollar spent on technology or library resources is a dollar that cannot be spent for other potentially worthwhile purposes. Ethically, we must spend every dollar in ways that will do the most good for our staff and students, keeping the entire school funding picture in perspective.

As informational resources become available both in print and digital formats, we need to carefully appraise which format best suits curricular purposes and our budgets. Collection development strategies are more important than ever as educational funds need to be stretched to cover ever-higher demands. Materials purchased "just in case" or for a "well-rounded collection" that remain untouched by human hands are not just unwisely, but unethically, acquired.

It is ethically irresponsible *not* to have a budget. Every library needs to have a written, goal-oriented, specific proposed budget. If students are to have access to the resources necessary for an effective educational program, all librarians must accurately inform decision makers of the cost of those resources. The greater outlays necessary for technology in schools, among other things, makes this more critical than ever.

Policies

The use and abuse of technology resources requires that the librarian must be able to create good policies and rules related to their use. While we are rightfully expected to enforce board-adopted policies such as the Acceptable Use Policy, each individual library has its own set of expected rules and consequences for their infractions that are set by the librarian.

Since technology may be an unfamiliar resource for many adults, our policies tend to be overly harsh in proportion to the importance of the act committed. Too often students lose "Internet privileges" for an entire year or semester for a minor or first infraction of a rule. When formulating consequences for rule or policy infractions, librarians need to:

1. Examine the existing consequences for other similar improper activities. If a student sends a harassing e-mail, for example, the consequences for harassment already in place should apply.
2. Graduate the penalties. Students should not be denied access to the Internet for an extended period of time for a first infraction of the rules. One might ask, "Should a child be banned from reading if he/she was caught reading something inappropriate?" If the inappropriate behavior happens again, the penalties can be increased.
3. Bring parents or guardians, the classroom teacher, and principal in on any ethical use violation.
4. Allow and encourage student personal use of the Internet. If the Internet-accessible computers are not being used for curricular purposes, students should be allowed to research topics of personal interest (that are not dangerous or pornographic, of course), use social networking sites, or send e-mail to friends. One reason for allowing this is that students are far less likely to risk loss of Internet privileges if it means losing access to things that they enjoy.
5. Make sure all rules are clearly stated, available, taught as part of library orientation, and consistently enforced.
6. Develop school-wide ownership of the rules. Having a site-based leadership team or library advisory committee that helps set the rules of technology for a school keeps the librarian from having to be the "heavy" and results in rules that more accurately reflect the culture of the school.

Access

The librarian has an ethical duty to advocate for liberal access to digital resources for all students in a school. Home access and public library access to information technologies alone will not close the digital divide. This means serving on building technology teams and advocating for:

1. *Access to technology for all students.* Too often technologies have been acquired and sequestered by certain departments, grade levels, or individual teachers within schools. Librarians need to voice the need for access to information technologies that are available before, during, and after school hours. Our "whole-school" view puts us in a unique position of knowing which children are getting technology skills and access in our buildings.

   Adaptive technologies have made more resources available to the physically challenged than ever before. The librarian needs to be the voice for awareness and adoption of such technologies. We also need to help schools understand and be in compliance with ADA regulations such as the mandate that all school webpages be machine-readable by providing alternate text descriptions of all visuals.

2. *The least restrictive use of information technologies.* The pursuit of information by students to meet personal needs should be encouraged in schools. Lifelong learning strategies, practice in information evaluation, and experiences in building effective communication strategies are all reinforced when students use information technologies to meet personal goals.

   As librarians, we need to be liberal in regard to what students are doing with the Internet in our libraries. The Internet has vast resources that are not directly related to the curriculum but are of high interest to students at all grade levels. Information about sports, fashion, movies, games, celebrities, and music in bright and exciting formats abounds.

   The use of the Internet for classwork must be given priority, but computer access should never go unused. And there are some good reasons to allow students personal use of the Internet:

   - It gives kids a chance to practice skills. After all that's why we have "recreational" reading materials in our libraries. Do we really subscribe to *Hot Rod* or *Seventeen* because they're used for research? If we want kids who can do an effective Internet search, read fluently, and love to learn, does it make much difference if they are learning by finding and reading webpages on the Civil War or Civil War games?
   - It gives weight to the penalty of having Internet access taken away. The penalty for misuse of the Internet is often a suspension of Internet use privileges. As a student, if I were restricted to only schoolwork uses of the Internet and had my Internet rights revoked, I'd pretty much say, "So what?" and wonder what I had to do to get my textbooks taken away as well. But if I am accustomed to using the Internet each morning before school to check on how my favorite sports team was faring, the loss of Internet access as a consequence of misbehavior would be far more serious.
   - It makes the library a place kids want to be. Many of our students love the library for the simple reason that it is often the only place that allows them to read books of personal interest, work on projects that are meaningful, and explore interests that fall outside the curriculum in an atmosphere of relative freedom. Kids need a place like that, and we should provide it—even at the Internet terminals (see chapter nine).

3. *The greatest range of electronic resources.* E-mail, social networking sites, and other Web 2.0 tools are often banned by schools, fearing their misuse by students. Yet such resources can put learners in touch with one of the best primary resources—the human expert. The ability to access sound and video and games is also often banned, even when there is demonstrated instructional need.

Accurate, unbiased, and courteous responses to all requests

One of my favorite *Calvin and Hobbes* cartoons has Calvin on the phone asking if the library has any books on "why girls are so weird." Frustrated when his question goes unanswered, he concludes: "I'll bet the library just doesn't want anyone to know." For some requests it is genuinely difficult to give an "accurate, unbiased, and courteous" response.

Anyone who has worked with children and young adults knows that they have as wide a range of interests and information needs as adults. While giving priority to requests for help with academic needs, we need to honor all information requests, keeping in mind that we do have a responsibility for providing guidance to our young charges as well. Personal interests can motivate reluctant readers to read, reluctant technology users to use the Internet, and library-shy students to use our resources.

And I sincerely hope we never forget that *courtesy* is a part of our ethical code. Opinions about libraries and librarians are formed at a young age and are often life-long. The kids we serve today will be our school board members and legislators of tomorrow.

> ***ALA Library Code of Ethics Statement II:*** *We uphold the principles of intellectual freedom and resist all efforts to censor library resources.*

As discussed in the previous chapter, technology has opened floodgates of information into schools by way of the Internet. Along with marvelous resources on topics of curricular and personal interest, the sewage and dangers of the Internet have become readily available as well. Materials and ideas that had been in the past physically inaccessible to students now can be viewed at the click of a mouse button.

The potential of student access to unsavory and possibly unsafe materials on the Internet has made the support of intellectual freedom both more challenging *and* more important. It is difficult to justify a resource that allows the accidental viewing of graphic sexual acts by second graders searching for information on "beavers" or communications by a malicious hacker with fellow hackers who encourage destructive behaviors. Defending unfiltered Internet access seems quite different from defending *And Tango Makes Three.*

Yet the concept of intellectual freedom as expressed in both the ALA's "Library Bill of Rights" and "Freedom to Read" statements is as relevant to information in electronic formats as it is in print. And as expressed in "Access to Resources and Services in the School Library Media Program: An Interpretation of the Library Bill of Rights":

> *Although the educational level and program of the school necessarily shapes the resources and services of a school library program, the principles of the Library Bill of Rights apply equally to all libraries, including school library media programs.*

While it must be recognized that preventing access to pornographic or unsafe materials is the reason given by those who advocate restricted access to the Internet in schools, there are political motivations behind such attempts to require blocking and monitoring software as well. The fight for intellectual freedom in schools is more important today than ever.

Librarians have the ethical responsibility to help ensure patrons use the Internet in acceptable ways by:

- Helping write and enforce the district's Acceptable Use Policy
- Developing and teaching the values needed to be self-regulating Internet users
- Supervising computers with Internet access and making sure all adults who monitor networked computers are knowledgeable about the Internet

- Educating and informing parents and the public about school Internet uses and issues
- Creating a learning environment that promotes the use of the Internet for accomplishing resource-based activities to meet curricular objectives

ALA Library Code of Ethics Statement III: *We protect each library user's right to privacy and confidentiality with respect to information sought or received and resources consulted, borrowed, acquired or transmitted.*

Privacy issues are a hot-button topic as citizens become more aware of how easily technology can gather, hold, analyze, use, and share personal data and how increasingly their own online activities can be monitored. As a society, we weigh our individual need for privacy against our need for security and convenience. Schools reflect the societal concerns, and the librarian is often placed in a decision-making position regarding privacy issues.

State and national laws are specific about the confidentiality of some forms of student information, including grades, health, and attendance records. State laws that address the confidentiality of library records can be found on the ALA's Office of Intellectual Freedom website. The Family Educational Rights and Privacy Act (FERPA) is a United States federal law that addresses student educational privacy rights. School board policies address student privacy rights, and these policies should be in compliance with federal and state laws.

While the librarian needs to be aware of the general laws and board policies regarding student data privacy issues, the ethical choices we must make about giving student library usage information may fall outside the parameters of legally or policy defined "education records." Circulation records, Internet use histories, and other professional observations generally do not fit the description of an "education record." State laws referring to library records may not be interpreted as applicable to *school* library records. (Please remember, I am not a lawyer although I sometimes play one on the Internet.)

Adding complexity to ethical choices that must be made in interpreting the general statement about a library patron's right to privacy, minors have traditionally been accorded fewer privacy rights than adults. To what extent do we as librarians reveal the information-seeking and reading habits of an individual student to other adults who have a custodial responsibility for the well-being of that student? Do I let a child's parent, teacher, or school counselor know if one of my students has been accessing "how-to" suicide materials on the web? Do I give information to an authority on a child's Internet use if it appears that the authority is just on a "fishing trip" with little probable cause for needing this data?

There are often legitimate educational reasons to share with a child's teacher information about that child's library resource use. Is the child selecting reading materials at a level that allows that child to practice his or her reading skills? Is the child using the online resources to complete a classroom assignment?

While most of us can agree that violating the privacy of our students for our own convenience (displaying overdue lists that link student names with specific materials on the library website, sending such information to parents directly, or blindly supplying information about student reading or browsing habits to any adult who requests such information) is unethical, finer guidelines need to be established if we are to act ethically in the broader context of student and school welfare.

I would suggest we ask ourselves as librarians when making decisions about student privacy issues:

- What are my school's policies and state and federal laws regarding the confidentiality of student information? Have I consulted with and can I expect support from my administration regarding decisions I make regarding student privacy? Is there recourse to the school's legal counsel regarding difficult or contentious issues?

- What is the legitimate custodial responsibility of the person or group asking for information about a student?
- How accurately and specifically can I provide that information?
- By providing such information is there a reasonable chance the information may prevent some harm to either the individual or to others in the school or community?
- Is there a legitimate pedagogical reason to share student information with a teacher? Am I sharing information about materials that students are using for curricular purposes or for personal use?
- Have I clearly stated to my students what the library guidelines are on the release of personal information? If the computers in the library are or can be remotely monitored, is there a clear statement of that fact readily posted?
- If student activity on a computer is logged, are students aware of this record, how long the log is kept, how the log may be used, and by whom?

As librarians, we must help students be aware of technology issues related to privacy so that they can both protect their own privacy and honor the privacy of others. Students need to understand that businesses and organizations use information to market products, and that information is often gathered electronically, both overtly and covertly. Students need to know that a stranger is a stranger, whether met on the playground or on the Internet and that personal information shared with a stranger may put themselves and their families at risk. Students need to know that schools have the right to search their files when created and stored on school-owned computer hardware. Students need to be taught to respect the privacy of others: that because information is displayed on a computer screen doesn't make it public; that information inadvertently left accessible does not mean that it is appropriate to access it.

> **ALA Library Code of Ethics Statement IV:** *We respect intellectual property rights and advocate balance between the interests of information users and rights holders.*

It's hard to remember, but intellectual property theft existed prior to electronic cutting and pasting, peer-to-peer file sharing services, and free term paper sites. It's just that the speed, availability, and ease with which property can be copied have all led to greater instances of piracy, plagiarism, and even disdain for copyright laws. The Internet has been rightly likened to a great copy machine.

The librarian has an ethical responsibility to help students understand that property is a two-sided issue: they need to respect the property of others as well as protect their own property from the abuses of others. Students need to know about the unethical practices of others and how to protect themselves from those practices. Students need to know that copyright laws protect their own original work and that they have a right to indicate how others may use it. Students need to know that passwords must be kept confidential to prevent unauthorized access to a student's data, as well as to help insure a student's privacy.

But the major challenge for librarians is helping teachers stem the tide of plagiarism washing through our schools that has been exacerbated by new technologies. One study reports that more than half of those high school students surveyed acknowledged downloading a paper from the Internet or copying text without proper attribution (eSchool News 2002).

While we need to acknowledge this is a serious problem, teachers and librarians are expending too much energy trying to "catch" plagiarism. Using various web services designed to detect plagiarism and techniques using search engines to determine if or how much of student writing is lifted from online sources is a primary means of addressing the plagiarism issue.

Ethically, we need to spend the greatest share of our time in preventing plagiarism before it happens. And this can and should be done in a number of ways:

- By teaching:
  - what plagiarism is
  - when and why to paraphrase
  - when using another's words is appropriate
  - how to cite all formats of sources
- By having a school or district-wide "cheating" policy that includes the definition and consequences for plagiarism

Our time as librarians is best spent in creating assignments that minimize the likelihood of plagiarism (see "Elements of projects that motivate" in chapter seven). We need to acknowledge that when students plagiarize, they are not just violating the ethical principles of intellectual property, but they also are not learning the skills needed to successfully solve problems and answer questions. If those critical skills are not taught and practiced, the librarian may have violated an even greater professional ethic.

Librarians must also be teaching students what their rights as information users are. Hyper-compliance to copyright laws may keep students from the fair use of intellectual property.

Finally, students must be taught that they need to determine how they wish to have their own intellectual property used, understand Creative Commons licenses, and be encouraged to control the use of their work by others (see "Creative Commons and why it should be more commonly understood" in the next chapter).

ALA Library Code of Ethics Statement V: *We treat co-workers and other colleagues with respect, fairness, and good faith, and advocate conditions of employment that safeguard the rights and welfare of all employees of our institutions.*

The introduction of technology into our libraries and schools has given an interesting twist to our collegial relationships. We have one role that has grown in importance, staff trainer, and another that has grown in complexity, staff counselor.

For many librarians, we are expected to teach not just students, but staff members the productive uses of technology. We have a responsibility to our coworkers to teach safe and ethical technology use along with simple "how-to's"—as we do with our students. Protecting one's privacy, guarding one's property, and stressing the safe use of technologies, especially the Internet, is now one of the most important ways we "safeguard the rights and welfare of all employees of our institutions." Sharing our expertise in the ethical use of information and technology is how we treat other educators with "respect, fairness, and good faith."

It has always been a part of our job to help ensure legal and ethical technology use by both staff and students in our district, not just through training, but by monitoring as well. This is not a task most of us would choose for ourselves, but one that is thrust upon us because of the resources we control. Being asked by a staff member to make unauthorized copies of print and digital resources, to load software on more workstations than for the number that the licenses permit, or to set up a showing of a movie that falls outside of public performance parameters is not an uncommon experience. In these cases, most of us have learned to quietly, politely, and firmly just say "no" and explain how such an action violates not only the law but also our personal and professional ethical codes. A gentle reminder of how our own attitudes and examples as educators toward intellectual property set a powerful example for our students is also usually in order. We should view our role as "copyright counselors" not as "copyright cops" unless the violation is so egregious that we need to inform an administrator of the problem.

Most schools' AUPs also forbid the use of school resources for nonschool uses. But more often than not, it may be best to turn a blind eye to personal use unless it is blatantly inappropriate and public. We need to strictly prohibit the use or distribution of pornography or any image that coworkers might regard as creating a hostile work environment. The librarian should not tolerate harassment or entrepreneurship conducted using school networks by anyone.

But we do need to recognize that teachers use school computers and networks to e-mail their kids in college, explore possible vacation destinations, or place an online order to Amazon now and again. We need to accept that these people are professionals and that lessons will be planned and homework graded whether at school during a prep time or at the kitchen table after supper. It's the nature of professionals. And professionals need to be accorded professional respect.

So why not take the hard-line approach to enforcing a school AUP? It has everything to do with climate. Unless it affects job performance, personal Internet use makes the school a more enjoyable place to work. Teachers have enough stress in their lives. A little humor lessens the stress, makes for a happier teacher, and this is a good thing. After all, would you want your child with an *unhappy* teacher?

We can't throw out the rules. We have a professional, legal, and ethical responsibility to enforce board-adopted policies. We cannot tolerate Internet use in schools that involves harassment, encourages malingering, or supports a personal business. But we can and should recognize that schools are comprised of human beings. And we need to do everything we can to make school a respectful, people-friendly place for both staff and students.

> *ALA Library Code of Ethics Statement VI: We do not advance private interests at the expense of library users, colleagues, or our employing institutions.*

In a school setting, I can't say that I've had much chance to violate this sixth standard. I've never been offered a huge sum of cash or an exotic vacation in exchange for purchasing a grossly inferior encyclopedia instead of the *World Book*. Probably just as well.

Is accepting vendor-purchased meals at conferences, adding vacation days to out-of-town conferences, or working on professional organization duties during school time a violation of this ethical standard? These infractions seem to be small potatoes in a world of political "contributions" and school boards being wined-and-dined in luxurious settings by big technology companies. But I also believe that there are no small lapses of integrity, so if any doubt exists, I will do nothing that may call my actions into question—or keep me awake at night with a guilty conscience.

Regardless of the amount of discretionary funds at our disposal, we do have an ethical obligation to practice open service and equipment procurement practices, thoughtful collection development, review-driven material selection practices, and detailed budgeting. When budgets are tight, the selection of resources for their specific value to students and the educational program becomes even more critical. Convenience, charm of salespersons, or the lure of that free calendar simply should not enter into the choice of one product over another.

A combination of new and expensive technologies, modest pay in the teaching profession, and a national spirit of entrepreneurship has created an environment in which some educators, including librarians, may be tempted to use school resources for personal gain. Establishing a website for a personal business on the school server, using school e-mail to close a deal, or using computer equipment to do nonschool projects for pay certainly qualify as advancing "private interests at the expense of ... our employing institutions." We need to carefully separate the time, equipment, and supplies we use as school employees from those we use for any private business or nonschool volunteer activities we may undertake.

Our time is also a resource. Ethically we are bound to use the time we are at work in the service of our school, our staff, and our students.

Most of us work in tax-supported institutions and have the obligation not just to be wise and honest in our expenditure of public funds, but to avoid the appearance of any wrongdoing as well.

ALA Library Code of Ethics Statement VII: *We distinguish between our personal convictions and professional duties and do not allow our personal beliefs to interfere with fair representation of the aims of our institutions or the provision of access to their information resources.*

Distinguishing between our personal convictions and professional duties is one of the narrower tightropes librarians walk. The addition of information technologies into schools and libraries has not made upholding this standard any easier. This statement should be addressed on two levels: policy and resources.

Policy. I hear many concerns and questions about information access policies, especially from teachers and librarians who believe their school guidelines are too restrictive. Should students have access to e-mail? To Facebook? To music and video files? How much printing should a student be allowed and for what purposes? Should students be able to use the Internet to play games? To check sports scores? To find jokes and pictures of questionable taste? Technology has made circulation rules (three books per student) seem quite simple.

As was stated earlier, good rules should reflect the philosophy of the institution and create ownership of the library program by staff, students, and parents. A good advisory committee that has as one of its charges oversight of library rules can help do this. The technology director whose responsibility includes network maintenance and security is an important member of such a committee. When the lines of communication open up between those whose expertise is in technology and those whose expertise is in education, intelligent, workable rules for student and staff result. If a teacher, student, or parent disagrees with a library policy, reconsideration of the policy by the advisory committee is an effective means of addressing such a difference.

Resources. We owe it to our students and staff to keep our personal feelings on issues from restricting their access to information, as well. *(Remember Ethical Statement I? We provide the highest level of service to all library users through . . . accurate, unbiased, and courteous responses to all requests.)*

I have political biases. Ask me about gun control, abortion, immigration policies, homosexuality, mass transportation, or global warming, and I will happily give you my opinions—some more informed than others. But as a librarian, I have prided myself in not allowing my personal convictions about specific topics to dictate the range of materials I make available to users.

This seemed to be relatively easy when our libraries offered users a limited range of print resources. If I ordered the SIRS Research folders, Facts-On-File titles, and Opposing Viewpoints books along with both *The Nation* and *The National Review* magazines, I thought I had all sides of most controversial issues covered.

But the Internet and online services have given us access to an unimaginable spectrum of opinions, now readily available to students and staff in even the smallest of school libraries. Scholars, pundits, wackos, and seventh graders all can and do publish "information" online, undistinguishable by appearance or availability. The information presented by businesses, non-profits, "think tanks," and other sites maybe be factual, but heavily biased. I am rapidly coming to the conclusion that there is no "supported" belief that cannot be found on the Internet. (Want a recipe for spotted owl? It's easily found.)

While the availability of misinformation or biased opinions is often confusing or can lead researchers to make choices or form opinions that are embarrassing, there is a profound and very serious dimension to this issue as well. Increasingly students are using the Internet to meet personal needs and for school assignments that ask them to solve genuine problems. Making good consumer choices, health decisions, and career choices are a part of many districts' curricula. Gaining historical background and perspectives on social, scientific, and political issues through research is a common task expected by many teachers.

Ethically, we cannot rely on the "free" Internet alone to meet the information needs of our patrons. The availability of resources that have been edited and selected for their authority is more essential than ever. It is our ethical duty to provide print reference and trade materials at reading levels accessible to the age of the student, a range of periodicals related to the curriculum and personal interests, and subscriptions to online resources such as content-specific databases and full-text periodical databases. We also must teach students about and facilitate their access to materials that are available through interlibrary loan.

But even more importantly we need to teach our library users to be able to evaluate information for themselves. Were I the Grand Panjandrum of Libraries, I would instantly add Johnson's IXth Statement to the ALA's Code of Ethics: *We teach our library users to be critical users of information* (see chapter seven).

Establishing the "authority" of information sources dealing with controversial social issues can be challenging if the librarian wishes to honor the religious or political views of a student's family, especially when those views differ radically from one's own. Commentaries on environmental issues, for example, offered on National Public Radio and on Fox News may be seen by some parents, some teachers, and by oneself as having differing degrees of value and reliability. This is compounded by the degree to which people at both ends of the political spectrum are ever-more reliant on dogma or doctrine than on a thoughtful review of evidence to help them make decisions.

Yet as ethical educators, we need to ask students to support their conclusions and be able to defend the sources of the information with which they have chosen to do so. If parents are sufficiently uncomfortable with the spirit of open inquiry as a part of education, they should consider enrolling their children in a nonpublic school that reflects their specific set of beliefs.

For countries like the United States, founded on democratic freedoms and individual choices, the ability to analyze information should be the most important goal of our schools.

ALA Library Code of Ethics Statement VIII: *We strive for excellence in the profession by maintaining and enhancing our own knowledge and skills, by encouraging the professional development of co-workers, and by fostering the aspirations of potential members of the profession.*

While we do need to practice and help others practice the standards of ethical behaviors I–VII, statement VIII, for those of us in education, supersedes them all. Our primary ethical responsibility is promoting meaningful change in our institutions.

Technology is being used as a catalyst for change in education in the best and worst senses of the word. It has opened avenues toward previously undreamt of information and communication opportunities. It is spurring some teachers to be more creative, more constructivist-based, and more individualized in their instruction. But the chance of technology being used badly is also great as many critics suggest. Technology can depersonalize education, divert funds from more effective educational practices, and overemphasize low-level skill attainment as the ultimate educational goal.

As librarians, we understand perhaps better than many in education that teaching is a moral pursuit. It is changing the world in a positive way through changing lives of our students in a positive way. Technology we must recognize as simply a tool that will help us achieve those changes.

Too many of our schools lack effective leadership for the positive changes that technology can foster or accelerate. In such situations, a clear vision of what technology can and should be doing, well articulated by the librarian, can have a tremendous impact. We can and should help fill such a directional void. The librarian makes an especially effective change agent because:

- Our programs affect the whole school climate.
- We advocate information skills and personalized learning for every child.
- We advocate for technology being used to promote problem-solving and higher-level thinking.
- We have no subject area biases or territories to protect.
- We're extremely charming.

While often uncomfortable, the librarian must challenge the system to be an effective agent for change. We do so by working on school governing committees, leading staff development activities, and personally exemplifying good teaching practices and technology use. We are involved in curriculum revision and fight for the effective integration of technology and information literacy skills. We write for district newsletters and talk to parent and community organizations. We hold offices in unions and other professional organizations. We write to legislators and attend political functions and school board meetings. We form strong networks with like-minded reformers inside and outside our profession. And throughout these efforts, we keep firmly in mind that technology's purpose is to empower our students.

Our role as the "teacher of teachers" has never been greater, as was alluded to in Statement V. We need to lead formal staff development activities, work on long-term staff development plans, and serve as mentors and peer-coaches in our schools. The librarian is especially effective in working with teachers on the meaningful integration of technology into the curriculum through instructional units that include information literacy skills and stress higher-level thinking and by designing authentic assessments of performance-based units of instruction. We are the team players, the hand-holders, the encouragers, the cheerleaders, the resource-providers, and the shoulders on which to cry. We help improve our institutions by helping to improve the performance of the people who work within them.

As the tools of our profession change with technology and our mission grows to encompass teacher training and leadership, our ethical duty to upgrade our own professional skills takes on ever-increasing importance. My formal education ended with a master's degree in 1979 from an excellent ALA accredited program. This was before personal computers of any usefulness; before popular use of OPACs; before online databases; before the acceptance of the Internet by the bourgeoisie; before multimedia encyclopedias; before the printing press (well, not quite).

It follows that our ethical duty also includes membership and participation in professional associations devoted to ongoing professional development and attending the conferences and workshops they offer. We must continue to read professional journals and books. We must take advantage of listservs, blogs, Nings, and other forms of electronic communication that help us establish professional learning networks that enable virtual conversations about our practice (see chapter thirteen).

As Statement VIII concludes, we must foster "the aspirations of potential members of the profession." A person recently commented to me that one must be mad to go into school librarianship. He's right, of course, on a number of levels. You have to be mad (passionate) for stories, computers, and especially working with kids. You have to be mad (angry) about how poorly our schools underserve too many vulnerable children. And finally, you have to be mad (crazy) enough to believe that you as one individual have the power to change your institution, your political systems, and especially, the lives of your students and teachers. It is a rightful part of our ethical code that we must recruit and mentor other madmen and madwomen to our profession.

We should all be on, as the Blues Brothers describe it, "a mission from God" *every day* to make sure technology use in our schools is actually improving the lives of our students and staff. Heaven knows that nobody goes into the profession to make money. As educators, our satisfaction comes from actually believing we are doing something that will make the world a more humane place in which to live. The ultimate ethic of our practice is improving the lives of the children who attend our schools. The addition of technology to our schools does not change this; in fact, it may just make it more imperative.

It is a dangerous thing to set oneself up as an "expert" about ethics. Others hold one to very high standards and there always seem to be folks sniffing about for hypocritical behavior on the "expert's" part. One runs the chance of appearing holier-than-thou and having folks feel uncomfortable in one's presence. But probably the worst thing is that one quickly realizes there are few ethical absolutes, and one is regarded as an anal-retentive or as a godless situational relativist depending on the audience. But ethics is an interesting and important topic that needs to be brought out into the sunshine and aired on a regular basis if we are to do our jobs well.

In the end the best thing we can do is to be thoughtful and listen to own consciences. As human beings we constantly make moral judgments, decide issues of right and wrong, and attempt to determine what behaviors are humane and inhumane. We want the decisions we make to not only not have a damaging impact on ourselves, on those we serve, or on our society, but improve our world as well.

I am proud to be a member of a profession that takes its ethical responsibilities seriously.

Knowing right from wrong in the digital age

Two worlds

Even very young children can quickly identify whether the behaviors in these examples are right or wrong:

- *A boy finds a magazine with sexually explicit photographs and brings it to school. He shows its contents to others in his class, who become upset.*
- *A student sneaks a peek at her grades and the grades of other students on the teacher's computer while the teacher is out of the room.*
- *A student locates a story, recopies it in his own writing, and submits it to the teacher as his own work.*
- *A student steals a book from a local store. She says the only reason she stole it was that she did not have the money to purchase it.*
- *A student visits with friends about the upcoming dance instead of working on schoolwork in the library.*

When students start using technology, especially information technologies, they start operating in a new world: a virtual world. Suddenly behaviors may not be as easily judged to be right or wrong. What would your students' responses be when given these situations?

- *A girl downloads a sexually explicit picture from a site on the Internet on a computer in the school library. Her classmates can easily view the computer screen.*
- *A student finds the teacher's password to the school's information system and uses it to change his grades and view the grades of other students.*
- *A student uses the copy and paste command to place large parts of a Wikipedia article into an assigned paper. She turns the paper in as her own work.*

- *A student makes a copy of a software program borrowed from another student to use on his computer at home.*
- *A student scans Facebook comments about the upcoming dance instead of working on schoolwork in the library.*

What's different about "computer ethics"?

Computer ethics, better labeled "information technology ethics," deal with the proper use of a wide range of telecommunication and data storage devices. Ethics is the branch of philosophy that deals with moral judgments, issues of right and wrong, and determining what behaviors are humane and inhumane. Most Western codes of ethical behavior describe actions as "ethical" that do one or more of the following:

- promote the general health of society
- maintain or increase individual rights and freedoms
- protect individuals from harm
- treat all human beings as having an inherent value and accord those beings respect
- uphold religious, social, cultural, and government laws and mores

A simplistic way of saying this is an "ethical action" then, is one that does not have a damaging impact on oneself, other individuals, or society.

In direct or indirect ways, children begin to learn ethical values from birth. And while families and religious institutions are assigned the primary responsibility for a child's ethical education, schools have traditionally had the societal charge to teach and reinforce some moral values, especially those directly related to citizenship and school behaviors. Most of the ethical issues that surround technology deal with societal and school behaviors and are an appropriate and necessary part of the school curriculum.

Why do technology ethics then deserve special attention? There are a variety of reasons. Using technology to communicate and operate in a "virtual world," one that only exists within computers and computer networks, is a relatively new and constantly changing phenomenon that is not always well understood by many adults who received their primary education prior to its existence. Both fear and romance usually accompany new technologies. Our mass media capitalizes on the unfamiliarity many adults have with communications technologies, often producing fearful and inaccurate views of its capabilities. Movies, books, and television programs often make questionably ethical actions such as breaking into secure computer systems seem heroic or at least sympathetic.

Our new technological capabilities also may require new ethical considerations.

- The ability to send unsolicited commercial messages to millions of Internet e-mail users (spamming) was not possible before there was e-mail or the Internet. Does the fact that the financial burden of unsolicited advertisements now falls on the recipient rather than the sender create the need for new rules?
- Digital photography has made the manipulation of images undetectable, an impossible feat with chemical photography. What obligations do communicators have to present an undoctored photograph, even if its message may not be as powerful as one that has been digitally "enhanced?"
- Prior to the Internet, minors faced physical barriers against access to sexually explicit materials. What safeguards do schools, libraries, and parents need to take to keep children from freely accessing inappropriate materials? Which will better serve our children in the long run—software filtering devices or instruction and practice in making good judgments?

- Intellectual property in digital format can now be duplicated with incredible ease. Do we need clearer definitions of property? Can an item that is taken without authorization, but leaves the original in place, still be considered stolen?

One of the most significant reasons that computer ethics deserve special attention is because of our rather human ability to view one's actions in the intangible, virtual world of information technologies as being less serious than one's actions in the real world. Most of us, adults and children, would never contemplate walking into a store and shoplifting a computer program or music CD. Yet the illegal duplication and downloading of computer programs and media files costs businesses and content creators billions of dollars each year. Most of us would never pick a lock, but guessing passwords to gain access to unauthorized information is a common activity.

Information technology misuse by many people, especially the young, is viewed as a low-risk, gamelike challenge. Electronic fingerprints, footsteps, and other evidence of digital impropriety have historically been less detectable than physical evidence. There is a physical risk when breaking into a real office that does not exist when hacking into a computer database from one's living room. Illegally copying a book is costly and time consuming; illegally copying an e-book can be done in seconds at very small expense. The viewed pornography on a website seems to disappear as soon as the browser window is closed.

Not that long ago, ethical technology questions were only of interest to a very few specialists. But as the use of information technologies spreads throughout society and its importance to our national economies and individual careers grows, everyone will need to make good ethical decisions when using technology, especially the Internet. Studies show that persons involved in computer crimes acquire both their interest and skills at an early age.

Ethical codes

Many organizations and individuals have written lists of ethical standards for technology use. One of the mostly widely used and easily understood sets of computer use principles comes from the Computer Ethics Institute. There are "Netiquette" guidelines long in use, helping determine polite behaviors online. Schools now have an Acceptable Use Policy that governs the use of the Internet and other information technologies and networks in a school with specific prohibitions of technology use.

A variety of guides should be made available to staff and students and one should either be adopted or an original set of guidelines written. While an entire school or district may wish to use a single set of guidelines, each classroom teacher needs to understand, teach, and model the guidelines. Simple and easily remembered rules are probably the best for children.

Johnson's 3 Ps of Technology Ethics:

1. *Privacy—I will protect my privacy and respect the privacy of others.*
2. *Property—I will protect my property and respect the property of others.*
3. *a(P)propriate Use—I will use technology in constructive ways and in ways which do not break the rules of my family, faith, school, or government.*

Educators need to be aware and understand that another, counter set of "ethical" behavior also exists—that espoused by hackers. Being described as a "hacker" once indicated only a strong interest and ability in computer use. Popular use of the word has changed, so that now "hacking" describes gaining unauthorized access to computerized systems and data. The term "cracker" is also used, but is often used to describe a hacker who has a malicious intent. Some common hacker beliefs include:

- all information, especially digital information, should be free and available to all people
- breaking into computer systems points out flaws in security features to those who are responsible for maintaining them and is a harmless form of learning about technology
- hacking helps monitor the abuse of information by the government and business

Librarians need to know and understand these counterculture beliefs and be able to offer reasons why they need to be questioned for their logic and ethics.

Major areas of concern

The scope of information technology ethics is very broad. This chapter will examine only some common cases where children will need to make ethical choices or have the unethical actions of other impact them. I have categorized the issues under the major headings of privacy, property, and appropriate use. These cases and others like them should be used to foster classroom discussion.

Privacy—Does my use of the technology violate the privacy of others or am I giving information to others that I should not?

John fills out a survey form on a computer game webpage. In the following weeks, he receives several advertisements in the mail as well as dozens of e-mail messages about new computer games.

Children need to understand that businesses and organizations use information to market products. Information given to one organization may well be sold to others. An interesting discussion can revolve around how much a person would like a company to know about him or her. Will a company who knows a lot about me use it to customize products for me or only to manipulate me?

Adele "meets" Frank, who shares her interest in figure skating, on a social networking site. After several conversations in the following weeks, Frank asks Adele for her home telephone number and address.

All individuals need to know that a stranger is a stranger, whether on the street or on the Internet. The same rules we teach children about physical strangers apply to virtual strangers as well.

The principal suspects Paul of using his school e-mail account to send offensive messages to other students. He asks the network manager to give him copies of Paul's e-mail.

Schools (and businesses) have the right to search student and employee files that are created and stored on school-owned computer hardware. Ask students if they know the school's search policy on lockers and book bags, and whether the same policy is extended to digital formats.

Helen is using a wiki on the classroom computer to keep her journal, but Mike keeps looking over her shoulder as she types.

Just because information appears on a computer screen doesn't make it public. Students who are accustomed to the public viewing of television monitors need to realize that student-created work on computer screens should be treated as privately as work created in a paper journal.

Ms. Jones, Terry's teacher, needs to leave the room to take care of an emergency. While she is gone, Terry finds that Ms. Jones had been working on student progress reports and that her grading program is still open. He checks to see what grade he is getting and finds the grades for several other students.

Information inadvertently left accessible does not mean that it is appropriate to access it. Ask students: "Is forgetting to lock one's home the same as allowing anyone to enter it?" While information may be about students (such as grades), that information does not necessarily belong to them. And students certainly do not have the right to look at information about other students. One question that might be raised is: "What right do I as a student have to check the accuracy of the data gathered about me and what would be correct procedure for making that check?"

Property issues—Do my actions respect the property of others and am I taking the correct steps to keep my property safe?

Jerry borrows Ben's game CDs for Monster Truck Rally II and installs them on his home computer. He says he will erase the game if he does not like it, or will buy the game for himself if he likes it.

Students need to know that computer software is protected by copyright law. It is unlawful, as well as unethical, to make copies of computer programs without permission of or payment to the producer of those programs. It also needs to be understood that when purchasing software, one is usually only purchasing the right to use the software. The ownership of the code that comprises the program stays with the producer. This means that one cannot alter the program or resell it. The vast majority of software licenses require that one copy of a program be purchased for each computer on which it is to be run. And no, the inability to pay for software is not a justification for illegal copying any more than the inability to pay for a book is any justification for shoplifting it from a bookstore.

Cindy finds some good information about plant growth nutrients for her science fair project on Wikipedia. She uses the copy function of the computer to take an entire paragraph from the article and paste it directly into her report. She also forgets to write down the title of the article and the source from which it was taken. When she writes her report, she does not cite the source in her bibliography.

Plagiarism is easier than ever, thanks to the computer. Students need to understand when and how to cite sources in both print and electronic formats.

Albert finds a site on the Internet that is a repository of old term papers. He downloads one on ancient Greece, changes the title, and submits it as his own.

Academic work is increasingly becoming available for sale or downloading from the Internet. Online services now offer help in writing "personal" essays requested for college admissions offices. How are such services like or unlike ghostwritten biographies and speeches of celebrities and politicians?

Fahad is upset with his friend George. He finds the flash drive on which George has been storing his essays and erases it.

Does destroying a file constitute the destruction of property? After all, the magnetic medium of the hard drive or the flash drive is left intact. All that has changed is the polarization of some magnetic particles. Students need to learn to treat intellectual property, existing only in virtual spaces, the same way they would treat physical property and that the theft or destruction of such property is unethical (and unlawful).

With her teacher's permission, Lucy uses the classroom computer to download an application from the Internet that has instructions on how to make paper airplanes. After using the program, the classroom computer does not seem to work very well, crashing often and randomly destroying files. Lucy thinks she might have downloaded a virus along with the paper airplane program.

Students need to know about the unethical practices of others and how to protect themselves from those practices. Computer viruses, often infecting a computer through downloading programs or opening websites, can be detected and destroyed by virus protection programs. Students need to know how to find, install, and use these programs.

Henry's older friend Hank, a high school student, has discovered the password to the school's student information system. Because Hank feels a teacher has unfairly given him a poor grade, he plans to install a hidden program that will erase all the information on the office computer.

Citizens regardless of age have the ethical responsibility for reporting wrongdoing, including destruction of property. And while there are lots of reasons why students are reluctant to do so, as adults we need to express our beliefs that reporting unethical or criminal behavior serves a social purpose. Younger students often believe that school property is owned by the teachers and administrators, and are surprised to learn that it is their parents' taxes or fees that must be used to pay for vandalized or stolen school resources.

Appropriate use—Does this use of the technology have educational value and is it in keeping with the rules of my family, my faith, my school, and my government?

Jack's class has been using the digital camera to take pictures for the school yearbook. Jack has found that he can use a computer program to modify the photographs. He has used the program so far to make himself look like the tallest boy in the class, to blacken out the front tooth of a girl he doesn't like, and to give his teacher crossed eyes.

While this example may seem frivolous or even like "good fun," journalistic integrity is a serious issue which even young writers and photographers need to be aware of. Deliberate distortion of events whether through words or pictures may harm both those involved in the event as well as the reputation of the reporter.

Just for fun, thirteen-year-old Alice tells the other people on a Facebook page that she is twenty years old and a nursing student. "Friends" have begun emailing her health-related questions.

Disguise, impersonation, and other forms of trying on new personalities are common childhood and adolescent behaviors. The anonymity of the Internet limits such impersonation only to the degree that the level of a student's writing skills or sophistication of thought allows discovery. Role-playing in a physical context is often seen as both healthy and educational. We need to help students ask when such activities are productive and when they might be harmful.

Penelope has found a website that has "gross jokes" on it. She prints the pages out and shares them with her friends.

A good deal of Internet content, if not obscene, is certainly tasteless, offensive, and lacking in educational value. Schools should define and teachers should help students understand the qualities and conditions under which an item becomes inappropriate for school use. Students need to understand the concepts of pornography, racism, and sexism. Students may be exposed to information produced by hate groups and political extremists. Such experiences may be springboards to meaningful discussions about propaganda and free speech issues.

Chang posts a message on a classmate's Facebook site. In this message he uses profanities, racial slurs, and belittles the classmate.

Most schools have harassment policies. Students need to understand that such behavior is wrong regardless of its medium and to whom it is sent.

The computers in the library always seem to be busy. Otis tells the librarian he is working on a research project, but actually uses the computer to access the latest soccer scores.

Most schools allow students to use free time in school to complete personal tasks—to read a book or magazine for enjoyment, to write a letter to a friend, or to draw for pleasure. Technology, too, should be available for students to use to pursue individual interests—to play a game, to send personal e-mail, or to search for Internet information of personal value. The ethical issue here becomes that of an allocation of resources. For most schools, the demand for technology has outpaced its acquisition. Computers and Internet access are often in short supply, and priority needs to be given to students who have an academic task to complete.

Just for fun, Nellie sets the print command on her computer to print fifty copies of a magazine article she's been reading, and then walks away.

Deliberate waste of school materials is not uncommon, and students again need to understand that it is wrong to waste finite resources. As with the vandalism questions, students need to understand that everyone is affected by such activities.

What students need to understand

It is quite obvious that students need to understand and apply both school rules and local and national laws that apply to information technology use, especially those related to privacy, property, and appropriateness as described above. They need to know the consequences, both immediate and in the long term for society, if they choose to act against school rules or their country's laws.

Students also need to know that the ability of officials to catch individuals breaking these rules and codes of conduct is growing. Network security systems are becoming more sophisticated in tracking who uses what resource at what time. Students need to realize that most web browsers keep a viewable log of recently visited sites, that most e-mail includes a return address, and that some schools are using programs that record all the keystrokes a student makes during a computer session. All of us need to understand that organizations have the right to search file server space and read the e-mail of students (and staff), especially if there is probable cause. Electronic fingerprints, virtual footprints, and broken digital locks are growing more visible each day.

Students need to understand both their rights and responsibilities related to information technology use. In your school is Internet access a right or a privilege? As the Internet becomes a more indispensable source of information and learning activities, it may become viewed as an integral part of one's right to an education. We have an obligation to teach students that they have a right to due process if charged with a violation of rules or laws. Our AUPs need to articulate what that due process entails. Pragmatically, students need to know how to protect themselves and their data from strangers, hackers, computer viruses, and unauthorized use.

What activities teach ethical behaviors?

Schools should be taking a proactive approach to dealing with ethical issues surrounding technology use. Teachers and librarians must:

- *Articulate and teach values.* Clearly display lists and create handouts of conduct codes.
- *Reinforce ethical behaviors and react to nonethical behaviors.* Technology use behaviors should be treated no differently than other behaviors—good or bad—and the consequences of student behaviors should be the same. It is important not to overreact to incidences of technological misuse either.
- *Model ethical behaviors.* Students learn more from what we do than what we say. All rules of ethical conduct we expect from our students, we must display. Verbalization of how we personally make decisions is a very powerful teaching tool.
- *Create technology environments that help students avoid temptations.* Computer screens that are easily monitored (no pun intended), passwords not written down or left easily found, and the habit of logging out of secure network systems all help remove the opportunities for technology misuse in a classroom.
- *Encourage discussion of ethical issues.* "Cases," whether from news sources or from actual school events, can provide superb discussion starters and should be used when students are actually learning computer skills. Students need practice in creating meaningful analogies between the virtual world and the physical world. How is reading another person's e-mail without their permission like and unlike reading their physical mail?
- *Stress the consideration of principles rather than relying on a detailed set of rules.* Although sometimes more difficult to enforce in a consistent manner, a set of a few guidelines rather than a lengthy set of specific rules is more beneficial to students in the long run. By applying guidelines rather than following rules, students engage in higher-level thinking processes and learn behaviors that will continue into their next classroom, their homes, and their adult lives.

Additionally, students' understandings of ethic concepts need to be assessed. Technology use privileges should not be given to students until they have demonstrated that they know and can apply ethical standards and school policies. Testing of appropriate use needs to be done especially prior to students gaining online privileges such as e-mail accounts or Internet access. The school should keep evidence of testing on file in case there is a question of whether there has been instruction on appropriate use.

Schools also have an obligation to educate parents about ethical technology use. Through school newsletters and websites, talks at parent organization meetings, and school orientation programs, the school staff needs to inform and enlist the aid of parents in teaching and enforcing good technology practices.

Finally, ethical instruction needs to be ongoing. A single lesson, a single unit, or a single curriculum strand will not suffice. All teachers, librarians, and staff members must integrate ethical instruction into every activity that uses technology.

For reflection: Guidelines for educators using social and educational networking sites (developed with Jen Hegna, Information Systems Manager, Byron (MN) Public Schools)

Social networks are rapidly growing in popularity and use by all ages in society. The most popular social networks are web-based, commercial, and not purposely designed for educational use. They include sites like Facebook, LinkedIn, and Google+. For individuals, social networking sites provide tremendous opportunities for staying in touch with friends and family.

Educational networking sites are also growing in use. These sites are used by educators for both professional development and as a teaching tool, and are usually restricted to selected users and not available to the general public. These include networking tools such as Moodle, educational wikis, specially created Nings, or district adoptions of online applications such as Edmodo, Microsoft's Learn360, and Google Apps for Education.

As educators, we have a professional image to uphold, and how we conduct ourselves online impacts this image. As reported by the media, there have been instances of educators demonstrating professional misconduct while engaging in inappropriate dialogue about their schools and/or students or posting pictures and videos of themselves engaged in inappropriate activity online. Mistakenly, some educators feel that being online shields them from having their personal lives examined. But educators' online identities are very public and can cause serious repercussions if their behavior is careless.

One of the hallmarks of online networks, both social and educational, is the ability to "friend" others—creating a group of others that share interests and personal news. Most districts strongly discourage teachers from accepting invitations to *friend* students within personal social networking sites. When students gain access to a teacher's network of friends and acquaintances and are able to view personal photos and communications, the student–teacher dynamic is altered. By friending students, teachers provide more information than one should share in an educational setting. It is important to maintain a professional relationship with students to avoid relationships that could cause bias in the classroom.

But schools should recognize the value of student/teacher interaction on educational networking sites. Collaboration, resource sharing, and student/teacher and student/student dialog can all be facilitated by the judicious use of educational networking tools. Such interactivity is a critical component of any online class and can greatly enhance face-to-face classes. Yet since this is a new means of communication, some guidelines are in order for educational networking as well.

For the protection of your professional reputation, consider the following practices.

Guidelines for the use of social networking sites by professional staff

- Do not accept students as friends on personal social networking sites. Decline any student-initiated friend requests.
- Do not initiate friendships with students.

- Remember that people classified as "friends" have the ability to download and share your information with others.
- Post only what you want the world to see. Imagine your students, their parents, your administrator, visiting your site. It is not like posting something to your website or blog and then realizing that a story or photo should be taken down. On a social networking site, basically once you post something it may be available, even after it is removed from the site.
- Do not discuss students or coworkers or publicly criticize school policies or personnel.
- Visit your profile's security and privacy settings. At a minimum, educators should have all privacy settings set to "only friends." "Friends of friends" and "Networks and Friends" open your content to a large group of unknown people. Your privacy and that of your family may be at risk.

Guidelines for the use of educational networking sites by professional staff

- Let your administrator, fellow teachers, and parents know about your educational network.
- When available, use school-supported networking tools.
- Do not say or do anything that you would not say or do as a teacher or librarian in the classroom. (Remember that all online communications are stored and can be monitored.)
- Have a clear statement of purpose and outcomes for the use of the networking tool.
- Establish a code of conduct for all network participants.
- Do not post images that include students without parental release forms on file.
- Pay close attention to the site's security settings and allow only approved participants access to the site.

Guidelines for *all* networking sites by professional staff

- Do not use commentary deemed to be defamatory, obscene, proprietary, or libelous. Exercise caution with regards to exaggeration, colorful language, guesswork, obscenity, copyrighted materials, legal conclusions, and derogatory remarks or characterizations.
- Weigh whether a particular posting puts your effectiveness as an educator at risk.
- Due to security risks, be cautious when installing the external applications that work with the social networking site. Examples of these sites are calendar programs and games.
- Run updated malware protection to avoid infections of spyware and adware that social networking sites might place on your computer.
- Be careful not to fall for phishing scams that arrive via e-mail or on your wall, providing a link for you to click, leading to a fake login page.
- If a staff member learns of information on the social networking site that falls under the mandatory reporting guidelines, they must report it as required by law.
- Please stay informed and cautious in the use of all new networking technologies.

References

American Library Association. "Access to Resources and Services in the School Library Media Program: An Interpretation of the Library Bill of Rights." 2008. http://www.ala.org/tools/guidelines/standardsguidelines (accessed Jan. 21, 2013).

American Library Association. "Code of Ethics." 2008. http://www.ala.org/advocacy/proethics/codeofethics/code ethics (accessed Jan. 21, 2013).

eSchool News Staff. Kentucky school finds seniors lifted text from the internet. eSchool News, July 1, 2002. http://www.eschoolnews.com/2002/07/01/kentucky-school-finds-seniors-lifted-text-from-the-internet/ (accessed Feb. 11, 2013).

Chapter Twelve

Copyright and Creative Commons

Expertise in copyright has long been an expected contribution of the librarian to the school. We teach students to cite sources, how to avoid plagiarism, and how to assign permissions to original work.

But as intellectual property has become almost entirely digital, our challenges and opportunities in this area have dramatically changed. This is a rapidly changing area of our practice as an increasingly large number of educators are asking serious questions of what seems like the overly restrictive protection of intellectual property. Be warned: I am not a copyright lawyer, and the ideas and opinions in the chapter may be controversial. The purpose of this chapter is to stir conversations and encourage librarians to stay abreast of all copyright discussions.

Make a copyright u-turn and other audacious statements about copyright

Few subjects engender more disagreement and confusion than intellectual property, copyright, and digital rights management. These are areas where I feel less and less certainty that as a professional I have a firm understanding and philosophy.

I am not alone. American University's Center for Social Media uses the term "hyper-comply." It means that some educators over-comply with copyright law, even giving up using legitimate teaching tools and techniques for fear of violating copyright laws. Along with hyper-compliance, the study found that "studied ignorance" and "clandestine transgression" lead to schools where teachers use less effective teaching techniques, teach and transmit erroneous copyright information, fail to share innovative instructional approaches, and do not take advantage of new digital platforms (Aufderheide, Hobbs, and Jaszi 2007).

How educators teach copyright and other intellectual property issues is overdue for an overhaul in our schools. The librarian's role as copyright cop needs serious attention. The mind-set that "if we don't know for sure that it is perfectly legal, don't do it" no longer meets the needs of either students or their teachers. Below are four changes our profession must seriously consider.

1. Change the focus of copyright instruction from what is forbidden to what is permitted.

As information professionals, we have as great an obligation to see that staff and students get as full access and use of copyrighted materials as possible as we do in helping make sure they respect copyright laws.

Our instructional efforts need to include teaching users that the use of copyrighted material in research, if properly cited, and if it supplements rather than supplants the researcher's product is perfectly legal. The question we should be asking is not "What percent of another's work did you use?" but "What percent of your product is of your own making?"

We also need to teach the concepts and tests of Fair Use. Both staff and students should be able to name and explain the factors surrounding Fair Use, "*for purposes such as criticism, comment, news reporting, teaching (including multiple copies for classroom use), scholarship, or research* [emphasis added] . . ." (Copyright Act of 1976, 17 U.S.C. § 107).

Fair Use states that these factors be "considered":

- the purpose and character of the use, including whether such use is of a commercial nature or is for nonprofit educational purposes;
- the nature of the copyrighted work;
- the amount and substantiality of the portion used in relation to the copyrighted work as a whole; and
- the effect of the use upon the potential market for or value of the copyrighted work.

Note the factors are to be "considered," not that each needs to be met. These are very flexible guidelines.

We need to be teaching that a copyrighted work's use is considered Fair Use if it is of a "transformative" nature. In "Recut, Reframe, Recycle," the authors define these uses of copyrighted works in online videos as "transformative" and meeting Fair Use guidelines:

- *Parody and satire*
- *Negative or critical commentary*
- *Positive commentary*
- *Quoting to trigger discussion*
- *Illustration or example*
- *Incidental use*
- *Personal reportage or diaries*
- *Archiving of vulnerable or revealing materials*
- *Pastiche or collage* (Aufderheide and Jaszi, nd)

All teachers and librarians need to understand every special right given to them as educators. Teachers can show personal copies of copyrighted videos to a class; off-air broadcasts can be re-shown to classes; and photocopies of copyrighted news and magazine articles can be given to students. (Some restrictions apply, but these are all legal uses.) The *Fair Use Guidelines for Educational Multimedia* (Consortium of College and University Media Centers, 1996) clearly state that educators may create educational multimedia projects containing original and copyrighted materials and may use those projects for face-to-face student instruction, directed student self-study, real-time remote instruction, review, or directed self-study for students enrolled in curriculum-based courses, and presentation at peer workshops and conferences. Educators also need to know that students can use copyrighted materials for educational projects in the course for which they were created and in portfolios as examples of their academic work for job and graduate school interviews.

Educators need to know the outer limits, not just the safe harbors, of the use of copyrighted materials—and allow their students to explore those outer limits as well.

2. When there is doubt, err on the side of the user.

A Singapore educator once shared with me that his countrymen tend to suffer from NUTS—the No U-Turn Syndrome—while Americans do not. When no signs are posted at an intersection, Singapore drivers assume U-turns are illegal; U.S. drivers assume they are legal. He felt the "assume it is OK" attitude gives our country a competitive edge. It really *is* better to ask forgiveness than permission.

An educator's automatic assumption should be that, unless it is specifically forbidden and legally established in case law, the use of copyrighted materials should be allowed.

A high-profile example of moving to a forgiveness-based approach came from Google's *Scan the Book* project. In its effort to transform all the world's books into a digital, searchable format, Google found that 15 percent of the world's cataloged books are in the public domain and 10 percent are actively in print, but 75 percent of the world's books are "in the dark" —neither being made available by publishers nor in the public domain. Since few publishers have shown willingness to investigate the actual ownership on these materials, the Google Scan the Book project decided to scan *first* and then remove the digital copies if requested (Kelly 2006).

Yes, current copyright law says that everything written in the Unites States is automatically copyrighted. Unfortunately, the will of the owner of the work is always assumed to be that she/he has exclusive rights. With the advent of Creative Commons (see below), an alternative means of describing a creator's level of control over a work, "exclusive rights" can or should no longer simply be assumed.

When copyright or use warnings are implicitly stated, teachers often disregard uses that fall under Fair Use provision. Most books contain the following standard warning:

All rights reserved. No part of this book may be reproduced, transmitted, or stored in an information retrieval system in any form or by any means, graphic, electronic, or mechanical, including photocopying, taping, and recording, without prior written permission from the publisher.

Yet as a researcher and teacher, one has the right to do all the expressly forbidden things listed in the warning provided Fair Use guidelines are followed.

Content creators or providers can impose any sort of restriction they wish without it ever needing to be vetted by a court of law. YouTube's Terms of Service read in part "You agree not to access Content through any technology or means other than the video playback pages of the Service itself, the Embeddable Player, or other explicitly authorized means YouTube may designate." To my knowledge, there is no U.S. court case to determine whether YouTube has the right to make and enforce such a condition. If I place a "Terms of Use" on this book that the reader must be drinking gin and wearing a pink bathrobe to read it legally, could I take my readers to court?

Until something is proven illegal, assume it is legal.

Schools and other institutions may place restrictions on the use of copyrighted information that go beyond legal requirements. One district's board policy on copyright states: "*All of the four conditions [of the Fair Use Doctrine] must be totally met to qualify a work for use or duplication under this clause* [emphasis added]." The law itself only reads that these are "*factors to consider* [emphasis added]."

Finally, consider that there is an inherent bias toward copyright owners when copyright "experts" offer advice about particular situations. A lawyer, a book author, or columnist who answers questions on copyright issues may be held liable for the advice they give and usually err on the side of the party most likely to be litigious. As one of my college-era T-shirts read, "Question authority!"

Some places to look for "expertise" that have a more user-centric bias include:

- Center for Social Media at American University
- Chilling Effects Clearing House
- Creative Commons
- Media Education Foundation
- Public Knowledge public interest group
- Stanford Law School Center for Internet and Society "Fair Use Project"

Place the onus of proof of wrongdoing on the provider, not the proof of Fair Use on the user. Assume the U-turn is legal.

3. Be prepared to answer questions when the law seems to make little sense, when a law is inconsequential, when a law is widely ignored, or when breaking the law may serve a higher moral purpose.

A few years ago, I found that my son had downloaded an illegal copy of one of the *Lord of the Rings* movies. I asked if he felt bad about depriving director Peter Jackson, one of his heroes, of his payment for making the film. His reply was, "Dad, I paid to see the movie twice and I bought the DVD when it came out in a regular version *and* will buy it again when it comes out in a director's cut version. I think I am paying Peter Jackson for his creative works. What harm does this digital version cause if only I use it to study his editing?"

Simple control over a person's intellectual property, even if there are no financial considerations, is a concept many find difficult to both explain and defend. And this is just a single example of laws that seem to be dated, overly restrictive, or just nonsensical.

As a result, there are intellectual property laws that are so routinely ignored that they have become meaningless—and enforcing them makes the librarian appear to be a martinet. These violations include showing movies in class for entertainment or reward without a public performance license, playing a commercial radio station that plays popular music in a public venue, using copyrighted or trademarked items on school bulletin boards or in locally produced study materials, converting 16mm films or videotapes that are not available for purchase into DVD or digital files, and making copies of materials for archival purposes.

Making copies of copyrighted materials of online resources that can be read online without cost for classes; downloading digital videos, such as those from YouTube, onto a local hard drive; and converting analog materials (text, pictures, video, audio) to digital formats to be used with interactive whiteboard or slide show software for whole group instruction are all regularly done by teachers. These uses have minimal impact on a copyright holder's profits. Overly strict enforcements of the letter of copyright laws will lead to creating scofflaws of not just students, but teachers, and make *all* copyright restrictions suspect.

We also must acknowledge that there is a growing movement that believes current intellectual property law, especially copyright, works against the greater good of society. "Free culturists" argue that everyone in a society benefits when creative work is placed in the common domain and everyone is allowed to use and build upon it, and that current copyright laws give the owner too much control and for too long a time. Building on the free and open source software movements, this group of thinkers at its most extreme insists that "intellectual property" is a meaningless term.

However, Lawrence Lessig, often seen as the movement's founding father, writes that a free culture is filled with "property" and rules and rights that govern it. The problem arises when property rights become extreme (Lessig 2004).

Contemporary experts maintain that applying Fair Use reasoning is about reaching a level of comfort, not memorizing a specific set of rules. This statement applies to all issues involving copyright and intellectual property.

4. Teach copyright from the point of view of the producer, as well as the consumer.

The librarian's role is to help teachers and students establish an informed, personal "level of comfort" in using other's intellectual property.

Few of us are comfortable at either extreme of copyright enforcement—playing the copyright bully *or* advocating total disregard of the rules governing intellectual property. Complicating the issue is that each of us is likely to arrive at his or her own personal level of Fair Use comfort, judgment of seriousness of possible use, and perspective of the morality of intellectual property use both personally and professionally.

And that's OK. Education is about teaching others to think rather than to believe. We need to help individual students arrive at personal comfort levels when using protected creative works.

Librarians can assume some practical stances toward copyright instruction and enforcement. They must insist that the enforcement of all laws and policies falls on administrators, not teachers or librarians, and rebrand themselves as "copyright counselors." And do what good counselors have always done—help others reach good decisions about their actions. Librarians should bring to the attention of administration the possibly illegal actions of fellow teachers only under a very narrow set of circumstances. Librarians need not commit any acts they personally deem illegal or unethical. In in-services and communications, the librarian should emphasize what *can*, not what *can't* be done with intellectual property.

The librarian should modify any commercial signs about Fair Use with a caveat. The popular charts like those produced by Hall Davidson, indicating very specific percentages of a work that can be used, should be amended thus:

This chart states only "safe harbor" guidelines and is not an authoritative legal statement. More flexible uses and amounts may apply for certain purposes.

We can certainly get a student to bubble in the "right" answer on a test about copyright, we can refuse to accept student work that may include copyrighted materials, and can say, "think hard about your actions, young woman." But I doubt any of those actions will stop the illegal downloading of materials once the child is out of sight.

Studies do suggest that teens are not amoral, but uninformed. One study conducted for Microsoft concludes that the more teenagers know about laws governing illegal downloading, the more the teens think it should be a punishable offense (Microsoft 2008).

We must allow the fair use of copyrighted material in student work, but expect students to be able to articulate *why* they believe it constitutes fair use. Only when students begin to think about copyright and other intellectual property guidelines from the point of view of the producer as well as the consumer can they form mature attitudes and act in responsible ways when questions about these issues arise. And as an increasing number of students become content creators sharing their work through YouTube, Flickr, social networking sites, and countless other Web 2.0 tools, this should be an easier concept to help them grasp.

Among the most serious misperceptions about copyright holders is that only big, faceless companies are impacted by theft. A popular view is that it is acceptable to steal from big companies but not from the small fry. Too often adults as well as students forget that many large companies are made up of small stockholders and employees also trying to make a buck. Publishing companies represent the interests of individual artists, writers, and musicians—whose ranks students themselves may one day join.

Students should be required to assign a Creative Commons designation to each piece of original work they produce—especially those items they will be publishing online or in print. By thinking about how one wants his or her own work treated, one is forced to consider the rights and wishes of other creators as well. Counseling teachers to use a Creative Commons designation on their work is a good thing as well.

Increasingly I am looking at the moral issues involved in intellectual property issues. Many states once had segregation laws that required African Americans to sit at the back of the bus. A brave woman named Rosa Parks defied the law and made history. Are our current copyright laws requiring our students and teachers to sit at the back of the intellectual property bus? How do we respond if a student's or teacher's actions seem legally suspect but morally correct? Do librarians and educators have the courage to be the Rosa Parks of the information age?

Creative Commons and why it should be more commonly understood

You've heard yourself countless times tell students, "Assume everything on the Internet is copyrighted!" Sorry. That's not exactly good advice anymore. Authors, videographers, musicians, photographers, well, almost anyone who creates materials and makes them publically available, has an alternative to standard copyright licensing: Creative Commons. As librarians, we need to understand this relatively recent invention and its implication for our staff and students.

Why Creative Commons?

The Creative Commons website explains its mission as providing:

> . . . a set of copyright licenses and tools that create a balance inside the traditional "all rights reserved" setting that copyright law creates.

In other words, Creative Commons (CC) is a tool that helps the creator display a licensing mark. The creator can assign a variety of rights for others to use his work—rights that are usually more permissive than copyright, but more restrictive than placing material in the public domain. CC makes sharing, reusing, remixing, and building on the creative works of others understandable and legal. While it has always been possible for a creator to grant rights for others to use his or her materials less restrictively than standard copyright's "All Rights Reserved," CC standardizes the process.

Inspired by the Free Software Foundation's GNU General Public License, the nonprofit Creative Commons organization was founded in 2001 by Stanford Law professor Lawrence Lessig. As a part of the "copyleft" movement, Lessig and others believe traditional copyright restrictions inhibit cultural and economic growth. A growing number of content producers want to allow others to use and remix their materials—and in turn be able to use and remix the content of others. CC licenses make this legal.

While Creative Commons was started in the United States, over seventy other countries and jurisdictions (as of this writing) have ported CC licenses to work with their copyright laws. More countries continue to be added. The "Affiliate Network" link on the CC homepage lists the cooperating jurisdictions.

Understanding Creative Commons licenses

While initially it looks complex, a basic understanding of the types of licenses and how they can be combined is relatively simple. There are only four "conditions" of a CC license. These four conditions can be combined to form six different licenses that specifically describe the conditions creators wish to apply to their works. These are, from least to most restrictive, as described on the CC website:

Attribution
This license lets others distribute, remix, tweak, and build upon your work, even commercially, as long as they credit you for the original creation. This is the most accommodating of licenses offered. Recommended for maximum dissemination and use of licensed materials.

Attribution-ShareAlike
This license lets others remix, tweak, and build upon your work even for commercial purposes, as long as they credit you and license their new creations under the identical terms. This license is often compared to "copyleft" free and open source software licenses. All new works based on

yours will carry the same license, so any derivatives will also allow commercial use. This is the license used by Wikipedia, and is recommended for materials that would benefit from incorporating content from Wikipedia and similarly licensed projects.

Attribution-NoDerivs
This license allows for redistribution, commercial and non-commercial, as long as it is passed along unchanged and in whole, with credit to you.

Attribution-NonCommercial
This license lets others remix, tweak, and build upon your work non-commercially, and although their new works must also acknowledge you and be non-commercial, they don't have to license their derivative works on the same terms.

Attribution-NonCommercial-ShareAlike
This license lets others remix, tweak, and build upon your work non-commercially, as long as they credit you and license their new creations under the identical terms.

Attribution-NonCommercial-NoDerivs
This license is the most restrictive of our six main licenses, only allowing others to download your works and share them with others as long as they credit you, but they can't change them in any way or use them commercially.

Two terms that may not be completely familiar are "remix" and "share-alike." Remix, which began as a recombination of audio tracks to create a new song, has become more generic and now implies using parts of many works (photographs, sounds, videos, and text) to create a new product. "Share-alike" means that others may use one's work on the condition that any work derived from the original carries the same licensing permissions as the original. In other words, if you borrow you must also commit to share.

How to use CC for one's own work

Determining which license one wishes to use has been made simple by Creative Commons. By answering just two questions on a form on the website—Allow commercial uses of your work? Allow modifications of your work?—the appropriate license will be generated for one's work, either as embeddable HTML code for a webpage or as text that looks like this:

This work is licensed under the Creative Commons Attribution-Noncommercial-Share Alike 3.0 United States License. To view a copy of this license, visit http://creativecommons.org/licenses/by-nc-sa/3.0/us/ or send a letter to Creative Commons, 171 Second Street, Suite 300, San Francisco, California, 94105, USA.

That's it.

Implications for K–12 education

Consider these scenarios:

- A student needs photographs and music for a history project but can't find what he needs in the public domain or in royalty-free collections.

- A teacher has developed outstanding materials that teach irregular Spanish verbs. She has posted them on a website and now regularly gets e-mails requesting permission to use the materials.
- The librarian is frustrated trying to help his junior high students understand the rights that intellectual property creators have over their own materials. The kids just aren't able to see the issue from the creator's point of view.

In each of the scenarios above, Creative Commons licensing may offer a solution. There are three primary uses:

1. Students and teachers need to be able to find and interpret CC licensed materials for use into their own works. Common advice given to both students working on projects and to teachers creating education materials is to abide by the fair use guidelines of copyrighted materials, search for materials in the public domain, and to use royalty-free work in order to remain both legal and ethical information users. But now understanding and finding CC licensed work is another source of legal materials that students and teachers can use in their own creations.

   There are three main ways to find Creative Commons licensed materials. CC has a specialized search tool. There is a list of directories by format. Google Advanced Search also allows searching by "usage rights." All can be effective.

2. Teachers should assign a Creative Commons license to materials that they are willing to share with other educators. As K–12 teachers produce and make available course materials on the web, they will need to understand how to give rights to others to use their work. (Check with your local school district to see who owns the copyright to materials that are teacher produced.) MIT's OpenCourseWare and Rice University's Connexions, two formal post-secondary learning materials repositories, are good models of using Creative Commons licensing.

3. Students should be required to place a Creative Commons license on their own work to increase their understanding of intellectual property issues. Only when students begin to think about copyright and other intellectual property guidelines from the point of view of the producer as well as the consumer can they form mature attitudes and act in responsible ways when questions about these issues arise. As an increasing number of students become "content creators" themselves, this should be an easier concept to help them grasp.

   Students need to know what their rights as creators and IP owners are. This may help combat the misperception that only big, faceless companies are impacted by intellectual property theft, and that it is acceptable to steal from big companies but not from the small fry. Too often students and adults forget that many large companies are made up of small stockholders and employees.

   Developing empathy toward content creators, who hope to profit by their work, helps everyone place copyright into context and perspective.

In recent years, the legal aspects of intellectual property sharing have been outpaced by the mechanical means of copying, distribution, and access. Understanding and using Creative Commons both as content consumers and content producers will help narrow the technology/acceptable use gap.

For reflection: Why students (and adults) satisfice

Satisficing (a portmanteau of "satisfy" and "suffice") is a decision-making strategy which attempts to meet criteria for adequacy, rather than to identify an optimal solution.

—Wikipedia

A common complaint about student researchers is that they "satisfice." They stop after finding the first possible answer to a question. I am guessing there is more to it than just laziness.

Consider this graph:

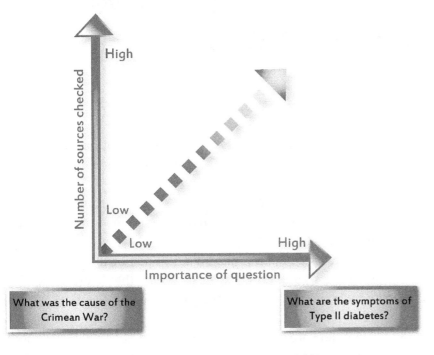

IMAGE 12-1   A cure for satisficing

Is there a direct correlation between importance of the question to the researcher and the depth of research he/she is willing to do?

Maybe, just maybe, if we made better research assignments, we'd get better researchers.

References

Aufderheide, Pat, and Peter Jaszi. "Recut, Reframe, Recycle: Quoting Copyrighted Material in User-Generated Video." *Center for Social Media*, nd. http://www.centerforsocialmedia.org/sites/default/files/CSM_Recut_Reframe_Recycle_report.pdf (accessed Jan. 21, 2013).

Aufderheide, Pat, Renee Hobbs, and Peter Jaszi. "The Cost of Copyright Confusion for Media Literacy." *Center for Social Media*, 2007. http://www.centerforsocialmedia.org/sites/default/files/Final_CSM_copyright_report_0.pdf (accessed Jan. 21, 2013).

Consortium of College and University Media Centers. *Fair Use Guidelines for Multimedia*. 1996. http://www.adec.edu/admin/papers/fair10-17.html (accessed Jan. 21, 2013).

Creative Commons website [creativecommons.org].

Kelly, Kevin. "Scan This Book." *New York Times*, May 14, 2006.

Lessig, Lawrence. *Free Culture*. New York: Penguin, 2004.

Microsoft. *Topline Results of Microsoft Survey of Teen Attitudes on Illegal Downloading*. Feb. 12, 2008. http://www.microsoft.com/en-us/news/press/2008/feb08/02-13MSIPSurveyResultsPR.aspx (accessed Feb. 11, 2013).

Chapter Thirteen

The Librarian's Role in Effective Staff Development

I was disappointed when AASL's *Information Power* standards dropped the term "instructional consultant" in favor of "instructional partner." My profession's charge to me of consultancy was my license to do staff training.

Oh, I understand why it was done. "Partner" is a far more modest sort of role than "consultant," and in our humble profession of librarianship we certainly wouldn't want to be seen as people who lord over others our superior intelligence, understandings, and skill sets.

And that is rather too bad. If ever the rank and file of education has been in need of the services of a good in-house "consultant" it's now. Education is changing at a rapid rate. No, I take that back. Education is being asked to change at a rapid rate. And using technology well is proving to be one of the most visible, costly, and frustrating changes.

Some schools are using technology well, while others are not. And the difference lies less in a school's finances than it does in its leadership and staff development efforts. In the ever-evolving role of the school librarian, "teaching the teachers" can play a huge part in increasing our value—to both our fellow teachers and our administrators. But serving as a primary player in staff development means more than just offering the occasional after school "Techie Tuesday" or "'Appy Hour" about new resources. We need to understand the big picture of improving teacher effectiveness with technology and problem-based teaching and carve an official role in it.

The why, what, and who of staff development in technology and the librarian's role

Judy has just come back to teaching after a ten-year stint as a stay-at-home mom. During new teacher orientation, she learns that she is now expected to keep her grades using a computerized grade book, take attendance online, read the staff bulletin as e-mail, use the district's "mapping" software when writing curriculum, organize all student materials using Moodle, and keep her classroom webpage current. There is also this strange-looking device called an interactive white-board in front of the room. "How, after only ten years," she wonders, "can I feel so out of touch? And how do I learn to do all these things?"

Tom's just about had it with the "personal narrative" unit in his writing class—he can't get the kids interested. But he's been reading that when students write for a wider audience than just the teacher, their level of concern and writing quality goes up. He thinks he'd like to try a class blog so students can post their narratives and get reactions from other students. Ah, but where to start learning how to create and use a blog?

Juanita is a part of the site team that is responsible for the building improvement plan. One of the big tasks this year has been looking at student test scores and disaggregating the data for specific groups of students like English-language learners. While the district uses a giant online data mining/data analysis program, its complexity baffles not just Juanita, but the rest of the site team as well—including the principal.

Few educators will dismiss the importance and need for teachers to have training that will help them successfully use technology for both professional productivity and to improve student learning. Yet as the examples above show, the scope of the needs of different teachers for training can be very broad, and teachers need ongoing support and training throughout their careers.

If a school is to develop a comprehensive plan to make sure all of its teachers can continue to improve their teaching abilities through the thoughtful use of technology, it needs to answer four basic questions:

1. Why is it important that the teachers in our district use technology?
2. What are the specific skills we believe our teachers should have and the minimum expectations of use?
3. Who should provide the training?
4. How can we provide effective staff development opportunities for our teachers? Who should provide the training?

This chapter will address the first three questions and suggest that the role of the librarian be expanded to the degree it largely answers the fourth question.

Why is it important that the teachers in our district use technology? The United States has done a poor job of teaching teachers to be productive users of technology. Walk through any school and you will certainly find "pockets of wow" where both teachers and students are using technology in exciting ways to meet curricular goals. But more often than not, there is a huge disparity among staff members in both attitude and skills related to technology, with many teachers only using it to complete required administrative tasks.

Yet both research and the observed experiences of schools with technology-savvy teachers shows effective technology use can:

- Improve teachers' professional productivity by automating routine administrative tasks and improve communications.
- Reach, challenge, remediate, and motivate exceptional students through the use of educational software targeted to specific learning objectives.
- Help teachers master skills taught to students to complete project-based units that rely on technology for research and presentation.
- Facilitate active, student-centered, constructivist learning.

Studies have long reported positive changes of a transformational nature in the classrooms of teachers who have entered the "appropriation" or "invention" stages of computer use (Dwyer 1991). The findings tell us among other things that these teachers expect more from students, spend more time with individual students, are more comfortable using groups, spend less time lecturing, are more willing to take risks, and collaborate with others in ways that improve learning opportunities.

Schools are looking for ways to improve the total educational environment so that more students perform at higher levels and see that the long-term benefit of teacher technology use will facilitate constructivist classrooms that use project-based learning experiences requiring problem-solving and higher level thinking skills.

What are the specific skills we believe teachers should have? While most administrators and parents when asked would say they'd like all teachers to be technologically literate, my sense is that few of these folks can define what being "technologically literate" actually means.

The National Educational Technology Standards for Teachers (NETS-T) is a respected, ongoing effort of the International Society for Technology in Education (ISTE) to help provide the definition of what a teacher needs to know and be able to do with technology. ISTE breaks the competencies into five broad categories:

1. Facilitate and Inspire Student Learning and Creativity
2. Design and Develop Digital Age Learning Experiences and Assessments
3. Model Digital Age Work and Learning
4. Promote and Model Digital Citizenship and Responsibility
5. Engage in Professional Growth and Leadership (ISTE 2008)

Individual districts often developed their own sets of competencies based on the ISTE standards. These tools help measure how well teachers have mastered basic computer use including using productivity programs such as word processors, spreadsheets, graphics programs, and a multiplicity of online tools to improve their professional work.

Even teachers who know all the fundamentals of computer use need help and guidance if they are to use the technology to fundamentally change the way they deliver instruction to assist all students and improve the degree to which problem-solving and high-level thinking is asked of students. "Information literacy" skills that rely on the effective use of technology are rapidly gaining prominence as the most important, whole-life skill that schools can teach. To help teachers create professional development plans that help them learn to use technology in new ways, these skill sets should be embedded in long-term goals reached through the successful completion of a variety of collaboratively planned and authentically assessed activities over the course of a school year.

Who should provide the training? Schools have relied on a variety of different individuals to provide staff training in whole or in part. As the chart below suggests, all types of trainers have their strengths and weaknesses:

Table 13-1
Strengths and weaknesses of technology trainers

Type of trainer	Strengths	Weaknesses
Professional trainers	Have expertise in specific product or skill, may have knowledge of successful use by others that will help in implementation, and have good interpersonal and communication skills.	Are expensive and may have expertise in technology but not in educational uses. They are not available for ongoing assistance to learners.
Technicians/Technology experts	Have expertise in hardware and software applications and are sometimes available for ongoing support.	May have expertise in technology but not in educational uses and may lack teaching or interpersonal skills needed.

District-level trainers such as computer coordinators or technology integration specialists	Have expertise in both technology and education, know district and personnel, and are available for some ongoing assistance to learners.	Are usually few in number, don't have time to work with individual staff members, and are often located in different sites than learners.
Classroom teachers	May have expertise in both technology and education, are located in same building for ongoing support, and enjoy high credibility with other teachers.	Are usually busy teaching. They may be unwilling to experiment with new educational methods.
Video/online instruction/ manuals/trial and error	Can be used at any time and in any place, allow learners to be self-paced, and are inexpensive.	Require a high level of commitment from learner and may be frustrating for beginners. Usually addresses the basic "how-to" level of technology use with more sophisticated practices and skills not taught.
Librarians	See following section.	May not see this as a part of their role and may not have had adequate training themselves.

Many districts have had wonderful success in giving librarians responsibility for staff development in technology. Here's why:

1. **Librarians have a healthy attitude toward technology.** I am afraid my latent sexism will show here, but the majority of our librarians are female, and females often exhibit a healthier attitude toward technology than do we males. On seeing a new box that plugs in, rather than asking "How fast is the processor?" or "How big is the hard drive?", a librarian tends to ask, "What is it good for?" Good librarians are neither technophiles nor technophobes. The librarian considers and teaches not just how to use technology, but why and under what circumstances it should be used. An old adage says that when your only tool is a hammer, every problem becomes a nail. For many technologists, technology can become the solution to problems that actually require traditional or human solutions. (Ever see someone spend forty-five minutes using a computer to address an envelope?)

2. **Librarians have good teaching skills.** Unlike technicians, they are more likely to use good pedagogical techniques and have more developed human relations and communication skills. We are understanding and empathetic when technologically related stress occurs in the classroom.

3. **Librarians have an understanding of the use of technology in the information literacy process and its use in fostering higher-level thinking skills.** We view technology as just one more, extremely powerful tool that can be used by students completing well-designed information literacy projects. "Technologists," it seems, are just now understanding this powerful use.

4. **Librarians have experience as skill integrators and collaborators.** Integration of research and information literacy projects has been a long-term goal of school library programs, and as a result many librarians have become excellent collaborators with classroom teachers, successfully strengthening the curriculum with information literacy projects. We know kids, know technology, and know what works.

5. **Librarians are models for the successful use of technology.** The library's automated library catalogs, circulation systems, electronic reference materials, and student-accessible workstations all showed up well before classroom technologies. Teachers rightfully see the librarian as the educator with the most comfort with technology as well, which in turn bolsters their own self-confidence.

6. **Librarians provide in-building support.** A flexibly scheduled librarian is a real asset to teachers learning to use or integrate technology. The librarian can work with the teacher in the library, computer lab, or classroom. The librarian is available for questions that might otherwise derail a teacher's application of technology. This is a primary advantage of the librarian as opposed to a classroom teacher having primary responsibility for staff development in technology.

7. **Librarians have a whole school view.** Next to the principal, the librarian has the most inclusive view of the school and its resources. The librarian can make recommendations on where technology needs to be placed or upgraded as well as on what departments or teachers may need extra training and support in its use.

8. **Librarians are concerned about the safe and ethical use of technology.** Students will need to have the skills to self-evaluate information, understand online copyright laws and intellectual property issues, and follow the rules of safety and appropriate use of resources. Who but the librarian worries about digital citizenship?

We need to remember that those responsible for staff development must have good opportunities for training themselves. Librarians can justify a need for workshops, conferences, and training sessions beyond that of the classroom teacher. And, accompanying the extra training must be the administrative expectation and acceptance that the knowledge and skills gained will be proactively shared with the rest of the staff.

Librarians must also commit to ongoing, self-directed skill acquisition by forming professional learning communities.

Whether called a consultant or a partner, the school librarian needs to be a major, if not lead, player in building staff development efforts. It builds our indispensability.

How can we provide effective staff development opportunities for our teachers?

Judy, Tom, and Juanita are all modeled after real teachers and can be found in any district across the country. Each of these teachers has a very real, but very different need for "technology" staff development experiences. To think that any one training program or approach will satisfy the requirements of all teachers in a district would be a mistake.

After helping teachers learn to use technology since 1980, I have seen a pattern of technology growth emerge—from Personal Productivity to Upgrading Current Practices to Restructuring the Educational Environment—and have discerned that each stage requires its own model for professional development. Let's look at each stage in a bit more detail.

Personal productivity

Easy-to-use word processing programs and personal computers have been readily available and affordable since the late 1970s—over 30 years. Wouldn't you think that any adult who needed to use a word processor would know how to use one by now?

Yet is seems some form of "basic training" is still needed to help teachers learn new programs and equipment. The recent adoption of online word processing tools like GoogleDocs, for example, requires some new skills such as knowing how to upload files and control how they are shared with others.

Computer boot camps have long been a staple of technology training in schools. Developing a series of often-required hands-on classes has been an efficient means of introducing teachers to fundamental computer operations and basic software such as file management, word processing use, editing digital video and still photographs, student information system use, working with online grade books, and sending and receiving e-mail. For a full list, see CODE77 Rubrics—Beginning 2009 version (Johnson 2009).

The aims of the Personal Productivity level of staff development training include:

- To give a novice computer user the fundamental skills needed to operate a computer and basic productivity software.
- To teach new teachers programs specific to the district such as online web authoring tools, computerized grade books, and the shared calendaring system.
- To acquaint teachers with new hardware, programs, and program features the district has adopted.
- To introduce programs to teachers that might be of value to them, developing an understanding of the software application's potential.

Teachers needing extensive training on basic computer operations are less common, but every teacher still needs some classes on a regular basis on new programs, new operating systems, and the advanced features of productivity programs. New teachers need a shorter version of the basic skills course that emphasizes technology use that is specific to a district. And when a new product or program is launched, such as a new grade book or the adoption of interactive whiteboards, special classes are needed.

Librarians can and should be helping design and teach these classes.

Simple rubrics like the one below can help the teachers determine their personal level of proficiency and know what skills are needed to become more proficient. They can also be used to assess the effectiveness of training efforts.

IV. Word processing

Level 1. I do not use a word processor, nor can I identify any uses or features it might have which would benefit the way I work.

Level 2. I occasionally use the word processor for simple documents that I know I will modify and use again. I generally find it easier to handwrite or type most written work I do.

Level 3. I use the word processor for nearly all my written professional work: memos, tests, worksheets, and home communication. I can edit my document using commands like copy and paste, find, undo, and save as. I can spell check, and change the format of a document. I can paginate, preview and print my work. I can use tables within my documents and insert graphics. I can save my document as a .pdf file. I feel my work looks professional.

Level 4. I can save my document as a text or rtf document so it can be opened by others who may not use the same word processor I use. I take advantage of collaborative writing/editing environments when available, including online word processors and wikis. I can suggest an open source word processor for those who wish or need to use one. I use the word processor not only for my work, but have used it with students to help them improve their own communication skills.

This is standard fare for most districts and is a necessary part of the staff development program. But it stops short of helping teachers recognize the real power of technology.

Upgrading current practices

As teachers become more comfortable with using technology for their own personal productivity, they want to start using it with students to help empower them. The first step that that usually takes is what I call "The Technology Upgrade." This is a traditional unit that is enhanced with the addition of a technology component.

For example, a teacher will add a multimedia presentation to a lecture to more clearly illustrate concepts and heighten student interest. Teachers often require that student writing be word-processed since it is easily edited and can be placed online to allow peer review. Or a teacher may ask students to solve a math problem using a spreadsheet in which formulas and operations are clearly visible and which can chart and graph numbers.

When teachers start seeing possibilities for enhancing lessons and activities with technology applications, the philosophy of teacher training shifts from just-in-case the teacher needs to know this to just-in-time for the teacher to use the skill. The just-in-time model of technology training relies not on district-mandated classes, but on personal, individual learning opportunities that are most often one-to-one. The librarian should be the key resource for helping teachers "upgrade."

The rudiments of most software programs can be learned in less than an hour—just enough to get one started. Online tutorials can be a convenient and effective supplement to face-to-face instruction.

Many teachers learn technology skills right along with their classes when the librarian collaboratively teaches the class. Librarians should always offer twenty- to forty-minute voluntary classes after school when there is an interest. And then some teachers are genuinely independent learners who would prefer to be given a program with a decent manual and simply be given time to learn through trial and error.

Find below eleven common activities that classroom teachers may be already doing and some ways technology can be used to "upgrade" the learning process.

Table 13-2
The technology upgrade

Current activity	Technology upgrade	Benefits
1. Teacher lecture	Add a computer presentation program	Graphics, sounds, movies, and photographs clearly illustrate concepts and heighten student interest. Easier for students to take notes.
2. Student writing	Word-processed, desktop published.	Easily edited, spell-checked, handwriting-proof. Illustrations or graphics easily added. Online peer review and commentary.
3. Student research	Require some online resources such an electronic encyclopedia, full-text magazine database, or websites.	Information is quickly accessed. Notes can be copied and pasted into rough draft. Sounds and pictures can be used in multimedia reports. Online citation tools ease creating bibliographies. Having access to large number of resources allows a topic's focus to be much narrower, adding interest.
4. Book reports	Use a spreadsheet or simple database with fields for title, author, publisher, date, genre, summary, and recommendation.	All students contribute to spreadsheet or database. Concise reports can be used as a reader's advisory by future classes. Easily printed and distributed to class.
5. Math problems	Use a spreadsheet to set up basic math story problems.	Formulas and operations clearly visible. Charting and graphing capabilities. Data from original surveys converted into understandable information. Numeracy, rather than math facts, is practiced.

6. Plays, skits, or debates	Video the presentations.	Record for later analysis, sharing with parents. Editing possible. Save as exemplar for future classes.
7. Create a timeline	Use a dedicated timeline creation tool like Timeliner, a mind-mapping tool like Inspiration, or a drawing program.	Fast, simple, and easy to read. Possible to add graphics and modify time segments.
8. Student speeches, demonstrations, or lessons.	Video record the presentation. Students use multimedia, incorporating media to accompany presentations.	Record for later analysis, sharing with parents. Editing possible. Save as exemplar for future classes. Graphics, sounds, movies, and photographs can be used to more clearly illustrate concepts, increase audience attention. Use slides in place of notes.
9. Drawings to illustrate concepts, create diagrams, or accompany writing	Use drawing or paint program.	Use features of drawing program to create meaningful original illustrations or modify clip art. Edit and use digital camera images or scanned images with writing for improved meaning.
10. Class discussion	Create a class blog with discussion questions.	Students can contribute outside of class time. Shy students might be more likely to contribute. Longer, more thoughtful responses may be given.
11. Games or simulations	Use computerized simulations such as SimCity or a title from the Choices, Choices series. Use online games to practice basic number facts, vocabulary words, or grammar.	Computer provides more realistic scenarios and visuals in simulations. Online "drill and practice" gives immediate feedback and increased attention.

The key to a successful upgrade, of course, is that there is *genuine* benefit to using the technology—not just adding it for its own sake.

From the examples above, some of the key "technology upgrade" benefits include:

1. Helping the teacher address multiple learning styles by allowing extensive use of multimedia in lessons.
2. Motivating reluctant students.
3. Allowing students to add elements of creativity, especially visually, to their work.
4. Allowing anytime/anyplace learning and access to information.
5. Allowing student performance to be reviewed and critiqued more easily and by the students themselves.
6. Increasing the audience for student work.
7. Increasing participation by reluctant students.

A final piece of practical advice for "easing into technology integration" is to make sure that technology integration is first implemented in units that are currently less than successful, rather than effective units that students and teachers already enjoy.

An old adage says that the way to eat an elephant is one bite at a time. The technology upgrade can be that first nibble teachers take to successfully and completely integrate technology into their classrooms in positive ways.

Restructuring the educational environment

The final and most powerful stage of staff development is paradoxically when technology becomes a means of achieving a larger educational goal. School improvement is not really about improved technology use, but about giving students more powerful learning experiences, making children more effective problem solvers, creating teaching methods that reach more students, and developing assessments and data use practices that inform instruction.

Learning technology is only a part of a larger professional growth target when the goal is restructuring some aspect of education—doing things in a fundamentally different way. Learning to use a database should be a part of learning to do more effective assessments. Learning to use mind-mapping software such as Inspiration should be a part of learning better writing instruction practices. Learning to more effectively search the web should be a part of learning to how to improve student research practices. In other words, the focus should be on improving professional practices, not learning to use a computer.

Staff technology training now becomes far more teacher-directed and personalized. At this stage we see professional development happening in two ways: as a part of an individual teacher's professional growth targets or at the request of our Professional Learning Communities, site teams, or curriculum departments.

Professional growth targets (or professional growth plans) have been a staple in many districts' staff development plans for some time. Teachers need to be encouraged when writing them to include a technology component that asks for the intended goal of the plan, activities the teacher will engage in to meet the goal, and the means by which the accomplishment of the goal will be demonstrated. Teachers themselves identify the skills and training needed to accomplish the goal.

The rubric below illustrates the change from using a technology (the word processor) as a personal productivity tool as described above to using it in more powerful ways to restructure the educational process:

II. Using technology to improve student writing

   Level 1. I am not familiar with any technologies that would allow me to help my students improve their writing skills.

   Level 2. I ask that the final draft of some student writing assignments be word-processed. I do not expect or encourage my students to compose or edit using the computer.

   Level 3. I help students use the computer in all phases of the writing process from brainstorming to editing to publishing. This may include the use of idea generators, graphic organizers, portable writing computers, outlining tools, spelling and grammar checkers, desktop publishing tools, and webpage generators. I use technology to help students share their work for a wide reading audience. I can find and use best practices data on improving writing with technology.

   Level 4. I store portfolios of my students' work electronically. I share successful units with others through print and electronic publishing and through conference presentations and workshops. I look for specific technology tools for helping my students improve their writing skills (Johnson 2010).

The emerging pattern of staff development comes from teams of teachers who believe technology can help them reach their building or curriculum department goal. For librarians this means helping serve the needs of Professional Learning Communities, each of which may have a different set of goals. But the common denominator among all goals is that they are tied back to a building or district goal.

Most educators, including me, are better teachers than students. I'll confess I have small patience with most classes and workshops whether they are about technology or anything else. Listening to a presenter often does little for me except help develop a strong empathy for our kids. But if we learn to structure technology training to suit individual adult learning styles and place it within the context of improving educational practices, teachers can and will become "technology-literate."

For reflection: Top 10 ways to increase your technology skills and knowledge (and the secret to being perceived as a technology guru)

1. Use your children and students as testers and experts. Let the students teach *you*.
2. Attend conferences, workshops, and seminars whenever possible. Take advantage of "virtual" learning opportunities through webinars. Make the case to your staff development committee that you will learn and share what you've learned, and should get funding priority.
3. Present at conferences. It's a compelling reason to become an expert. Write for a publication. It's a compelling reason to become an expert.
4. Order new and preview materials, but practice with two or three popular technologies. Be the expert, say, on search tools, GoogleDocs, and Smartboard operations.
5. Devote at least fifteen to thirty minutes a day to learning. Schedule it like you would a class or meeting. Learning so that you can teach others may be the single most important part of your job.
6. Form and participate in a Professional Learning Community (see next chapter).
7. Read journals, the business pages of your newspaper, and professional blogs. Read nonfiction related to both education and general social issues.
8. Visit other schools and see other school library and technology programs. You'll never visit a school without coming away with at least one great idea.
9. Get involved in your professional organization. You really do help yourself by helping the rest of the profession
10. Don't just give lip service to the expression "You only learn by making mistakes." Develop a tolerance for experimentation, ambiguity, and sometimes looking a little foolish in front of your peers. We expect that of our students. As poet Theodore Roethke describes, "I learn by going where I have to go."

Oh, the simple secret to being perceived as a technology guru? Here is how I answer probably 95 percent of the tech "how-to" questions I receive . . .

Uh, Doug, how do I add a graphic to my signature file in Gmail?

1. I type "Add graphic to signature file in Gmail" into the Google search engine box.
2. I select one of the first credible-looking hits.
3. I read the steps.
4. I try the steps out on my computer.
5. I reply to the person asking the question as though I already knew how to do it—no source of the answer cited.

Try it.

References

Dwyer, David C. "Changes in Teachers' Beliefs and Practices in Technology-Rich Classrooms." *Educational Leadership* 48, no. 8 (May 1991): 45–52.

International Society for Technology in Education. "The National Educational Technology Standards for Teachers." 2008. http://www.iste.org/standards/nets-for-teachers/nets-for-teachers-2008 (accessed Jan. 21, 2013).

Johnson, Doug. CODE77 Rubrics—Beginning. 2009. http://www.doug-johnson.com/dougwri/code77-rubrics -beginning-2009-version.html (accessed Jan. 18, 2013).

Johnson, Doug. CODE77 Rubrics—Rubrics for Restructuring. 2010. http://www.doug-johnson.com/dougwri/rubrics -for-restructuring.html (accessed Jan. 18, 2013).

Chapter Fourteen

Surviving Professional Transitions

Change will occur in our profession and our personal lives whether we like it or not. This chapter deals with proactive ways to face both voluntary and involuntary changes. The sooner librarians look at change not as something to resist, but to embrace, the more indispensable we will be.

Personal learning networks—Why you can't afford to wait for the next conference

LM_Net has been the mainstay electronic mailing list for an estimated 100 million school librarians in 2 million countries, on a dozen other planets, and within at least 2 identified alternative universes. It produces in excess of a trillion e-mail messages each day—10 trillion on "recipe day" (these numbers are rough estimates).

I was an early subscriber and participant on LM_Net using a university "vax" account back in 1992 when I first joined. This was 1200 baud modem dial-up, line interface, pre-WWW, uphill-both-directions-in-the-snow Internet days. Not soft and cushy like young'uns have it today with graphical user interfaces and wirelessness. The computer screen was hard to read by lamplight, too.

Anyway, LM_Net became my first Internet "continuing education" experience. And the learning began early.

It was my second year as library supervisor and I was getting lots of pushback from the district librarians I had inherited. I was determined to make them technology integration specialists, and they seemed just as determined to remain print-only librarians. After one particularly frustrating day, I turned on my computer, opened my e-mail, and just let rip about the reactionary, troglodytic, and myopic nature of school librarians, concluding that they had all better wake up and smell the coffee or they would all be replaced with technicians and not to let the door hit 'em where the good lord split 'em on the way out. And off the rant went to LM_Net.

Let me put it this way—I got some reaction. I knew librarians had good vocabularies, but even I learned some new words. I believe after that e-mail, other LM_Netters opened my messages simply wondering what idiotic thing I might say next. In this forum, I found my voice.

More importantly, I found colleagues who offered information, encouragement, and support. It was my first true "continuous learning" experience, not because I was the one doing the teaching, but because we were all learning together—as we do to this day. The virtual community built by LM_Net—a professional learning community before they were so named—was a lifeline and sanity-keeper for many of us.

Continuing education prior to LM_Net consisted of reading professional journals, attending library conferences, and taking college classes. These activities are still available and important. But given the pace and amount of change, they alone are insufficient to keep most of us current with the happenings in librarianship and information technology.

Over the past few years, perhaps without knowing it, connected librarians have assembled personal learning networks. It's an important by-product of the Web 2.0 social networking opportunities. We've become connected to learning we can access on a daily basis—at times most convenient to the individual. We can regularly read, listen, respond, and argue with the wisdom and points of views of colleagues in the world of school, public, academic libraries; technologists; classroom teachers; futurists; and visionaries.

This network creation using the resources listed below is not merely important for our own professional leadership and growth, but is important for us to model and share. Through our own professional connections, we model what is possible for classroom teachers, principals, guidance counselors, and students. We demonstrate the powerful new ways people build knowledge in the 21st century.

Thank goodness for these online continuing education options:

- Electronic mailing lists (aka listservs) continue to be valuable means of locating "primary source" information—human expertise. While LM_Net is the granddaddy of such resources, you might also consider joining AASLForum, ISTE SIGMS, WWWEdu, and your own state's mailing lists. A simple query to such lists often results in not just recommended published information, but in shared experiences and wisdom as well. Don't forget that some mailing lists like LM_NET archive messages for later retrieval. LM_NET has a wiki archive, allowing librarians to share materials that don't fit within the limits and format restrictions of discussion group threads.

- Web 2.0 "professional networks" such as the TeacherLibrarian Ning are complementing listservs by providing a media-rich forum with a means of sharing photos, videos, and other resources with fellow network members. These networks automatically provide members with their own home pages and allow smaller special interests groups to form within the larger network. Aimed at creating links and real-people connections for professionals, these operate much like the larger social networking sites Facebook and LinkedIn.

- Blogs and their aural cousins, podcasts, let librarians read or hear, react and converse on the latest thinking by leaders in the school library field, as well as leaders in related fields. Information on blogs tends to be timely, short, and often opinionated. Pick the ones that are fun to read and you *will* become addicted. If you have one favorite blogger, examine his or her blogrolls for leads to related bloggers worth following. The quickest strategy to manage your reading and keep up with those blogs you love is to subscribe to their RSS feeds and group them in one spot through an aggregator or reader. Consider becoming a blogger yourself. It's easy, free, and fun.

- For those of you craving a quick and organized introduction to many things 2.0, look for focused online tutorial efforts like "23 Things." Check with your local library organizations to see if such opportunities are being offered in your area. Choose to do it yourself or join the other librarians in meeting the challenges set forth.

- Webcasts, presentations, and workshops done via an Internet website like GoToMeeting or Elluminate are becoming increasingly popular. Watch your e-mail for these "web seminars." Webinars allow many of us to attend conferences we could never before consider to get inspiration from many of those keynoters with no need to invest in airfare or conference registration.

- TED Talks and other online presentations can delight, inform, and motivate. Some of the best minds in the world share their ideas in free lectures. Universities like Brown and MIT have placed their best courses online for free viewing. Expand your horizons and make connections by taking a class, say, on archaeology. Maybe you will understand some of your older faculty members a little better.

- Multi-User Virtual Environments (MUVEs) such as Second Life offer a number of opportunities to interact and learn with colleagues. Your Second Life avatar can attend or give a presentation, communicate with fellow professionals in real time, and even build virtual learning resources using this powerful information and communication interface.

- Twitter or microblogging allows users to follow other professionals' "tweets" (little posts of 140 or fewer characters) to see what they have been reading and thinking about. The real trick for success in Twitter is finding the right folks to follow. Those experts whose articles you read, whose sessions you attend, whose classes you take or have taken, inside and outside of the school library world, are likely Tweeters. Start with them. You'll find that tweeters will share their exceptional blog posts, their favorite web-based tools, their live experience from all over the world as they listen to or present as conference speakers. You'll find at least one great idea every day.
- Shared slide shows and videos allow conference and workshop presenters to share their best materials. Slideshare is one of the largest archives. Search by topic or by presenter's name. Many of the shows are downloadable. You will not only learn about the content of relevant presentations, you'll also see examples of good and bad slide design. TeacherTube and YouTube for Education are becoming major portals for teacher- and student-made educational videos. They're great starting places for seeking video relating to professional development, as well as video relating to curriculum. It's also a fine source for tech how-to-do-it films.

These are just a few of the growing number of "continuous learning" opportunities the Internet is making available to those of us engaged in the rapidly evolving field of school librarianship.

Librarianship can be lonely. As the only professional of your sort in the building, sometimes in the district, you likely crave the advice and sympathy of those who understand you best, as well as advice for colleagues who are out there moving and shaking. It's harder to learn alone. It's hard to collaborate alone.

Does your school's mission statement include the words "lifelong learning"? It should. And the sentiment should also apply to all of us as well.

Finding the time

Many of you are asking yourselves, "Where will I find the time for learning these tools and establishing my own personal learning network?" It's a great question. But try this:

- *Commit to just fifteen minutes.* Set aside that quarter hour from your lunch period, before you go to bed, or first thing in the morning for your PLN every day. Most of us find the time to accomplish those tasks that are most important to us. Make attending to your personal learning community a scheduled, regular activity every day.
- *Take it one tool at a time.* Many of us are overwhelmed when looking at a list of tools like the one above. Don't try to do it all at once. Pick one or two tools and try them for a few weeks or months. As their use becomes second nature, try a new resource. Eat the elephant one bite at a time. Remember that not every resource fits every individual's learning preferences.
- *One in, one out.* Keep the number of blogs or Tweeters you follow manageable by always deleting a feed whenever you add a new one. Too many of us continue to add more things to our lives without ever stopping to seriously consider the things we might choose to let go. This is never an easy task, but it is an important one.
- *Form a genuine community.* The thing about social networking is that, well it's social. Getting to know individuals and groups is a powerful way to stay committed and involved. Have conversations with the people you find interesting and knowledgeable. Most people are flattered to be asked for help or advice. One of the real pleasures of Web 2.0 communications is that the line between

personal and professional gets blurred. We get to know each other as individuals with real lives, not just people with similar jobs.

- *Give back.* The interactivity of personal learning networks is what gives them their real value. If you are only a "lurker" on discussion lists, blogs, or Nings, you are only getting half the value of the experience. Discuss, suggest, rant, praise, and question. It's all part of the daily PLN experience.

Indispensable librarians are leaders, and leaders share knowledge and visions. You cannot lead your school community, you cannot guide others in new and emerging information and communication landscapes if you yourself are not a continuous learner.

When your job is on the line . . .

Nobody likes his or her job being the possible target of budget cuts or reorganizations. However, given the ongoing state of inadequate or reduced school funding, staffing reductions are commonplace in school library programs.

These guidelines are for librarians whose jobs might be on the line as their school districts cut budgets. May you never have to use them.

Guidelines for librarians during budget reductions

If you are a librarian whose position may be reduced due to budget reductions or reorganizations in your school district, consider taking the following actions:

1. *Learn the timeline for your district's budget adjustment process.* Districts start planning for budget reductions for the next school year as early as November. (*Very* large districts may start budget planning in September.) Visit with your superintendent to see what the timeline and procedure for making budget reductions are. Don't rely on rumors—keep an open line of communication with your superintendent and building principal throughout the school year. If district budgets are the result of a collaborative decision-making process, make sure you are part of it. Every school district is required by law to have written budget policies and procedures. Find your district's official budget procedures and read specifically to find the timeline and which administrators have authority over budgets.

2. *Let your state school library association know as soon as possible when library staff cuts are considered in your district.* State library associations are willing to help you if your position is cut. Some even have an "emergency response" plan in such cases. Besides reviewing and clarifying such plans, state associations can provide advocacy materials, testify at board meetings on your behalf, and suggest strategies you might use to reduce the likelihood of your position being cut. Contact your association as early as possible. Contact the public and academic library directors in your region. They can be great allies. If the budget adjustment recommendations in your district are already final or even just approved by the administrative staff, there is very little anyone, including a state association, can do.

3. *Contact your teacher organization representative and check your state's laws regarding library programs.* Know what help your teacher organization is willing to give you. Understand your

teaching contract in terms of seniority and layoff notification deadlines. Find out the contract's role in the budget determination process. Many states mandate a minimum level of library programming and staffing. Check to see if the proposed reductions run contrary to state law.

4. *Distribute and discuss "library advocacy" information with your building administrators, superintendent, school board members, and site teams.* Compile and synthesize your local program statistics in a visual and easily understood format. While circulation, collection size, and usage numbers are important, also make sure to outline your information literacy curriculum and its specific skills, your literacy activities, and each of the collaborative units you team-teach within other teachers' curriculum. Discuss your role in teaching, supporting, and integrating technology uses in your building. Outline specific activities and skills you teach to both students and teachers. While the tools below are powerful, do not assume that just because the information gets in the hands of your school leadership that they read the material, understood it, or believed it to be applicable to your district. You need to find ways to *discuss* these materials with decision makers, not just distribute them.

   - Familiarize yourself with the professional association advocacy materials.
   - Get research about effective school library programs into the hands of administrators, including:
     o Any studies that may have been conducted in your own state or region.
     o Any program or skills standards developed by your state.
     o Summaries of the research done in various states and countries on the impact of school libraries on student achievement.

5. *Begin developing a short statement outlining the consequences to students and staff of the potential cuts to your program.* As soon as you know the degree of budget cuts, create a statement that describes in concrete and specific terms how the loss of services, learning opportunities, technical services, library access, and support for curricular and building goals impact students and staff. *Do not* frame this in terms of how *your* job will be more difficult, but in terms of how students and staff will be affected. Emphasize your teaching role. (What skills will students *not* learn if your program is cut?) Again—the more concrete, the better. Distribute and discuss it with all decision makers in the district.

6. *Begin getting commitments from district teachers, parents, and students willing to write and speak in opposition to the possible library staffing reductions.* Ask those who make use of your skills, your library's resources, and its services to speak on your behalf, either informally (to administrators), formally (at school board meetings), or in letters to the editor of the local newspaper. This is the most powerful advocacy you can have. Again, this action needs to happen during the budget reduction process, not after recommendations are already formalized.

7. *Arrange for a state school library association spokesperson to write and/or speak on your behalf to your superintendent, school board, and community.* If you feel that a state association officer speaking on your program's behalf to your administrative team or school board would be helpful, contact the association. This outside voice can be helpful under some circumstances, especially if the person speaking has knowledge of current research, best practices, and the state of libraries in your state.

8. *Keep doing your very best despite the possible cuts.* Your position may be restored if the school and community are aware that the roles, functions, and events you do may not happen the next year. Decisions and cuts are not always permanent. Don't burn any bridges.

You, as a school librarian, are too important to too many children to let budget reductions that affect your program just "happen." Get active and heed the words of Dylan Thomas—do not go gentle into that good night.

For reflection: Prevention

Of course, an ounce of prevention is better than a pound of cure. Ongoing efforts can make your library program less likely to be the target of budget reductions. Make sure you are already doing the things below, many of which have already been discussed in greater detail in other chapters of this book.

1. Build and maintain a library program that teaches critical information and technology literacy skills, improves student literacy rates, and supports all classrooms and curricular areas.
2. Serve the needs of your teaching and administrative staff through instructional collaboration, technology training and support, and filling requests for professional materials.
3. Establish a school library advisory board comprised of a wide range of stakeholders, especially parents, that meets on a regular basis to discuss goals, policies, and budgets.
4. Create long-term goals and annual objectives that are supported by the principal and teachers and are tied directly to your building's goals. Enacting long-range plans and multiyear strategies or projects makes it difficult to change horses in midstream.
5. Build a mutually supportive relationship with your principal.
6. Track and report to your administrator the use of your library program, especially units of teaching, collaborations, and specific skills you, yourself, teach.
7. Communicate regularly and formally with administrators, teachers, students, parents, and the community about what happens in your library program, through newsletters, websites, and e-mail. Communicate to individuals on "I thought you'd like to know about this . . ." topics. Present to your school board whenever you get the chance.
8. Have an ongoing involvement with your parent–teacher organizations.
9. Serve on leadership, curriculum, technology, and staff development teams in your building and district.
10. Be active in your professional teacher organization and remind officers that as a dues-paying member, you deserve as much support as the classroom teacher.
11. Be involved in the extracurricular life of the school, attending school plays, sporting events, award ceremonies, etc. Be visible. (I think it helps to be an active member of the community, belonging to a church or other religious organization, community service group, and/or volunteer groups. It's harder to fire a friend and neighbor than a stranger.)
12. Be active in your state school library association by attending conferences and regional events, reading its publications, volunteering for positions in the organization, and attending its legislative functions.

Chapter Fifteen

Libraries and the Future

A mind-set list for librarians

Beloit College annually publishes its Mind-set List that reminds faculty members of how the world entering freshmen grew up in is quite different from that of older persons. Our novice librarians also experienced libraries and education quite differently than many of us who have been in the field for a few years (or decades).

Librarians entering the field today . . .

- Have never typed a catalog card.
- Think "filed above the rod" sounds sort of kinky.
- Have never used the *Readers' Guide to Periodical Literature* or know the difference between the green and red ones.
- Don't know what a vertical file might contain. Is there a horizontal file, too?
- May never have attended an F2F graduate school library class.
- Have never purchased or rented 16mm films, VHS tapes, or laser discs and think a film loop is a ride at Disney World.
- Have never called Wikipedia's accuracy into question.
- Have always had the Internet as a resource but have never seen a C:/ prompt.
- Have never checked out 5¼-inch floppy disks of MECC games.
- Have never worked in a library without wireless connectivity.
- Have never used that flip-section thingy to sort book checkout cards.
- Have never had to rubber stamp a due date or re-ink a stamp pad.
- Is a "P Slip" something you wear?
- Think microfiche are on the endangered species list.
- Have never "shushed" anybody.

I suspect only a few readers of this book chuckled at any of the items mentioned above—indeed, even know what things like a vertical file or microfiche might be. Most librarians who have circulated film loops or "filed above the rod" are retired or soon will be.

But don't feel too smug, entering practitioners. Obsolescence is occurring at an ever-increasing rate. How many years, or even months, before flash drives, netbooks, Facebook, or Nooks will seem as quaint as floppy disks and rubber stamp pads?

My crystal ball is cloudy at best. Thankfully, futurists are rarely held accountable for their predictions, so I can boldly go on record here. The following narrative describes my hoped-for description of a school library program. My hope is that it inspires you to envision a future of school library programming—and your place in it.

Miles's library: A vision for school libraries

7:00 AM

"Miles . . . Miles, honey, time to get up," the librarian's voice whispered softly in the still dark bedroom. Miles, a senior in the graduating high school class of 2025,[1] slowly came awake.

"OK, OK, I'm awake, Marian. Schedule, please," Miles requested using the auditory interface to his school library portal,[2] accessed through a small device on his nightstand.

"You are meeting with your ecological science team F2F in Learning Space 17, Main Library at 8:45. Carlotta will be 15 minutes late. You've registered for 'Advanced Semantic Web Searching' with Head Librarian Baxter from 9:30 to 11:00 in Seminar Room B of the Main Library. Your IEP[3] Advisor, Dr. Li, wants to meet with you in her office at 1:00 about your senior project. And I have finalized the MUVE meeting schedule with Professor Shahada in Amman for 4:15 SLT this afternoon. Your lacrosse team practice has been cancelled, but time has been reserved in the simulation area of the gymnasium for team members wanting virtual practice."[4]

"Gee, that's all?"

"No, Miles, dear. Your report on theologian Reinhold Niebuhr is due tomorrow. Would you like me to reserve a video rendering terminal in the library for you?"

"Marian, you are a slave driver!" Miles cried, slowly crawling out of bed.

8:30 AM

"Looks like almost a full day in the library for me," Miles tells his girlfriend Jennie as they walk from the bus stop up to the school. Jennie is one of the main reasons that Miles still goes to his neighborhood bricks and mortar school at least three days a week.[5] "Let's grab a cup of coffee there while we have time."

"Seems like you've been living in the library this year," observed Jennie. "They should be charging you rent."

"Well my senior project, 'Can sims be programmed to exhibit free will?' has really been more involving than I thought. I mean, it's the perfect combination between my interest in religion and computer programming, but it's been a lot more work than I thought. And the library has been my primary resource for this project." Miles was embarrassed to admit that his presence in the school's physical library was only a fraction of the time he spent in the library's virtual spaces. "Just stamp 'nerd' on my forehead, I guess." Miles sighed.

The library Miles and Jennie enter might look cavernous were it not for the low ceilings and dividers filled with green plants that break up the space into small, intimate work areas. A combination of soft seating and small, easily rearranged worktables in coordinated colors make the library look both worklike and comfortable. There is a low hum of conversation, especially near the entrance to the library where a small coffee shop is located, but noise-cancellation technologies keep the main part of the library surprisingly quiet—

---

1. 2025 is the approximate year my youngest grandson, Miles, will graduate from high school, assuming children are still attending thirteen years of schooling beginning at the age of five or six—a big assumption.

2. Customizable portals are common, although still text based, as of today. iGoogle is a popular example. "Add-ons" in Internet browsers also exemplify the extensibility that users are beginning to require of any information accessing/processing tool.

3. An Individualized Education Plan is required by law for U.S. children having been identified with special needs today. By 2025, these will be required for all students and created with the help of sophisticated assessments and data-mining tools.

4. The Nintendo Wii gaming device currently allows users to participate in simulated sports and exercise.

5. Physical schools will still exist in 2025 since the societal charges placed on education of socialization and child containment will still exist. Inexpensive childcare will continue to be demanded by working parents—even if more are working from home.

considering there are over 200 students working here. The perimeter of the library has doorways leading to small conference and seminar rooms, faculty offices (this location is in high demand), and technology labs filled with powerful, specialized computers. Student work is silently displayed throughout the library space on monitors of various sizes with small signs indicating the channel on which the audio is being broadcast.[6]

Students and faculty alike carry or wear a variety of small portable computing devices that automatically connect to the data network via the library's portal interface.[7]

Miles says good-bye to Jennie and heads toward Learning Space Seventeen for his meeting with his team.

8:45 AM

"Hey, Juan. Hey, Liz," Miles says with a wave as he plops down on one of the sofas occupied by his learning team. "Any word from Carlotta?"

"She's having an emergency with some stuff at home and will be audio conferencing with us,"[8] Juan reports.

"Sounds like the emergency is a bad hair day." And with that, Carlotta's voice says, "I heard that. And just for your information, I *never* have a bad hair day. But I do have a little sister with the sniffles."

"OK, OK, I've got lots to do today," Liz chides. "I think at the last meeting we decided that our project was going to be looking at creating self-reporting devices for the green plants here in the library powered by the small voltage they themselves actually produce. Are we still agreed?" Heads nod. Eighty-five percent of all energy needed to power the school is generated by projects designed by the students themselves over the past fifteen years.

"So, Miles, what did your search on similar projects turn up?"

"Yeah, your creepy Marian avatar dig anything up?" asked Juan. "Do you still have her affection module running so she calls you sweetie, sweetie?"

"She's not creepy, just twentieth century," Miles replied. "She looks and sounds just like Shirley Jones's character Marian in *The Music Man*. If you weren't such a cultural Neanderthal, you'd appreciate the reference. As for her obvious and well-placed fondness for me, I'd say you're just jealous."[9]

Carlotta laughed, saying, "Miles and Juan, if you weren't such good friends, I'd say you couldn't get along."

Miles is the acknowledged expert at data acquisition in the group. Liz's strength is in leadership, organization, and historical knowledge; Juan's visual communication and math skills are outstanding; and Carlotta's interpersonal abilities keep the team moving and working well together—plus she is the acknowledged science whiz of the team. Miles considers each of these fellow students an integral part of his personal learning network.[10]

Miles himself does not conduct data searches—he programs bots that search for him. Ever since helping his older brother Paul create and modify creatures in the primitive simulation game Spore as a preschooler

6. David Loetscher and others have envisioned a "learning commons" that is user-centered with workspaces for a variety of groups with a variety of purposes.

7. Today's netbooks, tablets, and smartphones using 802.11x and EVDO wireless networks are early versions of those being used by Miles and his contemporaries.

8. Built-in laptop cameras and microphones along with simple programs like Skype are already making video conferencing commonplace in schools. The trend of more ubiquitous cameras and microphones, simple conferencing tools, and greater broadband connectivity will continue to grow.

9. Customizability in both ability and appearance are common in both MUVE (Multi-user Virtual Environments) such as Second Life and MMORPG (Massive Multiplayer Online Role-Playing Games) such as World of Warcraft avatars today.

10. Collaboration and group work skills are a part of every set of "21st-Century Skills" being promoted.

and later learning how to design custom Google Search[11] engines in elementary school, Miles has been devising ever-more sophisticated programs that help him meet his information needs. The librarians have been instrumental in helping Miles develop these skills. Several thousand other students—and adults—use some of the search bots Miles has created. Lately, he has been giving the bots physical forms as avatars and personalities using code from a new bank of 20th-century entertainer models.

"Marian only found about 750 gig of materials related to using plants' own electrical production properties to power sensors. I asked her to condense and audio-synth this data to five-, ten-, and fifteen-minute summaries. I've sent the audio and video files of the three top reports to you. In my view, this project is increasingly doable . . ."[12]

Encouraged by Miles's findings, the group discusses next steps, creates a timeline, and debates the format of the final report on the project. Their next meeting on the coming Friday will be virtual, using the library's video conferencing site.

9:25 AM

Miles hurries toward the seminar room on the other side of the library for his class with Librarian Baxter. Cutting around dozens of students working individually or in small groups, Miles glances up at the latest ALA's LISTEN campaign "poster" being displayed on one of the library's LED monitors. It features Tammy Fox, daughter of first decade hottie Megan Fox, displaying her favorite audiobook cover. Another LED promotes an ALA PLAY poster showing popular cartoonist Brady Johnson with his favorite video game. (The READ campaign was discontinued in 2020, along with the paper versions of the posters.)

Only one thing seems to be missing in Miles's school library—books, magazines, or *any* paper information source. The last print books—school yearbooks and some local history publications—were sent to Ghana to be digitized five years earlier. All those materials are now available online with the originals in the local history museum archives.

About 99.9 percent of intellectual property in all formats—text, visual, audio, and programming code—is in the world IP DataBank. On submitting work to the DataBank, a small identifying script is inserted into each work. Each time the creation is accessed, a nominal payment is made to its creator. Content users can pay either a flat monthly fee for unlimited access to the DataBank or pay per petabyte of data.[13] Miles's school library does not own or lease *any* information sources. But it has built, using freeware APIs, a powerful portal and guide to the DataBank.[14] And it allows its staff and students to customize that portal.

Miles enters the seminar room just as Mr. Baxter begins to outline the objective of the 90-minute lecture/demonstration/guided practice session on honing one's understanding of semantic web searching skills,[15] specifically dealing with language-specific idioms when doing multilingual searching with auto-translation tools. About ten students are attending in person while another fifteen are using the library's MUVE conference room. The virtual participants are not just from Miles's school but from other high

---

11. Customized search engines can be built now using Google Custom Search.

12. Full-text searching of millions of books is currently available as part of Google's Search the Book project. Google has reached an agreement with publishers to scan and make available not just out of copyright titles, but out of print titles.

13. Stanford Law professor Lawrence Lessig in his book *Free Culture* (New York: Penguin, 2004) advances the idea of such a compensation scheme for intellectual property creators, based on redistributing the proceeds from a tax on recording media to compensate musicians and videographers.

14. Subscription services to full-text magazine indexes, video collections, and e-book collections have been common since the 1990s.

15. The semantic web, a means of describing data on the Internet in ways that make it more easily searched by discriminating among homonyms and other word meaning discrimination techniques. Tim Berners-Lee, James Hendler, and Ora Lassila, "The Semantic Web," *Scientific American*, May 17, 2001.

---

schools, a university, and a home school. One participant is simply a retiree with an interest in the topic. The seminar will be recorded and added to the DataBank.

"Miles, what are you doing here?" Sergey backchannels using a primitive chat program. "You could be teaching this stuff."

"Thanks for the vote of confidence, but I heard Baxter just came back from an American Library Association conference with some beta code on idiom translation. I'm hoping that if I look interested enough, he'll share."

Mr. Baxter coughed. "Miles, would you Google Jockey[16] this seminar, just in case questions arise?" Miles nodded and made a mental note to find the etymology of that strange term.

11:00 AM

Miles uses the time between the end of the seminar and his meeting with Dr. Li to grab a sandwich in the school cafeteria with Jennie and then take a quick nap in the library. Research on adolescent sleep needs convinced the library advisory committee that napping is a legitimate use of library resources and that library policies should reflect this. After Marian again awakens Miles, he checks his TwitFace account and then listens to two audio reports—one a real-voice podcast and the other a speech-synth conversion—recommended by Mr. Baxter in the earlier seminar.[17] He reviews his progress on his senior thesis.

Miles's school is one of several operating in his small community. It is based on a highly individualized, project-based, collaborative learning model that uses performance assessment only. "Developing creative problem-solvers with a conscience" is the articulated mission of the school. All required classes end when students are twelve and have passed the national reading/writing/math proficiency test. After age twelve, each student works according to an individualized education plan (IEP), written by the student, his parents, a team of teachers and school librarians, and the other members of his formal personal learning network (PLN).

Another school in Miles's community is entirely computer-based, with each student using a structured, game-based programmed curriculum designed for his individual educational program. A third school retains the "traditional" classroom, 50-minute period, teacher-led, core content model. Neither of these schools have either physical or virtual libraries or librarians. (Miles's first podcast that earned him DataBank payments was a commentary arguing that sending children to traditional schools should be considered child abuse.) All families are given educational vouchers and are allowed to select which school to attend. Vouchers became politically feasible in 2017 when a law was passed that no school can charge more in tuition than the standard voucher amount and that all students, including those with special needs, are eligible for each school's lottery that selects the incoming class.[18]

---

16. Assigning a class Google Jockey is a current practice in higher education. See EDUCAUSE Learning Initiative, "7 Things You Should Know about Google Jockeying," May 2006.

17. Miles's library serves the "postliterate." Any number of recent studies are concluding that reading is declining—primarily the reading of novels and longer works of nonfiction. I personally define the "postliterate" as those who *can* read, but *choose* to meet their primary information and recreational needs through audio, video, graphics, and gaming media. Print for the postliterate is relegated to brief personal messages, short informational needs, and other functional, highly pragmatic uses such as instructions, signage, and time-management device entries—each often highly supplemented by graphics. The postliterate's need for extended works or larger amounts of information is met through visual and/or auditory formats. The term "postliterate library" may at first glance appear an oxymoron, but it is not. Our best libraries are already postliterate, increasingly meeting the needs of users who communicate, play, and learn using media other than print. And the attitudes we as professional librarians adopt toward the postliterate may well determine whether our libraries continue to exist (see chapter seven).

18. The societal demand for school "choice" has led to many different options beyond the traditional public school in the United States. Private schools, parochial schools, magnet schools, charter schools, online schools, open-enrollment—with a demand for government tuition vouchers controlled by parents—are all examples of the diversification of education. The reality is that not every type of school needs a library, even today.

1:00 PM

"I'm very pleased with the progress you've been making on your senior project, Miles," said Dr. Li with a smile. "Explain to me again why you believe that your sims are showing signs of free will."

"It's their preferences, Dr. Li!" Miles reports, "Kurzweil, one of my oldest sims, is choosing blue clothing at a rate outside statistical probabilities. In fact, even though he has a choice of several dozen colored garments from which to choose each day, he almost always chooses blue. He also seems to like anchovies on his pizza."

"And you are sure this is not a programming bug?" asked Dr. Li.

"I've gone over the selection routines about thirty times and asked three others in my PLN to do independent audits of the code. Everyone agrees that Kurzweil *should* be making random choices."

Dr. Li and Miles confer for nearly an hour, once bringing in Ms. King, a Hong Kong librarian who specializes in science fiction in popular culture and its treatment of religious and moral dilemmas. She quickly produces a qualitative list of works in which self-aware technologies are featured.[19]

"Here's one last dimension you might want to consider," suggests Dr. Li. "What might be the meaning of this discovery on how we as humans view ourselves? That we humans may merely be 'sims' in a great cosmic programming plan?"[20]

Miles checks to make sure his audio note-taker[21] caught this question, before agreeing that this was a good idea.

"Oh, before you go, I also want to check how the composition of your PLN is working for you. I understand that you did not accept my suggestion of dropping your grandfather's membership in favor of adding a second programming expert."

Miles considered his PLN. The school requires that all students have a "formal" personal learning network of twelve members. (Like other students, Miles's informal PLN has over one hundred members at any one time accessed by a variety of networking tools.) For their formal PLN, some students create expert groups from specialized fields of high interest; others form a group with as diverse a representation as possible. Librarians are a part of nearly every student's PLN and they take this responsibility seriously.[22]

"With all respect, Dr. Li, I did keep Grandpa Doug on my PLN rather than choose another expert. I recognize he knows little about my major areas of study and is hopelessly out of date on anything technology related, but because of his advanced age, he sometimes adds a sense of perspective that I don't get from other students or experts," Miles maintains. "He's also good for a joke now and then."

Dr. Li nods. "Perspective is valuable, I will admit. But I've heard his jokes—pathetic."

Miles thanks Dr. Li, and asks his librarian avatar Marian to send his advisor's last question out to his PLN for input, thankful his senior year and this project are nearly complete. Miles is looking forward to his first year as a North Dakota State University Bison. His older brother Paul, however, has warned him that his first year of college will be tough since many professors still lecture. He advises making sure his smartphone has a full battery charge for multitasking during the core courses.

---

19. The exponential growth of information will require the specialization of librarians into areas of interest.

20. Ray Kurzweil, in his book *The Singularity Is Near* (New York: Viking, 2005), suggests this explanation—that we are all part of some cosmic simulation game—for human existence.

21. A growing body of academic research shows that students who record instructions and classroom lectures get better grades, justifying personal MP3 player/recorders in schools.

22. Personal learning networks, a self-created set of experts, colleagues, and resources that can be relied upon to meet daily learning needs, usually dependent on networked technology, are currently being explored by educators.

2:00 PM

Miles uses the next hour putting the finishing touches on his report on Reinhold Niebuhr that's due the next day.

Luckily, Marian was able to schedule Miles a full hour of time in the 3-D rendering computer lab.[23] This is one of the few individual projects for which Miles is responsible this term so he has chosen to examine his favorite 20th-century theologian's influence on U.S. government policy. After listening to and viewing over 80 hours of materials on the topic, Miles's final project will be pseudo-discussion with Franklin Roosevelt, Lyndon Johnson, and Barak Obama, each discussing major Niebuhrian beliefs in relationship to their respective administrations' social policies.

Miles hopes that this project will be judged to merit inclusion in the school's student research "virtual museum." Miles's older brother Paul holds the record number of pieces of student work in the museum with three projects. Miles's goal is to get one more of his projects added this spring—giving him four. The permanent addition of student work to the museum is considered an honor.[24]

Like his fellow students, Miles writes very little, choosing instead to convey his ideas and research using the more natural communication methods of sight and sound. Technology makes it simpler to create audio and video reports than written ones. When a teacher does require a written "paper," Miles uses a speech-to-text conversion program to create his first draft and then edits that version. Most video and audio reports can be done using his personal computing device, but now and then Miles likes to explore more sophisticated modes of communication like the 3-D rendering software that requires more powerful processing. The library's labs supply equipment for this purpose. Miles and his fellow students can write very well; they simply choose to communicate in what they feel are more powerful ways.[25]

At one point, Miles get stuck on a highly complex task he asks of the rendering program. In answer to an online call, the support librarian pops up in a window in the lower right corner of the screen and efficiently helps Miles over the rough spot. Visual literacy is considered as important, if not more, than textual literacy for Miles and his classmates in this postliterate work environment, educational system, and society. Librarians view the communications portion of information fluency models as a critical part of their curriculum.

Satisfied at last, Miles stores his simulation in his digital warehouse along with all other work he has created since he was in elementary school.[26] He glances at the clock on his screen and decides that he has time to get home and do his MUVE conference with Dr. Shahada there.

---

23. Despite the ubiquity of personal computing devices, cutting-edge applications will continue to need very large processing capabilities, unaffordable by individuals, and therefore be housed in the library.

24. Educators have long known that the larger the audience for a student's work, the greater the level of concern by the student about the quality of the work. Permanent collections of student work, organized and managed by the library, should become a part of the school culture and contribution to the world's knowledge base.

25. Education and librarianship have a current bias toward print. This communication/information format has served civilization well for several millennia. Most professionals today demonstrate high levels of proficiency in print literacy skills and they can be expected to defend the necessity of such skills. Most educators are competent readers, writers, and print analysts, but neophyte video, audio, and graphic producers, consumers, and critics. It is human nature to be dismissive of those competencies that we ourselves lack. However, postliteracy is a return to more natural forms of multisensory communication—speaking, storytelling, dialogue, debate, and dramatization. It is just now that these modes can be captured and stored digitally as easily as writing. Information, emotion, and persuasion may be even *more* powerfully conveyed in multimedia formats. In Miles's school the bias toward print will fade as new generations of media-savvy educators take charge.

26. Comprehensive portfolios, managed with the help of librarians, will be under lifelong development by all workers of the "creative class." Cheap mass storage of materials in digital formats will allow creators to keep all work and never delete a project or file.

4:00 PM

As Miles walks in the front door, his dad calls out from his home office, "Supper's at six—I blocked it off on your calendar. Attendance is not optional. Oh, and when is that lawn going to get mowed? The grass gets any longer you'll not only have to mow, but bale as well."

Sighing at the hopelessly agrarian reference, Miles acknowledges his dad and heads to the family room. Rather than use the smaller, 54-inch screen on the computer in his room, he decides to go holographic for his meeting with Dr. Shahada. He grabs a cola from the fridge, gets comfortable in one of the big easy chairs, and opens the connection to the University of Jordan. The family room fades and is replaced by a holographic multiuser virtual environment. Dr. Shahada is already at his desk and Miles finds himself sitting across from him. The image is good enough to read the text on the diplomas displayed on the wall behind the professor's desk.

"*Salaam lakim*, Doctor," Miles begins, happy to have a chance to practice his Arabic, a language he has studied both formally and informally for ten years. (The rest of the conversation is conducted in Arabic.) One of the reasons Miles's parents chose his current school was that its staff recognize that multilingual professionals are at an advantage in the global economy.[27] In 2015 when Miles chose Arabic as one of his "focus" languages (along with Tagalog), his parents wondered if other languages would have been more beneficial. But the rise in democratic governments and a permanent peace settlement in the Middle East in the 2010s led to the region's growth as a world economic and educational leader.

"The blessings of Allah upon you as well, Miles," Dr. Shahada replies with a smile. "I've been looking forward to our conversation today. To get to the point, one of the librarians here at UJ spotted some of the avatar-represented search bots you've been creating and also noticed your proficiency in Arabic. Our library, in collaboration with the computer science department here at UJ, would like to offer you a summer internship with us. You would be working with our librarians to improve our own library portal by adding idiomatic Arabic-speaking avatars."

"It sounds exciting," remarked Miles. "Would I be doing this work in Amman or telecommuting?"[28] He and Dr. Shahada continue to discuss this opportunity until nearly six o'clock.

One of Miles's school library's major services is to provide and support "learning portals." While text-based portals have been a common library offering for many years, the virtual environment interface is relatively new. When Miles logs on to his library portal, he sees a 3-D representation of his physical school library. His avatar moves through it easily, looking far more natural than the funky Second Life–like creations of early MUVEs. He can see which members of his PLN network are online, check for messages (audio, video, and text), do real-time video/audio communications with those both in and out of the library, and view his selected and school-required news feeds. Around the library at various stations are librarian avatars with whom Miles can engage. While one sits behind a general information desk, others are subject-specific, offering guidance in languages, science, mathematics, history, communications, and other areas. Virtual doorways lead to teacher, advisor, and guidance virtual offices and to the school's virtual museum of permanent student project displays. There is also a doorway to Miles's "warehouse," a visual depiction of links to all the projects he has undertaken as a student.[29]

---

27. Thomas Friedman's book *The World Is Flat* (New York: Farrar, Straus, and Giroux, 2006) described a world economy and argued that cultural understanding would play an increasing role in successful business.

28. The continuing increase in fuel costs has led to a growing percentage of home-based workers. Home-based work has led to a greater need for "dispositions" as outlined in AASL's *Skills for the 21st-Century Learner* (Chicago: American Library Association, 2007).

29. An online presence has been of growing importance since the 1990s for all institutions, including libraries. The MUVE 3-D environment has been predicted to become the standard interface for web navigation.

What makes the portal especially valuable to Miles and others in his school is its customizability. Using open source APIs (Application Programming Interfaces) and programming scripts, Mile has rearranged the standard library layout, deleting some components like the annoying electronic posters and adding features like a real-time Arabic translation avatar, a collection of rare Tagalog documents, doorways to several research labs, and a hidden door to a representation of his bedroom at home where he can work on personal tasks.[30]

It is, however, Miles's work in creating custom-search bots represented by avatars that excites him. The library provides a set of tools that allow students to create "librarians" who will follow carefully composed search parameters that follow sophisticated semantic rules.

6:00 PM

During his conference with Dr. Shahada, Miles received a message comprised of several ideograms. It was Jennie keying from her phone, asking Miles if he wanted to meet her for a jog. He discretely replied that he was busy, but suggested they meet in the 20th Cent game after supper. After mowing the lawn with a push mower, Miles sits at the kitchen table where his mom, dad, and ten-year-old sister Maggie are already engaged in conversation.

Maggie tells about the latest version of Oregon Trail that she and her team are playing in their U.S. History class and about the research she is doing on animal rights of the 19th century; Dad shares his day of in-person pastoral visits to his elderly parishioners and how nice it was to get out from behind a computer screen. But it's Miles's mom's reflections about her day as the town's public library director that really interest him.

"I am always surprised at just how popular our 'Edit Yourself, Market Yourself, Support Yourself' workshops are—even after all these years of holding them. It seems it takes some people a long time to realize that the DataBank and payment plan changed the model of making money from one's intellectual property. While many creators choose to contract with editors and marketers—often people who once worked for large publishing companies—even more people have added editing and marketing to their own job skill sets. It's really gratifying to see the public library as an effective community and personal development resource."[31]

While Miles and Maggie visit their public library rarely, they both take advantage of its online presence. Maggie is a part of an active gaming group sponsored by the children's section and relies on its recommendations of new games. Miles attends the public library's online seminars and often consults its resident personal branding guru—"Purple Cow" Smith.

"I suppose it's time to hit the studies," Miles says after finishing his last bite of dessert.

"Time to talk mushy to Jennie is more like it," teases Maggie. "And don't forget, it's *your* night to do the dishes."

7:00 PM

After the last spoon is dried and put away, Miles spends thirty minutes playing virtual lacrosse—the cancellation of his regular athletic practice is making him feel a bit sluggish. He checks his vital stats on the game station after his workout and sends them to his data storage locker in the library.

---

30. One of the reasons for the popularity of today's Firefox and Chrome browsers are their extensibility. By using "add-ons," one can customize the tool to meet one's personal style of working. The expectation of extensibility will continue to grow.

31. Lulu.com, Apple's iBook, and other self-publishing sites are changing the relationship of professional editors and markets and writers.

Back in his room, Miles logs into the MMORPG, 20th Cent. His regular avatar easily moves from one virtual environment to another, quickly morphing when the situation calls for it. Jennie is already online.

"My friend Winslet just finished programming a challenge this afternoon and asked me to beta it." 20th Cent, like most popular games, relies on users to create quests, puzzles, and adventures for each other.[32] Both Miles and Jennie prefer "amateur" created content to that designed by self-designated professionals. "Think you can survive the sinking of the *Titanic* this evening?" Jennie asks. "You know, you look a little like Leo DiCaprio."

"Let's try it. If I am going down with the ship, I can't think of anyone I would rather have with me."

Jennie's and Miles's avatars, now looking like Kate and Leo, teleport to the White Star docks where they board the ill-fated ship—Miles playing steerage, Jennie, first class.

Jennie and Miles are capable readers. Due to early childhood educational programs, both, in fact, could read before entering kindergarten. But like the majority of their peers, they nearly always choose other media for nearly all their information and entertainment needs. Even video and audio are increasingly less popular than gaming. Miles and his peers demand engagement—not just entertainment—and engagement requires interaction.[33]

Games themselves have evolved, becoming an art form and are considered a medium of serious commentary on human nature. The Pulitzer Prize in gaming reflects the respect now paid to the creators of serious games for their plots, characters, settings, tones and themes.[34] And games, of course, are an accepted and effective pedagogical tool—especially for elementary students.

It takes Miles and Jennie almost three hours and a dozen attempts before both are rescued before freezing in the icy North Atlantic waters. Jennie notes several anachronisms that Winslet might want to fix before public release of this scenario. Miles gives Jennie a virtual kiss goodnight, logs off the game, and heads off to brush his teeth.

10:30 PM

There is a quiet knock on Miles's bedroom door.

"Hi, Mom. Come in."

"What are you reading, sweetie?" Miles's mom asks when she sees him propped up in bed with an actual paper book resting on his knees. As an avid reader herself, Mom is always a little disheartened by how little her two younger children read for pleasure and is delighted when one actually picks up a book.

"Oh, it's an antique paperback called *The Diamond Age* by a twentieth-century writer named Stephenson. Pretty interesting how he predicted the One Laptop Per Child movement that Negroponte and his cult began. Uh, Mom, can we talk a minute?"

"Sure. What's going on?" Mom asks, sitting on the edge of the bed.

"Don't faint, but I think I might major in library science next year instead of computer programming. Jennie was teasing me this morning about how much time I spend in the library and it got me thinking about how much I *do* like working there."

"Well, that is a surprise, Miles. The field and training has changed so much since I got my MLS twenty-five years ago, and it has really changed since your grandpa got his library degree almost fifty years

---

32. The MUVE Second Life is a model of an environment that is almost completely user-generated; the MMORPG World of Warcraft (modeled after the earlier analog Dungeons and Dragons game) relies on user-generated "quests."

33. The NetGen is spending more time in front of screens but less watching television—demanding entertainment be interactive rather than passive.

34. The library helps its patrons discover and understand this still relatively new medium, offering game discussion groups, organizing game fan clubs, and arranging game developer talks and seminars.

ago—long before personal computers were commonplace, let alone the Internet," Miles's mom observed. "My training seems obsolete, now. Good thing I'm in management where I don't need many technology skills."

"You know I talked to Grandpa just now, bouncing this idea off him. He said about the same thing—that the tools and roles of the librarian have changed dramatically, especially in the last twenty years or so. But then he added something. He said that the tools librarians use change, the importance of certain tasks that librarians perform changes, and even the services libraries offer to support their schools and communities change. But some things, like the librarian's mission and values, remain constant. Librarians still support intellectual freedom and fight censorship. Librarians are still about open inquiry and access to information and ideas. Librarians are still about helping people find and use information that is reliable and helping them use it to improve their lives. And librarians have always been about helping people help themselves by learning how to be lifelong learners and informed decision makers. And Grandma Annie, who was listening in, added that librarians have always wanted people to find enjoyment, fun, and excitement in learning *and* reading."

Miles's mom rolled her eyes. "Did Grandpa also go on about how librarians' people skills, not their technical skills, are the most important?"

"Yup. But you know he also said that he thought I'd make a great librarian and would be proud to have me in 'his' field."

"Well, that's your grandfather—always trying to recruit the best and the brightest."

Miles yawned. "Thanks, Mom. I need to get some sleep. My senior project is one day closer to being due so I need to really get cracking on it tomorrow."

As his mom left the room, Miles put down his book, switched off the bedside lamp, and spoke to his avatar,

"Please wake me up at seven, Marian. Goodnight."

"Goodnight, Miles, my love."

"I've gotta turn down those affection settings," Miles thought as he rolled over and closed his eyes.

For reflection: Prognostications for libraries and schools

As quickly as technology changes, it is almost impossible to predict or plan with any accuracy the specific challenges that will be facing us over the coming years. But we can speculate on some general trends:

1. Less emphasis on "technology" as a separate area of concern; more emphasis on technology as a means to achieve goals of other areas.
2. Greater need to train students and staff on ethics, safety, and civility (digital citizenship) when using technology, as well as the ability to evaluate the reliability of information found and to use it purposely.
3. Continued integration of technology skills into the content areas to meet specific state standards, accompanied by increased demand for individualized technology training by staff.
4. Continued, accelerated move to information in digital formats such as e-books, online databases, electronically submitted student work, web-based video conferencing, and video on demand.
5. More emphasis on anytime, anyplace access to personal information through web-based personal file space, calendars, and wirelessly networked handheld devices.
6. Increased desire by parents for real-time student information available via the web. Higher parent expectations of schools and teachers to provide comprehensive information about school programs (including libraries) and individual student achievement.

7. Increased ability for individual teachers to create and make available materials accessible from the web and increased need for help in doing so.
8. Increased importance of data-driven decision making by administrators, building teams, and individual teachers, with library needing to describe its efficacy in numerical terms.
9. Increased efforts to assure data privacy, data security, and network reliability.
10. Increased educational options for all learners including more choices of schools, more online course offerings, more interactive video offerings, and more computer courseware options. How will the library support this diversity of opportunity? Can the library help "market" its school?
11. Greater accountability for technology and library expenditures and impact on school effectiveness.
12. An accelerated blending of technology integrations specialists and librarians into a single job that takes responsibility for the instructional and curricular uses of technology.
13. Greater need for procedures that allow for joint decision making among all technology users.
14. Increasing in-school use of personally owned technologies due to the greater integration of technology into everyday life. The next generation of smartphones will become greater extensions of our "out-board" brains, increasingly powerful, convenient, and useful. Students and many adults will depend on them.
15. The increased importance of information professionals to help others make sense and use of the floodwaters of data. I hope they continue to be called librarians.

The ability to grow, to adapt, to anticipate, and to collaborate will determine the success or failure of each of us in the exciting years ahead. See you in the future.

References

American Association of School Librarians. *Skills for the 21st-Century Learner*. Chicago: American Library Association, 2007.

Friedman, Thomas. *The World Is Flat*. New York: Farrar, Straus and Giroux, 2006.

Afterword:
A Day of Ordinary Library Miracles

I wish you a day of ordinary (library) miracles and little things to rejoice in . . .

Eight hands that go up to request the title you've just book talked.

A computer that goes for an entire day without crashing.

A less-than-successful baking experiment taken to the teachers lounge, eaten before 10 AM.

A child asking for another book "just like this one."

Finding an "app" that saves you time.

Watching a student successfully use the newest database to find needed information.

A parking spot close to the school door.

The principal saying a sincere thank-you.

An unexpected larger amount on your paycheck or a smaller amount on your mortgage payment.

A new book just published by your favorite author.

A student who is actually concerned about the quality of his work.

A dozen doughnuts as "thanks" for service above and beyond the call.

A quick and pleasant response from a technician.

Kids who want to help you.

A teacher saying out loud in the lounge how much she uses the online tool you showed her.

A human voice on the phone when you expected a recording.

A student who wants to become a librarian when she grows up.

A chance to show a tech-tip to a teacher who thinks you are a "guru."

A library with windows and sunbeams in the winter.

A request to use the library for a meeting because "it is the most pleasant room in the school."

A smile of accomplishment from a student who shows you how to do something on your smartphone.

A quickly answered reference question asked by a teacher.

A library aid you like and who likes you.

A call from a parent thanking you for the information on your webpage.

A student so absorbed in a book, he doesn't hear the bell ring.

A call from a parent about a lost book found while cleaning.

A student who wants to hold your hand.

What strikes me as I read this list of "ordinary" miracles is how we, ourselves, often make them happen. It is by treating others well that good is returned to us.

Author's Note

Some of the ideas expressed in the *Indispensable Librarian*, 2nd edition, have appeared in my earlier published works. These materials have been substantially updated, revised, and edited. These works include the *Blue Skunk Blog*, the first edition of the *Indispensable Librarian*, and these publications:

Chapter One: The Roles and Missions of the Librarian

Johnson, Doug. "Are Libraries (and Librarians) Heading toward Extinction?" *Teacher-Librarian* December 2003.

Johnson, Doug. "Becoming Indispensable." *School Library Journal's Learning Quarterly* February 2003.

Johnson, Doug. "Curriculum Built Not to Last." *School Library Journal* April 1999.

Johnson, Doug. "Dangers and Opportunities: Challenges for Libraries in the Digital Age." *Minnesota Media* 2007.

Johnson, Doug. "New and Improved School Library Media Program." *School Library Journal* June 1995.

Johnson, Doug. "Seven Most Critical Challenges That Face Our Profession." *Teacher-Librarian* May/June 2002.

Johnson, Doug. "Vision for the Net Generation Media Specialist." *Leading & Learning with Technology* December/January 2005–2006.

Chapter Two: Program Assessment

Johnson, Doug. "Demonstrating Our Impact—Putting Numbers in Context Part 1." *Leading & Learning with Technology* December/January 2006/2007.

Johnson, Doug. "Demonstrating Our Impact—Putting Numbers in Context Part 2." *Leading & Learning with Technology* March 2007.

Johnson, Doug. "Linking Libraries and Literacy: A Review of *The Power of Reading: Insights into the Research*." *KQWeb* March/April 2005.

Johnson, Doug. "What Gets Measured Gets Done: The Importance of Evaluating Your Library Media Program." *The Book Report* September/October 2001.

Chapter Five: Managing Others and Collaboration

Johnson, Doug. "Collaboration and Reflection." *Minnesota Media* 2004.

Johnson, Doug. "Good Policy for Policies." *School Library Journal* March 2003.

Johnson, Doug. "Keep Your Building Technicians by Keeping Them Happy." *School Library Journal* May 2000.

Chapter Six: Managing Digital Resources

Johnson, Doug. "Libraries in the Cloud." *Library Media Connection* May/June 2011.

Johnson, Doug. "Managing Digital Resources." *Library Media Connection* September 2007.

Johnson, Doug. "Turning the Page." *School Library Journal* November 2004.

Chapter Seven: Curriculum

Johnson, Doug. "Libraries for a Post-Literate Society." *Multimedia & Internet @ Schools* July/August 2009.

Johnson, Doug. "Real Flexibility." *School Library Journal* November 2001.

Johnson, Doug. "Right Brain Skills and the Media Center: A Whole New Mind(set)." *KQWeb* March/April 2007.

Johnson, Doug. "Skills for the Knowledge Worker." *Teacher-Librarian* October 2006.

Johnson, Doug. "Survival Skills for the Information Jungle." *Creative Classroom* August 2001.

Chapter Eight: Budget

Johnson, Doug. "Budgeting for Lean Mean Times." *MultiMedia Schools* November/December 1995.

Johnson, Doug. "Politics of Money for the School Library Media Professional." *Minnesota Media* Fall 1994.

Johnson, Doug. "Weeding the Neglected Collection." *School Library Journal* November 1990.

Chapter Nine: Facilities

Johnson, Doug. "Changed but Still Critical: Brick and Mortar School Libraries in the Digital Age." *InterED*, Association for the Advancement of International Education, Fall 2010.

Johnson, Doug. "Some Design Considerations When Building or Remodeling a Media Center." ERIC ED425609, 1998.

Chapter Ten: Digital Intellectual Freedom

Johnson, Doug. "Are You Sure You Want an Internet Filter? Virtual Censorship Is Still Censorship." *TechTrends* May/June 1998.

Johnson, Doug. "Best Practices for Meeting CIPA Requirements." *EdTech Magazine* Q4 2005.

Johnson, Doug. "Maintaining Intellectual Freedom in a Filtered World." *Leading & Learning* May 2005.

Chapter Eleven: Ethics and Technology

Johnson, Doug. "Chapter Five: Ethics in Use of Technology." In *Ethics in School Librarianship: A Reader*. Ed. Carol Simpson. Linworth 2003.

Johnson, Doug. "Developing an Ethical Compass for Worlds of Learning." *MultiMedia Schools* November/December 1998.

Johnson, Doug, and Jen Hegna. "Guidelines for Educators Using Social and Educational Networking Sites." *Library Media Connection* March/April 2010.

Chapter Twelve: Copyright and Creative Commons

Johnson, Doug, and Carol Simpson. "Are You the Copyright Cop?" *Leading & Learning with Technology* April 2005.

Johnson, Doug. "Creative Commons and Why It Should Be More Commonly Understood." *Library Media Connection* May/June 2009.

Johnson, Doug. "Who's Afraid of the Big Bad (c)?" *School Library Journal* October 2008.

Chapter Thirteen: The Librarian's Role in Effective Staff Development

Johnson, Doug. "Just in Case, Just in Time, Just in Part: Three Levels of Staff Development." *MACUL Journal* 2007.

Johnson, Doug. "Why, What, How and WHO of Staff Development in Technology: The Growing Importance of Teacher-Librarian's Role in Helping Create Technology-Savvy Educators." *ISIS Conference Paper* Summer 2000.

Chapter Fourteen: Surviving Professional Transitions

Johnson, Doug, and Joyce Valenza. "Reboot Camp." *School Library Journal* May 2008.

Johnson, Doug. "When Your Job Is on the Line." *Library Media Connection* February 2005.

Index

AASLForum, 180
Accountability, 4, 17, 196
Advocacy, 44–55, 183
  brochures, 53
  ongoing, 54
  rules for effective, 53–55
  self-, 44
American Library Association, xviii, 10, 81, 128, 134,
Code of Ethics, 137, 140–148
Office of Intellectual Freedom, 141
American Association of School Librarians (AASL), 20, 37,
  81, 168, 192
American University's Center for Social Media, 159, 161
Americans with Disabilities Act (ADA), 118
Animoto, 52, 75
Ask.com, 94
Assessment, xviii, 17, 40, 67
  authentic, 6, 126
  collections, 70–71, 74, 79
  context and focus, 28–29
  data analysis, 22–23
  data-gathering, 20, 28
  follow-up action plan, 19, 25
  formal library, 18–26, 32, 39
  ongoing, 16, 25–26
  performance-based, 2
  program, 16–34
  report, 24–25, 32
  self-study plan, 20
  student, 66–67
  that help the learner, 90–91
  tools, developing, 87

Banned Books Week, 128
Berkowitz, Bob, 82, 85
Big6™, 82, 85–86
Blogging, xvii, 1, 9, 77, 95, 182
  micro-, xvii, 181
Books, print, 6, 102–103, 105, 134–135
Brain-based teaching, 2
Budgets, xviii, 4, 32, 50, 45, 53, 109–111, 105, 109, 138, 182
  as library ethic, 100–101
  maintenance and growth, 105–107
  open, 55
  outcome-driven, 103
  proposals, 101–102
  recognize sources of, 104–105
  reports, 107–108
  stakeholder ownership of, 103
  ten strategies of effective library budgeteers, 101–102

Card catalogs, 93, 185
Carlson, Gil, 44
Cator, Karen, 127–128, 134
Censorship, 127–128, 133
  reconsideration of banned books/e-books, 134–135
Children's Internet Protection Act (CIPA), 127–129
  meeting requirements, 132–134
Circulation, 50, 73, 183
  statistics, 26, 45
  systems, 12, 76–77
Cloud computing, xvii, 2, 110
  advantages of, 75–76
  e-books, 78
  how to take advantage of, 76–78
Collaboration, 57–68, 118
  codependency issues with, 66–67
  some concerns about, 66–67
  with teaching staff, 63–67
Collections, 26–27, 38, 50, 105–107, 126, 144, 183
  acquisition and access, 70, 72–73, 105–106
  assessment, 70–71, 74, 79
  promotion, 70, 73
  selection, 70–72, 144
  "weeding," 110–111
Communication(s), 9, 27, 32, 44–55, 98, 108
  "blasts," 52
  community, with, 50–51
  principles, 48–49
  program, components of an effective, 44–51
  skills, 11, 81, 109
Community involvement, 104
Computer
  boot camps, 172–173
  files, storing, 77
  hackers, 150–151, 155
  labs, 117, 120
  reconditioned, 110
  standardizing, 110
Computer Ethics Institute, 150
Conferences, 2, 6, 179–181, 184
Connexions, 166
Constructiveness education, 2, 6
Copyright, 115, 152, 159–167, 172
  Fair Use, xvii, 159–160, 163
  instruction, 159–160, 162–163

Covey, Steven, 16–17, 65
Creative Commons, xvii, 159–167
   license, 86, 143, 164–166
   understanding, 164–166
Cuban, Larry, 133
Curriculum, xviii, 17, 45, 81–99, 135, 184
   activities involving researcher, 89–90
   assignments that matter, 88
   building an information/technology literacy, 84–88
   committees, 67, 108
   information literacy, 82–88
   integration, 30, 183
   goals, 31–32
   projects that motivate students, 88–92
   programs, 71
   revision, 3
   technology, 82–88, 95, 168
   "teach-to-the-test," 4, 16
   "teacher-proof," 4

DVDs, 69–70
Data-driven decision making, xvii, 17
Davidson, Hal, 163
Department of Family Medicine, 131
Desktop publishing, 96
Differentiated instruction, 2
Digital citizenship, 82, 96, 195
Discussion groups, 9
Diversity awareness, 2
Drawing programs, 85, 175
DropBox, 75

E-books, 6, 71–72, 78–80, 105, 134–135, 195
   apps, 78
   cloud-based, 78
   costs, 79
   implementation plan, 79–80
   reader(s), 78–80, 102
   reader applications, 78
   unauthorized distribution of, 6
E-mail, 1, 12, 75, 83, 154–155, 166, 173
Eisenberg, Mike, 82, 85
Electronic Freedom Foundation, 130–131
Empathy, 96–97
Encyclopedias, online, 12, 85, 102
Essential Learner Outcomes, 13
Ethics
   assessing, 132, 155
   codes, 150–151
   information, 6
   modeling, 132, 155
   teaching, 155–156, 195
   technology, 6, 132, 137–158
Evaluations/evaluators
   employee, 68
   goal setting and, 41
   outside/professional, 19–20, 23–24, 40
   reports, 20, 24–25
   rubrics, 20

Facebook, 51, 81, 129, 134–135, 154, 156, 180, 185
Facility planning, xviii, 116–118
Fact checking, 103
Fair Use Guidelines for Educational Multimedia, 160
Family Educational Rights and Privacy Act (FERPA), 141
Federal Department of Education, 127
File storage space, 12
Focus groups, 20, 22, 27–28
Framework for 21ˢᵗ-Century Learning, 81
Free Software Foundation's GNU General Public License, 164
Fullan, Michael, 55
Fundraisers, 104

Garcia, Jerry, 4
Global citizenship, 2
Goals, 4–5, 14, 39, 55, 67
   long-term, 19, 184
   short-term, 19, 31–32
   timeline, 19
Google, xvii, 94, 97, 126
   +, 156
   Apps for Education, 12, 48, 52, 74, 76–77, 156
   Docs, 75, 77–78, 109, 172, 177
   Groups, 52
   Scan the Book project, 161
   Video, 78
Gorman, Michael, 10
Grants, 104
Graphing programs, 85

Hegna, Jen, 156–157
Humor, 96–97

International Society for Technology in Education (ISTE), 81, 170, 180
Information processing model, 85–86
Information Power standards, 168
Intellectual freedom, 140
   digital, 127–136
   maintaining, 130–132
International Society for Technology in Education (ISTE), 170
Internet, 7, 102
   access to, 133
   blocking, 130, 133–135
   database, 73
   filters, 72, 116, 128–132
   filters, myths regarding, 134–136
   policies regarding, 128, 129–130, 133–134, 151–152
   safety, 47, 72, 116, 127–136, 151, 155
   unblocking sites, 127–128, 135–136
   usage, productive, 131–132

Jobs, Steve, 97
Johnson, Doug, 11
John's 3 Ps of Technology Ethics, 150
Johnson's First Law of Effective Supervision, 67
Johnson's First Law of Schoolwork, 92
Johnson's Technology Implementation School of Hard
    Knocks, 122

Kelly, Kevin, 70
Kennedy, John F., 4
KidsClick!, 94
King, Martin Luther, Jr., 10
Krashen, Stephen, 33–34

LM_Net, 179–180
Learning commons, 113, 187
Learning groups, 112–113
Lessig, Lawrence, 164, 188
Librarian
    attitude, 91
    attracting new, 6–7
    challenges facing, 4–7
    collaboration, 38
    crowsnester, 2–3
    educational role of, 10
    enduring values of, 10–11
    information experts, remaining, 8
    interviewing new, 17
    leadership roles, 108
    learning opportunities, 38
    networking, 7
    opinions, 55–56
    professional development, 38
    professional teaching status, 6
    rabblerouser, 3–4
    roles and missions of, 1–15
    schedules, 68
    seven ways to remain relevant, 7–10
    training, 14, 105–106, 110, 168
Library
    advisory committee, 39, 41–43, 61
    annual objectives, 41–42, 45, 49, 184
    architects, 117–118, 120
    budgets, 32, 40, 53, 55, 100–111, 144, 182
    calendars, 12, 45, 55
    catalogs, 12, 31, 70, 73, 76–77, 102, 114, 171
    changes, long term, 16–17
    circulation, 12, 26, 45, 50, 73, 76–77, 183
    closings, 4
    collection(s), 26–27, 38, 50, 70–74, 79, 105–107, 110–111,
        126, 144, 183
    designing, 117–125
    economic rationale for, presenting, 4–5
    facilities, 1–2, 30, 38, 112–126
    future of, 185–196
    goals, 4–5, 14, 19, 31–32, 39, 55, 67, 184

    leadership team activities, 27, 31–32, 67, 184
    licenses, 74, 106
    marketing school through, 52–53
    mission and beliefs, 11, 35, 37
    plan, 16, 35–43, 45, 116–117, 119–120
    policies, 32
    postliterate, 97–98, 189, 191
    program management, 6
    progress reports, 14, 87
    purchasing strategies, 109–110
    record keeping, 87
    resource-based teaching, 31, 102
    resources, 8, 14, 22, 26–27, 38, 67, 69–80, 86–87, 135, 172
    role in digital culture, 70–74
    safety, 9–10, 30, 195
    special programs and activities, 27
    staff/staffing, 29, 38, 44–47, 67–68, 168–178, 184
    student visits to, 27
    study carrels, 119
    subscriptions, 74, 103, 106
    supervising, 122–123
    support staff, working with, 57–60
    teaching staff, working with, 63–67, 169
    teaching spaces in, 115
    technology advisory committee, 36
    technology, long-term goals, 36–38, 40, 69, 122
    technology, short-term objectives, 36, 39–40
    technology department, working with, 60–63, 85
    technology program, integrated, 13–14, 87
    traffic, 26–27, 38, 45, 123–124
    transparency, 55–56
    virtual, 1–2
    web pages, 1, 51, 53, 73
    welcoming environment in, 9–10, 114, 124–125
    workspaces, 120, 171
Lightweight directory access protocol (LDAP), 73
LinkedIn, 156, 180
Loetscher, David, 28, 113, 187

MIT, 166, 180
Mankato Public Schools
    Media program, 11–14
Managing others, 57–68
Merriam-Webster Online, 66
Microsoft Office365, 77
Minnesota Educational Media Organization (MEMO), 26
Mission statement, 11, 35, 37
Moodle, 12, 168
Multi-User Virtual Environments (MUVEs), 180, 187, 192,
    194
Multimedia productions, 9, 96, 113–115, 117, 120, 175
MySpace, 156

NETS for Students, 81
National Educational Technology Standards for Teachers
    (NETS-T), 170

Net Generation/NetGen, 7–10, 194
  Learning preferences, 8, 70, 112
Netbooks, xvii
NetLibrary, 73
Networked learning tools, 2, 116
Newsletters, 156
  district, 3, 51, 53
  e-mailed, 51
  library, 46–48
No Child Left Behind Act, xvii, 28
Noah Principle, 3

Open houses, 51
OpenCourseWare, 166

Parent(s), 44, 46–48, 104
Parent-teacher organizations, 3–4, 28, 108, 182–183
Partnership for 21st-Century Skills, 81
Peacefire, 130
Personal Learning Networks, 30, 180–181, 189–190
Pew research, 9
Phaedrus, 98–99
Photographs, 9, 28, 49, 173
  of students in libraries, 49
Pink, Daniel, 96
Plagiarism, 142–143, 148, 152–153
Planning, 16, 35–43, 119–120
  critical elements of a library/technology plan, 35–40
  documents, 35, 45
  plan, implementation timeline, 36, 40
  process, 40–41
  purpose and directive, 35–36
  team and procedures, 35–36, 116–117, 120
Plato, 98–99
Power of Reading, 33–34
Principals, 41, 44–46, 66, 105, 120, 184
  12-point library program checklist for, 29–32
  conference with, 39
  reports, 45
Privacy, 11, 141–143, 150–153
Productivity tools/programs, 12, 71, 85, 172–173
Professional Learning Communities, 13, 30, 176–177, 181–182
Project Achievement, 28
Public domain material, 86, 161, 165
Purchasing strategies, 109–110

Readers Guide to Periodical Literature, xvii, 14, 70, 93, 185
Reflective Practice to Improve Schools, 64
Relationship building, 17, 54, 67
Reporting, 17
Research, 92, 95, 102, 117, 120, 121, 174
  motivational projects, 88–92, 95
  question rubric, 92–93, 167
  sources, 93
Resources, 38, 67, 135, 172
  analog, managing, 74

counting, 22, 26–27
digital, managing, 14, 69–80
identifying, 86–87
online, 8, 27
Rice University, 166
Roethke, Theodore, 177

Safety,
  Internet, 47, 72, 116, 127–136, 151, 155
  library, 9–10, 30, 195
Satisfice, 166–167
Schlossberg, Edwin, xvii
Search engines, xvii, 15, 94, 97, 127, 177
Service organizations, 50, 108
(The) 7 Habits of Highly Effective People, 16
Sexually-explicit materials, 148–149
Shaw, George Bernard, 25
Skills, 10
  communication, 11, 81, 109
  creativity, 82
  grouping, 86
  higher-level thinking, 170–171
  information, 11, 27, 81, 95
  interpersonal, 104
  layout and design, 1, 96, 97, 109
  print literacy, 98, 191
  problem-solving, 17, 82, 95, 126, 170
  reading, 11, 32–34, 38, 47, 66, 184
  "right brain", 96–97
  teaching meaningful, 85, 119, 171
  technology, 13–14, 27, 81–82, 85, 109, 119, 184
  writing, 96, 174
Social networking, 2, 85, 156–157, 179–180
  guidelines for staff, 156–157
Staff/staffing, 38, 44–47, 67–68
  development, 168–178, 184
  development in technology, 168–172
  newsletter, 46
  support, 29
Standards, 19, 41, 111, 125
Standards for the 21st Century Learner, 81
Stevenson, R.L., 7
Storytelling, 96–98
Student
  achievement, xvii, 17–18, 25–26
  achievement, measuring, 17–18
  extracurricular activities, 17
  graduation rates, 18
  networked, 12
  postsecondary success, 17
  reading abilities and attitude, 38
supervision, secret to successful, 67–68
surveys, 19, 27–28
  alumni, 18
  employer satisfaction, 18
  library, 20–22

parents, 21–22
"Thirty-Second", 49
Synthesis, 96–97

Teachers, 63–67, 91, 169
    staff development opportunities for, 172–177
TeachingBooks.net, 74
Technology,
    10 ways to increase skills, 177
    appropriate use of, 153–154
    concerns about, 151–154
    directors, 132–133, 135
    obsolete, 110, 185
    policies regarding, 138, 154–155
    skills, 13–14, 27, 81–82, 85, 109, 119, 184
    student access to, 113–115, 139, 154–155
    teachers and, 168–172
    training, 4, 6, 13–14, 31, 170–171
    upgrades, 174–175
    workshops, 2
Textbooks, xviii
Thoreau, Henry David, 57
Time management, 16
Thomas, Dylan, 184
Transitions, surviving professional, 179–184

Transparency, 55–56
Tumblr, 127
Twitter, 51, 181

Unions, 4, 182–183
University of Michigan Medical School, 131

Valenza, Joyce, 8, 113
Vandalism, 154

WWWEdu, 180
Webpages, 70, 166
    library, 1, 51, 53, 73
    making, 94, 96
(A) Whole New Mind:..., 96
Wikipedia, 39, 70, 127, 166, 185
Wikis, xvii, 1, 9, 77, 151
Work groups, 9, 112–113, 156
    online, 15, 156

Yahoo!, 94
    Mail, 75
YouTube, 52, 70, 97, 127, 129, 135, 161–162, 181

Zoho, 109

About the Author

DOUG JOHNSON has been the Director of Media and Technology for the Mankato (MN) Public Schools since 1991 and has served as an adjunct faculty member of Minnesota State University since 1990. His teaching experience has included work in grades K–12, both in the United States and in Saudi Arabia. He is the author of six books, including *Teaching Right from Wrong in the Digital Age*; *Machines Are the Easy Part; People Are the Hard Part*; and *The Classroom Teacher's Survival Guide to Technology*. His long-running column "Head for the Edge" appears in *Library Media Connection*. Doug's *Blue Skunk Blog* averages over 50,000 visits a month, and his articles have appeared in over 40 books and periodicals. Doug has conducted workshops and given presentations for over 160 organizations throughout the United States and internationally and has held a variety of leadership positions in state and national organizations, including ISTE and AASL.